AM I LYING TO MYSELF?

AM I LYING TO MYSELF?

How to Overcome Denial and See the Truth

DR. JANE GREER

ROWMAN & LITTLEFIELD
Lanham • Boulder • New York • London

Published by Rowman & Littlefield
An imprint of The Rowman & Littlefield Publishing Group, Inc.
4501 Forbes Boulevard, Suite 200, Lanham, Maryland 20706
www.rowman.com

86-90 Paul Street, London EC2A 4NE

Distributed by NATIONAL BOOK NETWORK

British Library Cataloguing in Publication Information Available

Library of Congress Cataloging-in-Publication Data Is Available

ISBN: 978-1-5381-6423-5 (cloth: alk. paper)
ISBN: 978-1-5381-6424-2 (electronic)

♾™ The paper used in this publication meets the minimum requirements of American National Standard for Information Sciences—Permanence of Paper for Printed Library Materials, ANSI/NISO Z39.48-1992

To My Father

CONTENTS

Acknowledgments ix

Introduction xi

Part I 1

Chapter One: Are You the One for Me? 3

Chapter Two: You Need Your Space; I Should Be More
Understanding 25

Chapter Three: Your Love Is Smothering Me 45

Chapter Four: You Told Me You Were Just Friends 67

Chapter Five: I Can Wait—For Us 89

Chapter Six: Maybe Tomorrow We'll Have Sex? 113

Chapter Seven: I Thought You Said You Would—Or
You Wouldn't. 135

Part II. **159**

Chapter Eight: Are You for Real? 161

Chapter Nine: You're Driving Me Crazy 183

Chapter Ten: Why Are You Always So Angry? 207

Chapter Eleven: It's Always Yes, But, with You—. 227

Conclusion 245
Index 253
About the Author 255

Acknowledgments

This book came to life because of three people: to my dearest friend, Lynne White, for the gift of your universal guidance, I treasure our cosmic bond; to Karen Dougherty for the remarkable gift of my father's message; and to Amelia Appel for the gift of your laser vision, belief, and dedication. I also want to thank Dr. Uwe Stender and everyone at Triada US for your ongoing commitment. Thank you to my steadfast and tremendously supportive editor, Suzanne Staszak-Silva, for seeing the value in uncovering the problem of not seeing the truth. To Hannah Fisher, my production editor, for your enthusiastic attention to detail. To Elizabeth LaBan, for the awesome gift of our magic with words and music, your amazing alacrity, and your incredible devotion. To Maria Papapetros, for our kismet connection, your astounding spiritual intuition, and the trust you've shown me through the years. To Heather Zarnoch, for becoming invaluable right out of the gate and being all hands on deck with your savvy skill and tenacity; you are my secret weapon. To my patients for the gift of your faith in letting me help you get to higher ground. To my amazing family, including sister of my heart Carol April and Dr. Richard April for so many reasons, my cornucopia partner. To all my magical friends, in particular Rae Schabel for a half century of navigating life together and the gift of your wisdom; Vicki Mintz, my first and forever PK friend in life; Dr. Doris Day for your talent extraordinaire, your heart of gold, and for being my saving grace; and Nicole Bilzerian for our special shared kindred spirit. To my innately wise husband, Marc Snowman, for being my safe haven and filling every day of my life with your infinite wit, laughter, joy, and love.

INTRODUCTION

Denial is the new buzzword. It is what everyone is trying to wrap their head around and make sense of both personally and politically because, really, one is connected to the other. Denial is all around us, more than ever before. We have seen it on the news, in social media, in our daily lives, and even in the White House. It is the subject of our favorite shows on many of our most-watched streaming services. But the truth is, it has always been here; sometimes it is just more visible than other times.

For most people, it has long been a part of their conversations with family and friends as they deal with other people's Denial. When you are up against someone else's Denial, it can be confounding to grasp how they can cling to their beliefs even in the face of the facts that refute them. It can be equally as insurmountable for you to recognize your own Denial. So often it is that stubborn voice of Denial that prevents people from finding a way out of their unhappiness. How many times have my patients sat across from me after their Denial was finally recognized, asking, "how did I miss the signs?" I will help you reach that point, too.

I will show you how to squelch the tendency to let Denial rule your life by answering the important question "AM I LYING TO MYSELF?" Remember when George Costanza famously said to his good friend on the hit sitcom *Seinfeld*, "Jerry, just remember, it's not a lie if you believe it"? Well, I am here to tell you that is not true. So much of what you allow yourself to believe in the name of Denial might very well be a lie. I will guide you toward recognizing that sneaky voice of Denial, which I sometimes refer to as the Houdini of the heart. That voice can perform magic. It can make things disappear in the blink of an eye. It can also convince you that you are seeing what you want to see even when it isn't there, leading you to believe in non-sense, i.e., nonsense, along the way.

Denial makes your life easier in the moment. It even makes it better, the way you would like it to be, the way you wish it was, rather than what it actually may be. From small nuisances like traffic and weather—when you say *I don't believe it*, and ignore the sign that says traffic is backed up on the bridge so you don't have to be inconvenienced going out of your way with an alternate route, or tell yourself *it's not going to rain* despite the weather report because you don't want to be bothered carrying an umbrella all day—to the major league problems like infidelity and addiction, Denial reassures you, tells you not to worry, it's not that bad, it could be worse. But the truth is, without Denial in your life it could all be so much better.

Merriam-Webster.com defines Denial as a statement saying that something is not true or real—in other words, a statement in which someone denies something. The same dictionary's definition in terms of psychology is a condition in which someone will not admit that something sad or painful is true or real. To put it simply, Denial is refusing to acknowledge that an event has occurred. The person who is affected basically acts as if nothing has happened. To take that one step further, Denial is when people seem unable to face reality or admit an obvious truth, which can appear to other people as an outright refusal to acknowledge something has occurred or is currently occurring. Alcoholics and drug addicts often deny that they have a problem. Along the same lines, victims of a traumatic event may deny the event ever took place. That's because Denial is a defense mechanism that everyone has and that functions to protect the ego from things that the individual cannot cope with. While it helps save people from pain and anxiety, it requires a substantial amount of energy to keep up. In many cases, there might be overwhelming evidence that something is true, yet the person will continue to deny its existence or truth because it is too uncomfortable to face. This can run the gamut from someone knowing it to be true but then forgetting it, to never registering it in the first place. By allowing it to happen in any form, though, you are blocking your path to a happier life where you no longer must hide from the truth.

Similar to the famous children's story *The Wizard of Oz*, Denial tells you to ignore that man behind the curtain who is manipulating the truth so you can't see what is real and what isn't. But, like the wizard, Denial is also pretending to have all the power and is a fraud. I will expose it for what it is and help you see there is no great and powerful Oz. Once you understand that, the smart voice in your head will help you make better choices, instead of feeling paralyzed and controlled. It requires work, stamina, and courage to ultimately tune out that voice of Denial and tune into reality. But first you have to recognize it so you can talk back to Denial with clarity and strength. Why is it that so many people are tone deaf to reason, but will listen to that voice of Denial day in and day out? How does Denial succeed in pulling the wool over our eyes? And the most common question of them all: why don't we trust our guts? I will help answer those questions and guide you to a way to recognize Denial and face reality.

So often we find ourselves having to deal with family and friends—be it on holidays, birthdays, special occasions, or during simple visits—and realize we have a completely different set of beliefs from them. Whether they are about religion, politics, or something else, not only can those differences ruin the occasion; they can threaten to compromise the relationship itself. It used to be that whom you voted for or what causes you supported remained private if you wanted them to. But now more than ever it has become everyone's business as simple, everyday choices can make a political statement. I will help you figure out how to navigate these conflicting beliefs, which may be clouded by Denial, so you have more options than just turning your back on the people you look to for support. Can you get them to see where you are coming from and understand your beliefs and what your thinking is, or is it possible to find a way to accept and make room for their beliefs? If so, how do you begin to do that? And if not, then what?

How is it that people ignore what they know? Whether it is that their brother does drugs, or their mother drinks too much, they keep approaching the situation as though that is not an established fact. People ignore the obvious, sweeping things under the rug, to avoid unpleasantness and push away the facts that are staring them in the face. You may face denial from others, when a friend or family member pretends they have not done something wrong, or failed to do what they said they would. Consequently, you spend lots of time and energy banging your head against the wall trying to get them to face reality. It upsets you when they repeatedly vent their troubles, and you always feel compelled to swoop in with advice to improve their situation, doing whatever you can to get them on the path to change. I will help you understand that in this case you are dealing with what is clinically known as the *Stay-Stuck Complainer*. They want only to complain and will reject any suggestions you offer. You will always come away feeling frustrated and overwhelmed. You will learn to recognize this characteristic in other people, and acquire tools to deal with them, ultimately gaining the strength to untangle yourself so you don't let the Denial this person is in continue to weigh you down and keep you stuck, too. You will learn how to "see the light" yourself, rather than continually trying to enlighten the other person, which is as futile as yelling in an empty forest, hoping someone will hear you.

You will learn from the stories of my patients, people I sit across from each week who, like everyone, struggle to face the hard truth about themselves and their lives. I'll show you what typically trips and traps people in their misery, frustration, and disappointment with their relationships. In the same way, I help them finally let the voice of reason in—that voice that says *he is drinking too much* or *he is probably never going to call* or *she is being unfaithful*—the one we don't want to hear but must in order to be honest with ourselves and live a healthier emotional life. I will help you be open to it. I will guide you to finally be able to balance that dominant voice of Denial with a strong voice of reason. I will help you handle the people who upset you so much. I will offer perspective and enable you to see the whole picture. Each chapter will conclude with an important takeaway skill and, in the end, will amount to a session in my office as I analyze and explain what is going on and let you know what you can do to finally be honest with yourself and stop lying. I will hone in on poor but common coping mechanisms and help you find new ones that will serve you better. I will professionally offer the voice of reality to counter Denial's voice because this is what I do every day. With this new knowledge you will be able to wipe out that nasty loud voice of Denial and finally be on your way to an enriching and satisfying emotional life.

Part I will focus on dealing with your own Denial and offer you methods to manage it in all areas of your life. Denial most often shows up in a relationship, be it dating, infidelity, sexual intimacy, or just the nitty-gritty of commitment where all the problem behaviors that can derail people exist. I will show you how Denial runs on a few basic elements, including *Wishing and Hoping*, when you delude yourself with fantasy; *Missing the Signs*, when you give someone the benefit of the doubt while dealing with lying, controlling, manipulating actions and broken promises; *Believing What You Are Told*, when you make the unbelievable believable; and *Turning a Little into a Lot*, where you are so deprived that you are grateful for anything you receive. You will see how the expectations that you have of yourself lead to low self-esteem, excessive guilt, and self-blame when you don't measure up to them.

Part II will look at dealing with Denial in others and give you tools to cope with their disapproval. The differences people have in politics, religion, ethnic values, beliefs, and their personal opinions can divide families and end relationships. This part will look at the demands you experience from family and friends, what is reasonable to attempt to give to them, and how much you are really responsible for. It will evaluate the expectations other people have of you, and the anger and disappointment you experience from them when you don't satisfy their requests. You will see Denial's hand at work when you are subjected to constant criticism and blame that you're the problem, and you buy into it.

After you read this book, you will have the skills to identify Denial when you or someone else is experiencing it, and to uncover your own and others' true motivations and actions. My goal is that in giving you the up-close views, the takeaway skills, and the ability to distinguish Denial's voice you will finally be able to recognize reality and deal with what is making you unhappy head-on, not sideways or backward, or, as is the case with so many people, not at all. There will be nothing left to hide behind. Come on, let's get started.

PART I

CHAPTER ONE

Are You the One for Me?

As Sophie waited for Lou to arrive for their first date, she let herself daydream a little. Maybe she had finally met The One. He was incredibly handsome and had a hugely successful ice cream company known for their whacky and wildly popular flavors, which he founded and ran. She really couldn't think of anything cooler. She laughed to herself as she realized her unintended and corny play on words. Maybe she would even share it with him later. It was true. Everyone in town knew his name; he had been written up in numerous magazines and newspapers. She couldn't believe she was lucky enough to be the one he asked out on a date after they met at a recent fundraiser. She couldn't wait until he arrived. She thought they had said they would meet at 7:00, but at 7:15 she was still waiting. She must have been wrong about the time, she told herself, continuing to sit up straight with just the right smile on her face, which, frankly, was getting tiring. When he walked into the restaurant at 7:20 he was looking at his phone. She kept up her posture and facial expression until he finally saw her and waved, looking down again quickly and running his thumbs over the keyboard before he approached the table.

"Hi!" she said, noticing once again how cute he was. He was wearing a light blue shirt that made his eyes look like a tropical ocean.

"Oh, hey," he said, meeting her eyes and then glancing quickly at his phone before looking up again.

"Busy day?" she asked kindly. She was truly interested.

"Crazy," he said. "One of the machines is down and we planned to do a drop tomorrow so now we might have to postpone. We advertised a peanut-free chocolate combo this week and now we think there might be some cross-contamination, which will really mess up the orders."

"Oh, wow, that sounds hard," Sophie said, finally sitting back a little. "How do you decide which flavors you're going to do each week? Zombie Crunch is my favorite, by the way."

"Well, we—" he began just as his phone rang. He looked at the screen then put a finger up in the air as if to say *hold that thought*. "Hey, I have to take this. I'll be right back."

"Sure," Sophie said, glad to be privy to some of the ice cream secrets. She watched as he stood and walked back toward the front door of the restaurant.

***

Across town, Abigail was also on a first date, but she was not yet seated at a restaurant. Instead, Abigail and Joe were walking around looking for one that had space. She had met Joe on a dating app, and after weeks of texting, he finally suggested they get together for dinner. She accepted his invitation right away. She was very eager to find a nice guy and finally settle into a relationship. They set up a meeting place at a small park not too far from her apartment because she wasn't ready to let him know exactly where she lived. She figured they would find each other and then he would tell her where they were having dinner. She was starving and had let him know during the course of their texting that Italian food was her favorite, so she secretly hoped he had picked up on that and planned accordingly.

He was waiting when she got there. She recognized him immediately from his picture, although, if possible, he was even better looking in person. He had thick blond hair and green eyes. It was hard not to think how cute their kids would be.

"Where to?" she asked pleasantly after they said their hellos.

"I don't know," he said. "I thought we could decide together."

"Oh, okay," she said, ignoring the pang of disappointment she felt. Hey, she told herself, this is a good thing. Maybe he won't be as controlling as the last few guys she dated. "Which direction should we try?"

"Up to you," he said with a shrug.

"Let's try west, there are a lot of good places on Tenth Avenue," she said.

An hour and fifteen minutes later they were still looking.

"Things are busy on a Friday night," she said for the third time after a hostess told them she could seat them at 10:15.

"I'm thinking maybe we should just get coffee," Joe said. "I'm not even really hungry anymore."

"Sure," she said. She could get a pastry or something. She had had a fairly big lunch. Plus, all she really wanted to do was sit down and get to know him. They found a small coffee shop that was quiet. The pastry counter was empty. Oh well, Abigail thought, at least they still have coffee.

* * *

In a suburban town about twenty miles north of the city, Flora and Christian were on their third date. Each date so far had been on a weeknight, and tonight was no exception, even though Flora would love to see Christian on the weekend. So far that hadn't worked out because he had a family commitment the first weekend and a work commitment the next; they hadn't talked about this weekend yet, but Flora was hopeful. Also, he was inconsistent about calling and making plans. For example, he didn't call her for a few days, then he called today to ask her out tonight. Now they were at a bar that was known for its burgers. Up until that moment they had been laughing and having fun. A server walked by and placed two plates in front of the people directly across the bar. The woman picked up the sandwich on her plate, took a bite, and moaned.

"What do you think she's having? Do you think that's the cheeseburger?" Christian asked Flora.

She leaned closer and looked. It didn't look like a burger.

"I think she's having the fish sandwich," Flora concluded. "It was at the top of the menu, locally caught trout or something."

Christian furrowed his brows.

"No way," he said. "Nobody would enjoy a fish sandwich that much. Hey, bartender, what is she having?"

The bartender looked; they all smiled at each other since it wasn't a very big bar.

"It's the fish sandwich," the lady called across the bar. "It is delicious."

Flora expected Christian to say *you're right* or high five her, but instead he had no reaction and turned toward the bar and farther away from her. It reminded her of how last week when they were out, they had a big conversation about the benefits of planting bee-friendly flowers in a yard. He said there was no such thing. She looked it up and showed him, having fun as she loudly read the list of all the plants that might attract bees to your garden. He didn't seem to think it was funny at all, nor did he acknowledge that she was right then either. In fact, he had turned away in a similar manner. Oh well, she thought to herself, maybe she shouldn't be so forceful, even when she is sure she's right.

* * *

Sophie, Abigail, and Flora have a few things in common. The first is that they are all my patients. The next is that they are each looking for a healthy romantic relationship. And while it is immediately clear to me that there are what I call the *Watch-Out Signs* with each of these dating situations that could likely lead to disappointment down the road, the three women want it to work out so much, at least at first, that they are willing to over-look many of them by justifying the guy's behavior, looking to be accommodating on their part, or telling themselves the guys are just quirky or loosey-goosey. If they were more open to the *Watch-Out Signs*, they would know that ultimately these guys were not going to give them what they want and deserve, and they could save themselves a lot of heartache. But they can't yet see that or admit it to themselves. At this point, they have welcomed Denial into their relationships—a third wheel in each of these situations—allowing these otherwise smart women to explain away one questionable behavior after another: being late and not apologizing for it; spending more time on his phone than talking to her; not putting enough or any time into planning a date; never being available on weekends; not being able to admit he is wrong and instead blaming her.

Another thing these women have in common is that soon they will each ask me a similar question that goes something like this: *It's too early to give up, right? I mean, the chemistry is great so I should at least give him a chance, don't you agree? Maybe he had a bad day, maybe he's nervous and shy. How do I know what to look for and when to get out—or even when to start at all?* Whatever words they choose to ask this, whatever reasons they give for sticking with it longer than they probably should, they are still in the thick of it. They are not quite ready to kick Denial out of the equation and see these men for who they really are. But I will show you how they get there, and then how they eventually come to what I view as a good conclusion. Even more importantly, they will begin to recognize the *Watch-Out Signs* more quickly so they can stop wasting so much time and energy on an emotional roller coaster that is not going to get them where they want to go.

Let me pause here to ask if any of these scenarios sound familiar to you. They might, in one way or another, be similar to a beginning or many beginnings of relationships you have had. Should I tell you now that anything resembling these dates probably won't work out? That at the first *Watch-Out Sign* that something is amiss, these women or you should stand up and call it a night? My answer to both those questions is no. There is a chance each issue really does have a plausible explanation, or that he will do better next time. There is the possibility he is under a lot of pressure at work, or that he has a sick family member who took a turn for the worse right before he met you. Also, he could be anxious and wanting to impress you and that, too, can get in the way by making him interrupt or seem to not listen to you. There is also the chance that you can nip the problem in the bud and work it out, that you can voice your concern early on and he will respond in a satisfying way and work to find a solution. But there are ways to decipher whether these are truly character flaws or unfortunate moments. I will help you do that. One question I always ask is, considering everything you know about the person and about your connection to him, if you continue to give this relationship a chance will you be playing with matches that you can blow out if you want to or need to, or will you be playing with dynamite and it will likely end up blowing up in your face?

Let's flash ahead to Sophie's next visit in my office. She has seen Lou for one more date. She tells me about it. It was similar to the first; he was a little late. But she gave him the benefit of the doubt because he is so busy, and in her eyes, so glamorous. She loved hearing about the ice cream; all her friends wait eagerly for the emails each week since they sell out almost immediately, and she feels lucky to have an insider's view. Also, he promised her a tour of the ice cream factory at some point. *I mean, how cool would that be?* She wishes he wouldn't be on his phone so much, but before I have a chance to ask anything she follows it up with: *If I just remain patient, I know it will all fall into place. Clearly he's being pulled in a million different directions; you really can't blame him for being distracted.*

Sophie has been here before. The details were different, but the feelings she is expressing are almost exactly the same. Adam, whom she dated about seven months ago, wanted to see her only in the afternoons, which immediately struck me as a *Watch-Out Sign*. At first, though, Sophie thought it was sweet and romantic. Plus, he always had what seemed like a good reason. They had coffee, high tea, very early pizza dinners. After a few dates they would end their time together by making love back at her apartment or, if they were in another part of the city, sometimes at a fancy hotel, and every time he would have to leave before 6:00 p.m. He told her repeatedly that he planned to see her at night, but he never followed through. Sometimes he would be out of touch for a day or two, but he always came back. Finally, one week, he stopped calling and texting completely.

"I feel just awful," she said at the time. "Like I'm all alone. I really loved him."

"I'm so sorry you feel that way," I said. "But let's give this a little perspective. Did he ever made you feel like you were a priority? Or did he make you feel more like he was fitting you into his life?"

She thought for a minute. She knew the answer, and she was ready to admit it; she was just a little embarrassed that it had taken so long.

"I didn't feel like a priority," she said.

"So really, even when you were together you felt alone because you never knew when the next time would be," I said. "It was an unwelcome mystery."

She was quiet for a minute. Then I heard her take a deep breath.

"Yeah," she finally said. "It was an unwelcome mystery."

This was a breakthrough moment.

A week later he got back in touch with her. He apologized for disappearing and explained that he was going through a divorce but he wanted to keep seeing her the way they had been. Suddenly it all made sense to her. Of course he couldn't spend time with her in the evenings since he was dealing with his marriage—whatever shape it was in. Despite what he said, he was not free to truly pursue a relationship with her. I was proud of her when she told me she said no, she didn't want to keep seeing him. A few weeks later she asked what was wrong with her, why was she the one who never got the guy?

"This wasn't about you," I said. "This was about him. Really, this is his problem—he knows he's unavailable and based the relationship on his terms with no regard for the impact it had on you."

"Yeah, well, it became my problem," she said.

"That's true," I said. "But you don't have to let that happen. And ultimately you didn't let it happen. You said no."

As we continued to dissect her time with Adam, Sophie realized there had been glaring *Watch-Out Signs* that things were not as they should have been, signs that she had missed or that Denial had helped her overlook. Basically, I saw many similarities now with Lou even though the details were different. It was unavailability served up in different varieties with each of them. And Denial was part of the equation each time, helping her explain each bad behavior away, helping her make it all seem okay.

All these guys had something very important in common, and once Sophie and everyone else could recognize it, they would be in a much better place. They were all what I call the Not About You Guy. This is the guy who is narcissistic and thinks only of himself. They are typically thoughtless and never factor in your needs, whether it is about timing, location, frequency of spending time together, or anything else. Because of that, you are often left feeling unimportant, as if you are just an afterthought, or even forgotten about. It might look like they are doing nice things, but in truth they are doing those things only when it is easy and convenient for them and they don't have to go out of their way. Women get fooled by the seemingly generous gestures they make, without realizing they didn't actually have to extend themselves at all.

Understanding this helped Sophie keep her boundaries so she didn't get too involved. With the echo of her relationship with Adam still in her mind, I was confident Sophie was going to see Lou's *Watch-Out Signs* soon and realize that she was with someone who was not emotionally literate, someone who was displaying narcissistic behavior. Whether it was that they are being forgetful, noncommittal, or not interested, the knee-jerk reaction was to think it was about you and that they were behaving this way because you were not good enough. But as I told Sophie, that was all standard when you're with a Not About You Guy—it has absolutely nothing to do with you. That detail is, in fact, the defining factor of their personality. This behavior is their signature statement, and it gives you a look at their true identity and who they really are. The good news is that it's not about you, but the bad news is also that it's not about you, which can sometimes feel even worse in the moment because you don't feel considered, thought about, cared for, or important, all the things you wanted in a relationship.

"When Lou took that call that first night, how long was he away from the table?" I asked, trying to get her to remember that moment and to lead her to see he was focused only on what he needed and not at all on her.

"He came back about fifteen minutes later," she said.

"Fifteen minutes?" I emphasized. "That's a long time to sit alone on a first date after you have barely even said hello. Was that okay for you?"

"I think so," Sophie said.

"And when he got back, was he all in?" I asked. "Did he stop looking at his phone?"

"No," she said. "But he was clear about having a work crisis. I mean, he could have canceled the date altogether, but he didn't, so he must have really wanted to see me."

Instead of arguing with her, I shared an example of a loud-and-clear message a newly single friend of mine had recently with a Not About You Guy. I set it up by explaining that before Simone went out with him, she asked me what to look for to determine whether it was worth moving on to a second date.

I told her, if he helps himself to your food be wary, because it illustrates that he has no boundaries and is comfortable helping himself to what's yours. That can be a problem—more so, if he does that and doesn't offer you a taste of his food; it is a double whammy because it indicates he has no intention of reciprocating. In other words, what is hers is his and what is his is his. He is not looking to share. Let me tell you, her mouth fell open when they were on their date and he reached across the table and took a forkful of her pasta, and then he didn't give her any of his. And yet, she moved right on by; basically, she asked me, heard it, witnessed it, and knew it, but she ignored it—it is really the perfect snapshot of Denial. She told me how nice she thought it was that he felt so comfortable with her, that they didn't have to stand on formal practices. A few weeks later things got worse. He told her he wanted her to walk his dogs even though she had an important appointment at the same time. She canceled her appointment and took his dogs out. When she came back and told me she was walking the dogs I said, really? He's been living in the city six years; surely he's had arrangements for a dog walker. Why did he ask her? She passed right over the first *Watch-Out Sign* and their relationship continued in exactly that vein. He pulled on her to take care of him but gave nothing back.

It turned into what seemed like a never-ending list of things he wanted her to do, and he never gave what she hoped for any thought at all. There were other *Watch-Out Signs*, too. He didn't listen and relate to the stories she told; instead he matched them. If she told a story about a summer vacation as a child, he didn't even acknowledge it, he simply waited until she was finished talking and told his own story with no connection at all to what she had shared with him. She never felt heard or related to, and frankly it felt empty. When she was finally able to see it, she realized that he had told her exactly who he was and how he was going to behave at that first lunch. Basically, he had clearly spelled out that he was going to take but not give. He was a Not About

You Guy, and when you were with someone like that everything you shared was about the other person's needs and what they wanted. You became a piece they moved around in their life to fit in when it worked for them.

"I can see that Adam was a Not About You Guy," Sophie said. "But do you really think Lou is, too? I mean, he's busy and distracted but it all seems reasonable. Everything he does and says could be true. Maybe he really wants a girlfriend, but nobody hangs around because of all these things. I wouldn't want to do that to him."

Ah, Denial.

"I just want you to start to pay attention," I said. "Sometimes it's easy to be swept away by the possibility of what might be, as well as what can be superficial romantic gestures, like his offering to take you on a tour of the factory. The question really is, does he seem interested in you and in getting to know you better?"

"There really hasn't been much time," she said.

"I don't doubt that he likes you," I said, trying again. "The question is, how much is he able and willing to give to you? Will he ever choose you over a work crisis? How long are you going to wait for it to turn into more than it might ever be in his eyes?"

"I don't know," she said honestly. "How can I figure that out?"

"The best way to figure it out is to use the skill I call *READ THE SMALL PRINT*—*it can be hazardous to your emotional health* if you don't. This means you have to know there is information right in front of you that looks small and insignificant but is really incredibly significant. When it comes to dating, the logistics—the where and when you are going to meet and dine—are quite important, but a lot of the time women don't realize that. They don't know how to interpret them. They know there is something there and they don't know what it is, and they aren't looking closely enough to see what it means. That's because these little details pale in comparison to the fact that he is so handsome, or he is a successful stockbroker, or he has his own business. They are so blinded by these characteristics, and the fact that he wants to spend time with them, that they overlook any and all *Watch-Out Signs*. So, paying attention to the little behaviors that are so telling of his personality and how he is going to interact with you in an ongoing relationship will make a huge difference in how long you are going to remain stuck. How often is he on his phone? Is he late to meet you? Does he repeatedly leave you alone at the table to deal with a work crisis? Did he put any effort into planning your date? It can be so easy to make excuses for him or sweep those things under the rug, thinking he means well or he'll be different next week, but it can just leave you in limbo and keep you hooked on and living for the fantasy of what you want him to be, as opposed to who he really is."

"But he seems so appealing," Sophie said, not defensively but firmly. "And impressive."

"If you're happy with this being it, his showing up but being distracted and having to take calls when you're together, being ignored by him, sitting at the table alone for periods of time while he steps away, then okay, that's perfectly fine. I mean that. What is going to be hard for you is if you're always wishing for more, always feeling like you're settling for now with the hope things will change. That could end up being frustrating for you."

"For now that might be enough," Sophie said.

"Okay, but if I can leave you with one thought it is to pay attention to his actions and the way they make you feel, because that's the small print that will turn into the big picture eventually."

"Deal," she said.

That is always easier said than done. Abigail was having similar issues in her new relationship. She came to see me after her second date with Joe. We had already talked about her first date. This time they agreed to meet at a restaurant near his apartment and when she got there it was closed. She stood outside the locked door and googled it, finding out it is always closed on Tuesdays. He arrived ten minutes later.

"It's closed?" he asked as he approached her.

"Yeah," she said, not wanting to sound annoyed even though once again she was hungry and eager to eat.

"So, we ended up walking around again for about twenty minutes," she told me. "Not nearly as long as last time."

"Do you think he could have checked to make sure the restaurant was open before planning to meet you there?" I asked her.

"It's so easy to forget to do that," she said, excusing it away. "I forget all the time. Plus, he held my hand the whole time we were walking. It was really nice."

I shared the same skill I had shared with Sophie, to *READ THE SMALL PRINT*, to really pay attention to the *Watch-Out Signs* he is giving her. For example, is it possible, I asked her, that his failure to plan ahead or even call to make sure a place is open reflects his level of interest? She doubted it, but she agreed she would try to be open to noticing details like that.

Now, let's take a look at how Flora and Christian are doing. Their scenario is a little different because it has gone on for a while longer than the other two. Flora wanted it to work out so much she was willing to put up with much more than she should have. There is something to be said for people showing you who they are right away, and really, Christian did that. He kept asking her questions, starting debates, egging her on, and then not being happy when she was right. Sometimes he was correct, and she didn't mind, she acknowledged it and praised him. But every single time she was right, about silly things like how many miles ten big city blocks equaled or whether there were direct flights from New York to the Bahamas, he would shut down and turn away. Other times, though, he was so nice. He even said he knew her birthday was coming up in a month and he wanted to plan something special, although he didn't offer any details. She hadn't had a boyfriend on her birthday since high school, which was a long time ago, so she really liked that idea.

There were a few times, too, when she didn't hear from him and she couldn't reach him. When she finally did, he said he was busy at work and that he would call her later that day. When he didn't call by six, she texted, saying she knew he was working so hard and she would like to bring over dinner. He thanked her immediately but said no, he didn't have the time. When he was still working on the same project two days later, she offered to bring him breakfast—she loved that idea, it was sort of romantic and he had mentioned he loved croissants—but again, he said no, he didn't have time. When she told me about this it was clear to me that he didn't want her to come to his place, that he was putting up an invisible fence to keep her off his property and out of his heart, so to speak.

Still, he always came back and reached out, and she was eager enough to move on and say yes, she would see him again. They would have a great time, and then get into another silly debate and things would go downhill. When that happened, he always pitted his judgment against her and told her she didn't know what she was talking about. A few times he even said to her, "How does it feel to always be wrong?" It became a pattern.

"Hold on a second," I said at our next session after she told me about one of their interactions that ended this way. "Do you think it's okay for Christian to treat you that way? To tell you that you're wrong even when you know you aren't?"

"I mean, no," she said. "But it's just one part of a bigger picture. The thing is, and this is going to sound strange since things have been moving along and we are seeing each other at least once a week, sometimes more, but here's the thing: I don't really feel any closer to him than I did after our first date. Do you know what I mean?"

I told her I thought I did, but I wanted to make sure she was ready to unpack this a little, so I asked her to explain exactly what she meant.

"You know," she said, sitting back, then scooching forward again. Clearly, she was restless. "I just feel that despite the time we've spent together since our first date I don't even know that much more about him."

I nodded. I have heard this so many times in different ways in my office. Two people meet, they seem to hit it off, and many of my patients jump ahead in their mind and heart to what they think is the ultimate goal: commitment, the perfect house with the white picket fence, spending the rest of their lives together. Remember how Sophie let herself daydream about what could be before she even spent any time with Lou? And how Abigail immediately thought she and Joe would have cute kids together? In other words, they think in those very early days that they may have found their soulmate. Sometimes it really does happen that way. But more often than not it goes along for a few dates, or weeks, or even months, and all the while, despite the reality of what is happening in front of them, they keep *Wishing and Hoping*, deluding themselves with fantasy. This is one of the striking elements of Denial, and happens when people keep imagining the good that they want the relationship to be, instead of recognizing the reality of what it really is. With Denial by their side, they truly believe it will all turn out in their favor.

At some point my patient comes in and says exactly what Flora said, that she doesn't know him any better than she did after their first few hours together, that something is missing, although they are not sure what. Another thing my patients talk about in these scenarios is not feeling connected to them, or, at least, like they are not connected to my patient. Even after this moment of questioning, it can still take them a while to get to the point where they actually begin to face the fact that this guy might not be who they think he is or, more importantly, who they want him to be. It takes time before they begin to *READ THE SMALL PRINT*.

"It looks like he could have all the goods, right?" I said. "He is handsome, spends time with you, he's interesting, he knows your birthday is coming up."

She nodded as I said all of this.

"He appears to have this full backpack," I say. It's an image that I think a lot of people can relate to. "What I want you to think about is, how full is it? Does each thing hold up when you scrutinize it?"

"I think so," Flora said slowly. "I mean, we always get past those weird moments. Oh, and he did mention spending my birthday with me again. And the sex is really good."

There she went again, convincing herself he was as great as she wanted him to be. The thing about so many of these guys is that they look great on paper, they check all the boxes—they are handsome, they have great jobs—but when you hold them up to the light, they are paper thin.

The image of the backpack stuck with Flora. Was it full or was it not so full? What was even really in there? And she finally began to pay attention and *READ THE SMALL PRINT*. The next time they had a disagreement over a silly bet they made, she knew she was right but he insisted she wasn't. For a split second she thought that if they simply stopped disputing information, things would be okay. And then she realized how unrealistic that thought was, and how he was, in fact, showing her that he couldn't stand to be wrong, and he would never give her the satisfaction of being right. For the first time she doubted if this was going to work.

Flora shared all of this with me the next time we spoke.

"Good for you," I said.

"And that backpack?" she said. "I'm starting to wonder if it's empty. If he might actually not have any of the goods it takes for what I want."

"Okay let's be clear, what is it that you want?"

What she wanted was a guy who made her feel good about herself, made her feel understood, made her feel she mattered by following through on plans and not canceling them.

"Okay, you have your backpack," I said. "Make sure you hold onto it."

I encouraged Flora to look out for herself by addressing the relationship. Very often, women want to avoid speaking to what is going on for fear that by confronting it, it is going to scare the guy off, so they avoid it. But the truth is that checking things out can put you in control, because you move from being in the dark and anxiety ridden to at least having understanding and becoming enlightened. This can all be done with a simple question that does not have to be antagonistic at all. You just simply say, "I'm curious, do you see us becoming more involved with each other?" Another way to put it is "have you thought about spending more time together?"

The next time we talked, Flora told me she finally asked Christian where he saw their relationship going.

"And?"

"Not good," she said.

She relayed the conversation to me.

"You just don't seem to be as interested or committed as I thought you were at first," she said to him. "You don't even seem to really want to get to know me better. What are you hoping for here?"

"My bad," he said casually. "Actually, I wasn't looking for a relationship really, more of a situationship."

"A what?" Flora asked, having never heard the term before.

"You know," he said. "Like I like to see you sometimes and all, but I don't want to, you know, feel like I have to or like we owe each other anything."

"Oh," she said. She had never heard of that. She rolled the word around in her head, situationship, which sounded a lot like relationship but clearly wasn't. In fact, it seemed to her, it might be the exact opposite of what she wanted with Christian.

"Have you heard that term?" she asked me. "Situationship?"

"Unfortunately, I have," I said. It had come up a lot recently in my reading and in my talking to patients.

"What does it mean to you?" she asked.

"It is something I call the *Not About You Relationship*, which all begins with the Not About You Guy. It's like taking all the left-over food out of the fridge, throwing it into a stew, and presenting it as a meal when it's really just a bunch of all the things you were going to throw away. Basically, it has no originality or backbone, nothing to hold it up. There is often no consistency and no con-text since sometimes the dates are sporadic, the connection never gains momentum. There is often a lack of commitment or any accountability, so you can't count on them to 'be there' in any way or be held responsible for anything. As a result, when they let you down, you are left to deal with your disappointment by yourself."

I continued by telling her that in my opinion when you are in a situationship you are on a sinking ship, and you are going to go down in it. It can be a recipe for anxiety.

"They hook you and keep you hopeful by trying to make you feel you are special to them because they offer to spend your birthday with you, or plan a visit, or take you to your favorite restaurant, but it never actualizes," I said. "Another *Watch-Out Sign* that this is what is going on is if he keeps you at a distance from his own life. In other words, he doesn't introduce you to his family and friends. You are not welcome in his world. It is like a one-lane highway; there is no expansion and broadening of lanes whereby your life and his life come together. It is a constant state of uncertainty as to when you might see each other again or even if you might see each other again. The time in between texting can be four hours or four days."

Still, many people are willing to stay in a *Not About You Relationship* with the hope that things will get better, or that the relationship will continue to grow even if it has appeared to slow down or stop progressing. That's because Denial prevents them from seeing it is not about them, so they think they can still make it work. I tell my patients to shift their focus from what he's bringing to the party to, instead, how they are feeling. Are they feeling angry, sad, blamed, unappreciated, unloved, uncared for, or devalued? And then, with that in mind, to think about why they would want to continue to feel that way. I asked Flora to consider this.

"Can you take a pulse on how you're feeling?" I asked her.

"Constantly up in the air," she said. "Like I can't even look forward to seeing him the next time because he is so unpredictable."

"Is that how you want things to continue to be?" I asked.

Flora hesitated.

"I like him," she said. "He's prickly, sure, but he's handsome and, as I've mentioned, he's really good in bed. But I'm starting to wonder. The thing is, every time I think of ending things I feel like I have wasted so much time."

"Not nearly as much as you could, though, if you keep going," I said. "And next time, if there is a next time like this and hopefully there won't be, you'll try to make wiser and healthier choices even sooner. You won't let Denial take you for that up-and-down roller coaster ride again."

At our next session Flora told me she had ended things with Christian. It was hard, like pulling off a Band-Aid, but she did it.

"I *READ THE SMALL PRINT*, finally," she said.

"What exactly did you see?" I asked.

"That he was shallow, that he didn't care at all about what I had to say, that all his overtures to make me feel special, like spending my birthday with me, were just lip service to keep me hopeful, that he always had to be right at my expense."

"I think you're correct about all of that," I said. "Well, you are definitely seeing him for who he really is."

"I just don't get it," she said. "Why do these guys bother to make a connection if they don't really want one?"

"He does want something, companionship," I said. "To date somebody familiar, to have someone to have sex with when he wants to, but what he was clearly telling you was that he never wanted anything more."

Flora got so good at paying attention to the small details that when she met Mike, who seemed amazing at first, but then began to cancel dates, she became suspicious. They finally had a plan to get together, but Flora got a migraine a few hours before. The original plan was that he would pick her up at 7:00. She texted saying she would still like to see him, but staying in and watching a movie at her place would be better, and could he please bring some Tylenol? She wore cute but cozy clothes and waited. It got later and later and there was no word, no arrival. That time she just shook her head and happily crawled into bed alone. He texted the next day, apologizing and offering an excuse that his phone had been acting up, but she had already had enough. She texted back to say it wasn't going to work out, that she was no longer interested.

When I saw her the following week she said, "I *READ THE SMALL PRINT*, faster this time."

"I'm so glad," I said. "What did the Small Print tell you?"

"That he didn't really care about me, that it didn't matter that I was in pain and feeling bad, that he was not dependable and I couldn't count on him for any support." By being able to see the Small Print, my patients can see the big headline that ultimately it is not going to be what they want it to be and is *hazardous to their emotional health.*

"Good for you," I said. "It's a pretty big headline, isn't it?"

"What is it about me?" she asked. "Why do so many men end up disappointing me? Do I have 'mislead me' written on a piece of paper pinned to my back?"

"No, you were misled because you didn't see them for who they are—Not About You Guys," I said. "Now you will spot them more quickly."

"I hope so," she said.

Without Denial by her side Flora was not willing to put up with any questionable behavior and no longer missed the signs. She took each personal explanation as a statement about how each guy would likely behave in a relationship. When Sam told her before they even met in person that he would never get a pet because it was a seven-year commitment, she saw the *Watch-Out Sign* and didn't bother to set up a first date. When Jonah ignored her suggestions for restaurants on two dates, that was it and she let him go, too. When Isaac seemed put off by her knowledge of the business world and made condescending remarks to her, instead of making excuses for him or giving him another chance, she ended the first date early. None of these men was going to be the man she wanted him to be, no matter how many tries she gave him. She could see now that it had almost been as if she were a passenger in an out-of-control car with Adam, Christian, and the few who came after until she began to put her own foot on the brake. She had been letting them take her for an unpleasant ride and was not exercising any control because she wanted the relationship to work so much. Sophie and Abigail reached the same conclusion, too, and are now each able to *READ THE SMALL PRINT* before things progress too far.

In my experience, a *Not About You Relationship* never turns into one that is about you, and a situationship never becomes more than that. They each might have the appearance of promise but no substance at all. However, if you don't pay attention or get out before you spend too much time being unhappy and unsettled, if you continue to ignore that man behind the curtain, the *Not About You Relationship* can turn into the *Going Nowhere Relationship*, which can be even more draining and disappointing. We'll talk about it in the next chapter. Come on, let's take a look.

CHAPTER TWO

You Need Your Space; I Should Be More Understanding

SUSAN AND RALPH MET AT A PARTY. SHE WAS MORE THAN READY to have a steady boyfriend after years of bad dates and many situationships. She noticed him sitting quietly across the room, not awkwardly, just quietly. He looked approachable. He appeared to be nice and, there was no denying it, he was good-looking. But she had been through it so many times before, talking to someone at a party, hooking up that night, and never seeing him again. She didn't know if she could go through that another time.

She decided she would refill her drink, and if he was still sitting there when she got back, she would approach him. One month later, Susan and Ralph were just where she hoped they would be in her dreams, seeing each other almost every day, talking on the phone constantly, sneaking away for lunch together whenever possible. They had barely had a fight. She couldn't believe it. *See?* She told herself. *All it takes is finding the right person and then all the craziness and negative energy melts away.* She finally started to trust that this would be different. If things kept going this way, she couldn't imagine what might prevent them from going all the way and getting married. She stopped playing even the most subtle games and threw herself in full force. She called when she wanted to, said whatever came into her mind. The other day she even talked about her desire to have children.

During this period, Ralph introduced her to his friends. There was no question that Susan was pretty, and he knew it. His pals all told him how lucky he was. She loved being invited into his circle and his world, and she started to feel really important. She didn't notice yet that he was never able to make time to meet her friends. On a rainy night almost five weeks after they met, something shifts. Ralph doesn't call after work the way he said he would. That isn't such a big deal, she tells herself, maybe he got caught up in a meeting. She waits about thirty minutes and calls him. No answer. A little strange—this has never happened before—but anything is possible. Maybe he got stuck on the subway. Maybe he's out with friends. She doesn't consider that he could be sitting on the couch, looking at his phone and deciding not to answer her. Unfortunately, Denial, which has been lurking in the wings for a little while now, recognizes an opportunity and takes it. I hate to say it, but I have seen it many times with my patients. Susan didn't notice any *Watch-Out Signs* for the first month they were together, so she let down her guard and thought she was out of the woods. Now what might have been considered *Watch-Out Signs* as a relationship began or in a situationship have turned into *Hazard Lights* as Susan and Ralph get more involved. The problem is, despite her history with one previous bad relationship after another, she isn't seeing them.

Denial allows Susan to explain it all away, her doubt, her nagging feeling. It helps her forget that this feels an awful lot like when things started to go downhill with her last relationship. She decides to wait to open the bottle of the wine, even though she really wants it now, because surely he'll call soon or come over, any minute now. Here is what Denial is making her think: *He'll call, of course he will. There couldn't possibly be anything really wrong. Things have been so great between us. I'll take a shower and get ready. I'm sure he'll come through. He always has before.*

But the night goes on; there is no call and he doesn't answer her calls or her texts. As she goes to bed that night alone, Denial settles onto the pillow beside her head. She is so afraid that this will be the turning point when things are no longer great, which she has encountered repeatedly in her other relationships so it is more familiar than she would like to admit, that she refuses to even consider it as a possibility. In fact, she can't bear the thought of that. So, she lets Denial in—she welcomes it in, really. As she finally drifts off to sleep, she thinks: *Tomorrow will be different. Tomorrow he will explain what happened with a perfectly logical reason. Tomorrow everything will be okay again.* Tomorrow, tomorrow, tomorrow.

And the next morning he does call.

"Hello?" she answers, trying to sound cool but unable to keep the eagerness out of her voice.

"Babe, I am so sorry," he says. "I got totally caught up at work. My boss—not Sid—the other one—the real boss—was in from San Fran. I literally could not get to my phone. I promise, I'll make it up to you. He's flying out tonight around eight. What do you say to dinner at Amore? We can share a whole fish."

Susan hesitates, for a second, maybe not even a second, a tenth of a second. Denial is right there beside her, erasing all her uncertainty.

"Sure," she says, softening. "Should I meet you there?"

"I'm counting the hours," he says.

Okay, she thinks, *that's a relief*, which is really her Denial talking. *Nothing is actually wrong. His real boss was in town. Everyone can have an off night. Even I could. Tonight, we'll go to our restaurant. We'll share the fish like we always do, and everything will be fine.* She is accepting his explanation even though there are so many reasons not to. She doesn't let herself think about the fact that sharing the whole fish is less expensive than buying two entrees. Instead, she buys his romantic notion of it. Otherwise, she might wonder if he is hesitant to invest any more money in

27

their relationship now than he has to. But Denial doesn't let her see that; it allows her to miss all the *Hazard Lights* so she doesn't question any of it. Really, she makes it easy because that is the last thing she wants to realize. With Denial's help, she carries the thought *He is so romantic* with her, and that's how she gets through her day, how she gives him another chance.

In Ralph's defense, it doesn't happen again for a while, giving Susan enough time to really settle back in and stop being afraid the other shoe will drop. But it does. Eventually, Ralph has to go on a business trip for a week. He explains that he won't be able to call while he is away—something about roaming charges and being in constant meetings from dawn to dusk. Hmmm, she thinks.

"Can't I call you?" she asks. She is at work, he is at the airport. While she waits for him to answer she hears a boarding announcement being made.

"No, babe," he says. "It's better if you don't. They really want us to unplug and be 100 percent present. If this goes well, I'll get those bonus days off and we can plan something great. Maybe a weekend in Vermont."

"Come on," she isn't exactly whining but there is a higher pitch to her voice now. "Please? A week is a long time."

"I don't think I'm even going to have my phone turned on," he says.

"What if I call you really early in the morning? Before you're even awake?" she asks. "That won't count as taking you away from your workday."

"Like I said, babe, I really want to be focused," he says. "It'll be worth it for both of us in the end. Just think about that weekend I mentioned. That's what's going to get me through. Don't you know by now I'd rather be with you than working? Trust me on that."

The words *trust me on that* sound funny in her ears for the briefest moment. Again, she feels a slight nagging, but before she even realizes it, Denial is back. And you know what she does? She *Believes What She Is Told.*

"A weekend in Vermont would be really nice," she says, smiling to herself. She has to be more understanding, she tells herself. She doesn't want to seem needy. "I totally understand. Try to take a few breaks for yourself, though, and don't get dehydrated."

"Thanks, babe," he says. "The plane is boarding. I better go."

"I'll miss you," she says, but he has already hung up.

When he gets back, he wants to see her right away. She is thrilled and makes herself completely available. They see each other most nights that first week. The second week things slow down a tiny, almost imperceptible, bit. He stops calling twice a day and now calls only once. When he starts to call later in the day, she can barely stand it sometimes and ends up calling him before he has a chance. There is one night he says he has to work late, and she shows up uninvited to surprise him with a picnic dinner—fried chicken and homemade coleslaw. She thinks she notices him look irritated for a second when he sees her get off the elevator before he smiles, just a split second. *No*, she tells herself. *I was imagining that. Of course he's glad to see me.*

After that he starts to call even later in the day, not until he is about to leave the office. He never calls her first thing in the morning anymore. They have a few more weeks together but he keeps making their dates later and shorter, and he cancels plans more frequently. What is going on? She wants to know. Nothing, he assures her. I'm just overwhelmed at work. One night he doesn't even ask if she wants to have dinner. He tells her he has a meeting and can come by after, but only for an hour or so. She doesn't like it, but she tells herself *it will all work out, she just has to be patient; at least he wants to see me so much he is willing to come by for the one hour he has free tonight!* She has now reached the stage where she is doing what I call *Turning a Little into a Lot.* That happens when you look only at what you receive from the person but not at what you don't get. So instead of feeling deprived, you

are just grateful for anything they give you. This is a major component of Denial, and one of the ways it frequently tricks you. With
Denial's help Susan sees Ralph as caring. She has become so used
to coming up empty more often than not, that any time she does
get to spend with him feels positive.

As she explained all this to me in my office, I could see the
bubble starting to dissolve and I knew their relationship wouldn't
last; it was going to evaporate soon. Each reason he gave made
sense and was conceivable, but it was also upsetting. What she
couldn't see is that there were too many excuses, changes in plan,
and disappointments. If there are lots of big chunks of time
missing—excuses around having to work or helping a family
member—things that are difficult to refute, it is a *Hazard Light*
that should be considered. Ralph was too often missing in action,
promising her future time together, and she was in that pattern of
accepting much less under the illusion that it would pay off in the
long run. If this happens once or twice, fine, that's reasonable over
the course of a months-long courtship. But piled one on top of the
other they were clearly building up to something. It was no longer
a single happening; it was THE happening. She couldn't see the
big picture. This had now turned into his statement that he is not
going to be there for her. While she had moved away from the
Not About You Guys, it was clear to me that she had moved into
what I think of as a *Going Nowhere Relationship*. She could spend
weeks or even months—for some it can be years—driving down
this same road of fewer calls and plans coupled with big promises,
but it is going to lead her to a dead end. It is never going to be the
relationship she hopes for.

Susan refuses to see it, though, even when I suggest she start
to look at the bigger picture. *No*, she tells me, *it is just a busy time
for him*. And then one night he tells her he wants to take a break.
That dreaded break. Nothing serious, he says, just a big project
coming up. It has nothing to do with her, he swears. She can't help

wondering, though, does it have something to do with her? Had she said or done something to turn him away?

And once again Denial sneaks into view from stage right, and with that Susan accepts that Ralph meant what he said. *If it had to do with her, he would have said so.* She starts to wonder, *hadn't she been pretty needy lately? Of course, he needed his space. If she gave it to him, if she believed what he said, if she wasn't such an annoying, demanding girlfriend, she would be rewarded. He would love her.* This is where she starts to feel guilty that she isn't being supportive or caring enough. *She thinks she should be more accepting. If only she could be, he would see how trusting and, most importantly, how independent she was because she could handle the space, just the kind of woman he would want to marry since she is so understanding.* When he finally calls again and is ready to see her, even though she had been lonely and couldn't help but dissect their last few times together to try to remember if anything happened to make him need his space, she takes his call.

"Babe, how are you?" he says, like he's been out of touch for a few days, not almost an entire month. "Things are slowing down. I'm finally feeling some relief at the office. Do you want to meet tonight for dinner?"

"Sure," she says hesitantly, she wants to see him, that isn't the issue. *He had said he wanted a break, after all, not to break up. Now that break was over. Why shouldn't she see him?*

"Listen, I'm really sorry, I was overwhelmed with this project," he says like he means it. "I was in a real funk."

What is missing in his tone and in his words is any expression of emotion or disappointment in not seeing her for all this time. There is no mention of missing her, or of their time apart being a mistake or at the very least something he is rethinking. There is no discussion about what may have changed for him that makes him want to see her again now. All she is getting here are basic, impersonal explanations and excuses. But she takes what she can get.

"That's okay," she says, because Denial is right there, holding her hand, helping her explain away all the *Hazard Lights*. "We all get into funks. I'm glad you're feeling better."

This is the perfect instance of another striking element of Denial, which is *Believing What You Are Told*, making the unbelievable believable. Susan's expectations of herself are that she should be tolerant, understanding, and patient; her self-esteem is based on it. Because of that, she goes along with what Ralph tells her because it fits into the caring image she has of herself, as opposed to pushing back, questioning him, and possibly appearing to be combative, which would lead her to feel guilty and also to self-blame if things didn't work out between them. Consequently, she allows herself to remain in the dark.

The whole "he or she needs their space" scenario plays out in my office almost every day and Denial is almost always the culprit. It might seem to make things better for an instant in the moment, because who wants to deal with sadness or rejection? But the fact is Denial makes everything worse and prolongs the problems. If we could just clear the scrim a little, move Denial back into the wings, we can see what is really going on here. In any relationship you will inevitably have to deal with the question of space, and it will have to be negotiated to some extent. Sometimes it's hard to know what is reasonable to expect and ask for on both sides—the side who wants to spend as much time together as possible and the side who is jockeying for some time alone. I have talked about this before, and I often think of it as the *Me Versus We* time. What is the right balance and how do you avoid the slippery slope of too much or too little? There are no real guidelines and therefore one push either way can sometimes set someone off. Ralph did want to be with Susan; he was drawn to her the minute he saw her at that party. He loved hanging out with her, having sex with her. But then things took a turn as they have always done when Ralph got too close to someone.

Based on the information she shared with me about Ralph's previous dating patterns, it appeared to me that he has intimacy issues. He is thirty-eight and he's never been married. He allows himself to get close until the relationship starts to feel serious and then that's it, that's all he can stand. When they have reached the point when the other person clearly believes she is having an exclusive relationship with him that is going to lead to love and marriage, thoughts he actually encouraged at times along the way because a part of him always hopes this time will be different, that's when the monkey wrench is thrown into the works. To further complicate the matter, it isn't always just the one person who is dealing with intimacy issues. Often both are grappling with them one way or another, which contributes to the complicated recipe of being involved and committed. While it appears that one person is more willing and wanting to be close and intimate than the other person who pulls away, in fact they are each wrestling with their own trepidation of being really close to somebody. Even the person who presents as wanting to be more intimate often has their own concerns about being deeply connected to someone, and that's why they continue to pick unavailable people. Somewhere deep down, Susan knows that if Ralph married her, if anybody married her really, she would have to deal with her fear of losing her independence, as well as being responsible for taking care of someone else. Additionally, she would have difficulty because then she's afraid she would have to give up the things she does now, such as take care of her parents, see her friends, go for long runs alone on the weekend.

Often this tug of war with intimacy begins when people experience disappointments early in life because of one circumstance or another—a divorce, an unreliable or absent parent—and they adapt and learn to change their expectations in order to attempt to protect themselves from being let down again. The challenge is that every child wants to love their mother and father no matter how badly they behave, and they want to feel loved by that parent.

They will shift and adjust accordingly to achieve that. In doing so they lower the bar on what to expect and what makes them feel loved because getting anything, sometimes even negative attention, is better than getting nothing. The reason these women go for men who clearly want space is that they are continuing to try to connect in the same way they struggled to as children. That connection, however tenuous, was what defined their self-esteem—and it still does. They had to work hard to obtain the love they desired from their parents, and that continues to be their modus operandi as an adult. It almost seems that if they don't work hard it doesn't feel like love because they don't recognize it. If they can just secure the attention of a distant partner, it will make them feel better about themselves. People are always looking to get what they didn't have and feel they missed out on in the past.

Take, for example, Susan's fear of intimacy, which stemmed not just from the knowledge that she would have to make permanent space for him in her life—which means also being accountable and making changes to accommodate him—but from the fact that she didn't trust that he would really care about her. I see this often with my patients. They worry about being so deeply connected to someone that the possibility of that person's not holding up their end of the bargain can be terrifying, and often not worth taking the chance to let it play out. They wonder, will he or she take care of me? Will they be there for me?

Consequently, when somebody disappoints them, as Ralph has done repeatedly to Susan, even though it is hurtful, it actually makes them feel strong because they can handle it. Since they have experienced it so often, they are not surprised, and have even come to expect it. It is a familiar pattern. It's the *Turning a Little into a Lot* element of Denial at work again. *He didn't call at all last week, at least he called yesterday!* Or *he might not have helped at all when I was sick, but he texted me today!* The most basic gestures seem like a huge deal because their partners give so little overall. People are afraid to give up what they have with the hope of finding a more present or giving partner because in their world it might be more than they ever got before—it is pretty good.

So, understanding that—even if you think you are ready for a more committed relationship—can help as you move forward and make decisions about what you will and won't accept from your partner. Your own anxiety, fears, and past experiences have all taken a toll on your self-esteem and might be getting in the way of seeing things clearly. Denial is all over this scenario, causing Susan to continue to explain the *Hazard Lights* away while letting Ralph try once again to enter a serious relationship. It is a snow job. Once things really look solid, and they both get snowed in for better or worse, it is almost impossible to get out without emotional damage and pain.

Most people can't see this coming. It's hard to see when you're in the middle of it. Everyone wants, or thinks they want, it to work out "this time." They think it will be different with this person. Acknowledging the complications would be like admitting defeat, so they tell themselves things they don't necessarily believe—*not this time, this time it is going to work out.* In this way, people are more willing to deceive themselves, and are therefore more ready to accept the dishonesty of others.

Until you can become truthful and stop believing your own lies, you are likely to continue to encounter people who will lie to you, deceive you, and betray you. That's because in order to maintain the untruths you tell yourself, you tolerate hurtful, devaluing behavior from others that makes you feel bad about yourself. In order to raise your self-esteem, you need to shut the door on Denial so you can feel better about yourself and the way people treat you. You have to raise your expectations and hold people to a higher standard, so it is no longer okay to cancel plans, leave you waiting, and not call you. To do that you have to be honest with yourself and face the fact that their behavior really is a problem and is unacceptable, and then be willing to confront it.

Of course, this is much easier said than done, and can take longer than either partner would hope to reach the inevitable end of their relationship. It takes a lot to face the facts, and where they each start and what they each hope for often has a lot to do with how long it takes to run its course. Susan came to this relationship wanting to settle down, but, in reality, Ralph didn't. On paper he wants to get married and have kids, but that's as far as it goes. His life is completely structured around remaining single. If he were willing to do anything that would take him out of his comfort zone—going to her neighborhood, meeting her friends and family, or not always putting work first—then this whole package would start to look different. But that was not the case with Susan and Ralph. There were *Hazard Lights* everywhere, but she wasn't even slowing down. Even without that wanting to have a family comment, he was inevitably going to start to pull away and create more and more space between them. He was not going to marry her, or anyone, for a long time. He isn't going to get married for six years, in fact, to another woman. But before any of that is known, they are both going to plow ahead, hoping and ducking and generally disappointing each other. Even with all these clear obstacles they are not ready to give up. They are still invested in believing that this is a *Going Somewhere Relationship*.

At our next therapy session, I set the groundwork for the important skill I wanted Susan to embrace—I call it *DO THE EMOTIONAL MATH*. I did this by helping her focus on the *Hazard Lights* that were right in front of her, add them up, and avoid the prolonged heartbreak that was facing her. The big picture was there—he was thirty-eight years old, never married, successful in business, traveled a lot, was generally unwilling to come to see her. He was living his life, tailoring it to his own creature comforts, unwilling to extend himself unless it was convenient for him. The nights he met her on time it just so happened that his meeting ended early and it worked for him; there was no extra effort involved. Otherwise, he would have run two hours late like he did the night before. But when it did go well, when he was there to meet her, she took it as a sign that he really wanted to be there, that he had moved mountains to be there for her.

All of this feeds into what happens next. Susan and Ralph do go out to dinner. He takes her to a new place—although he doesn't tell her he discovered it during their "time out"—and they have a lovely meal. Once again, they settle into a pretty regular pattern of spending time together, and once again Susan relaxes and stops worrying. But the *Hazard Lights* are there. The problem is, she can't see the light. He is often distracted by his phone when they are together. A few times he cancels a date just before they are supposed to meet, blaming work. And one night he mentions that a job has come up in Pittsburgh, which, of course, is about six hours from New York, but she doesn't think anything of it. *He is so settled here; he isn't going to pick up and move.* She even kids him, you would never leave me, and he smiles. He waits until after her birthday to tell her. He has taken the new job. It was too good an offer. They will still see each other, of course they will, it is barely a six-hour drive! Every weekend, one of them will make the trip. She'll see, it will be great. And really, it is all about their future, isn't it? If he gets a better job now it will serve them both later. Talk about making space for himself!

Susan has a moment of panic, maybe a few days of panic. But he keeps telling her the same things, and with Denial's help she starts to buy it. *It won't be so bad. We'll talk every morning and every night, not to mention we can text all the time and Facetime as well. We'll always say goodnight to each other. In fact, things will be even better than they have been because every moment together will be special.* She agrees to continue the relationship long distance. Did she really even think of it as a choice? Once he leaves, she thinks about him all the time and wants to dissect every word they spoke to each other. She is always obsessed with when they will talk next; she can never relax. She tries to find answers without really facing the facts. Is he worth waiting for? Can I really expect him to move back here to live with me at some point? How serious is he about me? When he first moves away, she learns he is casually dating other people. He promises her it is no big deal, just a way to meet people in his new city—he is looking for friends more than dates really—so she thinks *maybe if I date other people too it will make me feel better, put us on an equal playing field*. Denial helps her deal with her insecurity that he will replace her by instead making her wholeheartedly believe that nobody is better than she is, that she is irreplaceable, and therefore he will always choose her over someone else.

Denial moves slowly onto the stage and works his way back into her thoughts, helping her continue to go down that path for a while. She convinces herself that this will just bring them closer because as they meet and casually date others, they are going to see how much they want to be together—that they will find there will be nobody better than each other. Plus, of course, she wants him to be happy. *If he's happy, she's happy, right?*

In my office the next week she tells me all this. I listen and then without my prompting she asks, "How long should I wait for him?" It is the opportunity I was hoping for, and I know the previous adding up of the *Hazard Lights* has helped to get her here. She is on the brink of being able to untangle herself from Denial, recognize the *Going Nowhere Relationship* for what it is, and let go. She is finally ready to *DO THE EMOTIONAL MATH*—in other words, write down all the facts, add them up, and integrate them with the options she has and the actions she will decide to take.

As I have done before, I encourage her to look at the facts, really consider them. We begin to add it up together. He moved to another city, away from her, after they had been dating for months. He is not talking about making any changes now or in the near future. He has never said he wants to come back to live in New York. He has been dating other people. He doesn't call or visit as often as he once did. And through it all he has never shared any feelings of yearning for her, sadness, or disappointment at not being able to see her. And, for the record, she has yet to consider why she has agreed to continue to date someone so far away. For the first time she allows herself to think about what she could lose if they moved in together or got married. She was so focused on thinking that was all she wanted that it took until now for her to really imagine it. It isn't that she doesn't want to be close to Ralph, she understands that; it is that she's also dealing with her own fears about what would happen if she does get what she has long believed is her end game. Would she lose herself completely if the relationship becomes even more serious? Would she be the one who would ultimately have to move and give up her life and her world? "Oh my gosh," she says with wide eyes, "is that why I accepted this as a long-distance relationship?" I want her to answer that question for herself, but I do point out that it's funny how having space can make you feel independent, but in reality it really hides your needs and keeps you more dependent because you remain hooked on trying to achieve the togetherness that seems so unattainable. It can complicate things and make it hard to see the clear picture.

For a long time, Denial says *it's all okay. So-and-so would never lie. What's-his-name means what he says. It will all work out.* People give their partner space and it becomes so wide there's soon room to put another relationship in it. The fight for space comes in a million different colors and excuses—from having to train for a marathon or care for a sick parent to taking care of their kids and everything in between. They are steadfast in how they have to spend the weekend time with their kids, but suddenly you realize they don't have their kids every weekend, or they have a night away from them but still don't make plans with you.

The whole caring-for-a-sick-family-member routine always makes me wonder. It is not impossible that someone is doing just that, but I have found in my years of offering therapy that this excuse often comes up when space becomes an issue and it turns out to be just that, an excuse, and it is a very common one at that.

The person in crisis is looking to provoke sympathy, patience, and understanding so you don't hassle them about breaking plans and not being able to spend time with you. How could you put demands on them and make them feel guilty for having to take care of their grandmother, their kids, their sick mother, whoever it is? When that happens, they are turning the guilt around on you, trying to make you feel bad about expecting anything from them or putting pressure on them when they are dealing with a difficult situation. Sometimes they might even look to coerce you into helping out and involve you in taking on some of the caretaking, whether it is bringing a meal to their mother or walking their dog, to help make their life continue to run smoothly. Instead of rightly feeling put upon, like *why am I the one taking care of his mother?* Denial changes it into *aren't you lucky that he wants you to do this? That he is including you in this private part of his life? How could you refuse to help? How could you be so uncaring?* With Denial in your head, it can seem like a good thing. You tell yourself, *He needs me! See how important I am? And he is bringing me into his family!* What you aren't seeing is that he has dumped the burden of responsibility into your lap.

Another *Hazard Light* that alerts me that someone is carving out their space is when they refuse to see their partner on the weekend, any weekend. There can be all sorts of reasons, work commitments, family responsibilities. But usually it is an indication of lack of commitment, seeing someone else, or cheating on a spouse, and with Denial by your side you will have a hard time determining what is real and what is not. When you look to spend ongoing time with your partner to have a consistent connection, he generalizes it and blows it up as if you are asking to be with him all the time, every day. I can't spend 365 days a year with you! he says. What he is really saying is that no matter how much time you want to spend with him it is just too much. You are asking too much of him. Denial will help you see that *of course he's right, what are you thinking? See how needy you are?* But, in fact, what you are asking of him is very reasonable. It's called involvement; it is not neediness. You are asking to be involved, which is exactly what he is trying to avoid with your help. He is looking for you to cooperate and go along with his thinking, and to stop asking so much because he just can't give you what you want.

I encourage my patients to stop letting the person off the hook for their bad behavior, such as making them feel they are asking for too much, or not calling, or canceling dates, as Susan did when Ralph called after their month apart and continued to do throughout their long-distance relationship. She said *it was okay, she understood, everyone gets into a funk now and then, everyone gets busy and distracted.* By reassuring him that it was okay, she was reassuring herself. If she called him on it and admitted to herself that it was not okay, then she would be really calling it a problem and that can be scary.

This is where the skill *DO THE EMOTIONAL MATH* can help you make sense of it all. In column one you're going to make a list numbering each excuse and reason that you've been told to justify his behavior. Next to that write down how it has made you feel, about him and about yourself. For example, if he said his mother is sick and why can't you help him with something you might write sad for him and guilty about yourself. You've heard people say go with your head, not with your heart, right? In order to get there, you've got to move past your heart. Emotion and Denial blind you to the facts and cause you to move forward with your heart and your feelings. Using your head allows you to make decisions and choices based on knowledge. On paper, almost all the excuses make sense—I have to work late, I was sick, my dad is in the hospital, I can't turn down this great, better-paying job. They make less sense, however, when you put them all together and see what they equal. If, for example, your longtime boyfriend has never spent a Saturday night with you but often promises he will, the timing just hasn't been right and each specific reason seemed legitimate enough, chances are he never will so stop pretending he might. It's time to start to question the things you're being told.

To do that, it's vital to look at the amount of time you are together and how often you get together, versus the amount of time you would like to spend with him. In other words, how does the literal frequency of your shared time compare to the quantity of the time spent longing to be with him? Do you actually see each other one in every two times you initiate plans? Or one in three? One in four? Why spend time waiting for something that is probably never going to happen? If your girlfriend cancels every other date you have, even though she has good reasons, you can pretty much stop counting on that alternate date to ever happen. If you are finally able to stop making his or her nonsense sensible, you will be in a far better place.

You do this with column two, which is where you start to question what you've been told by listing all the facts as you know them to be. By doing this you see the whole picture as opposed to each single instance that alone seems understandable. Really look at the quality of your connection; is it all by text or phone even if that isn't how you want to do it? His side—what he tells you— always ends up being the minus column and always comes out a loss. Your side—what you know, your truth—is the plus column. If you add up all the statements with the whole picture you will always come out on top. This will give you the strength and the courage to make choices for yourself so you can feel free to put boundaries in place to look out for your own needs and stop getting lost in his. As I said before, when you stop lying to yourself, you stop tolerating and accepting bad behavior from others, and that changes everything.

After I add up the facts here, my emotional math problem equals zero for Denial and a perfect score for me. When I am in my office, my usual working method is quite different from Denial's. While Denial flat-out tells people what to think and say, my professional hope and way of working is that with my guidance my patients will come to their own realizations when they are ready. My job is to help them get to that point where they can take a clear stand on their own behalf, which I then support. My objective is for each person to reach their own healthy conclusions after reflecting on our therapeutic work together. Now that she has done her emotional math, she is ready to hear my voice of reason. Watch as I help Susan overpower Denial's voice, kick it offstage and steal the mic once and for all.

Susan had convinced herself that she was finally over Ralph. With Denial there she believed that she rarely thought of him anymore. The truth was, she thought about him all the time! After months of no contact, he called her and told her he was going to be in town and suggested they meet. *Why not? Maybe things will be different this time. Maybe he's grown up.* Old habits die hard.

Susan comes into my office seriously considering getting together with him again. As she flounders on the brink of longing, I remind her of her emotional math equation and I ask her, "Has he indicated that anything has changed? Did he say he feels bad about what happened? Did he say he wants to get back together with you? That he has made a mistake?" He made it seem like the visit would be starting over, but there is nothing to support that. For Ralph, it is just a matter of picking up where he left off and continuing in the same old way. With an already tried and proven escape hatch in place, he has nothing to lose; he only wants some company when he is in town. She uses her emotional math equation and this time he is now the one who ends up with zero, not Susan. She is able to grasp this reality, and finally say no to him. Sorry Denial, this time you are out of luck.

I have been talking about Denial in action to help you cope with when you are experiencing too much empty space in your relationship. Now let's look at how Denial can be just as effective when dealing with the opposite—no space at all.

Chapter Three

Your Love Is Smothering Me

Joe resisted the urge to look at his Apple Watch as it lit up on his wrist, even though the pull was strong. He tried to stay in the moment with the client as he presented his plans for the living room of a huge beach house he had been hired to design. He had saved the best for last and was just unrolling his drawings onto the large conference room table in front of him when the first text came through. He felt it and saw it out of the corner of his eyes, thinking he could speed this up and get back to Ellen before she freaked out—at least he hoped he could.

"And here is the place you will be spending all your time," he said proudly, but his voice wavered ever so much. He really felt the clock was ticking now. He wanted to get on with it. He cleared his throat, trying to will away the sudden dryness he felt. "You'll notice the kitchen moves right into the large room; they are separate, but also quite connected and—"

This was his big moment. He had rehearsed it in the car on the way into the office. But just as he said the word *connected*, another text came in and he knew it was also from Ellen. This one said URGENT. Damn. Their seven-year-old daughter Sydney had been sick this morning with a slight fever and she had stayed home from school. But it didn't seem like anything more than a stuffy nose and a low-grade fever. He hoped that hadn't changed.

Whatever it was though, he knew Ellen would say Sydney was the priority above all else, and, of course, she wasn't wrong. Still, it seemed he could barely get through a meeting, any meeting, these days without a text from Ellen. This internal dialogue played out for just a little too long. He sensed the client was looking at him, as was his boss. He tried to shake it off. All he needed were five uninterrupted minutes to finish the presentation. He took a deep breath.

"And," he said, trying to act like he had simply paused for dramatic effect. "As you walk up the stairs, notice the rounded walls here, and the shape of the two decks just beyond the floor-to-ceiling windows, so as you enter the room you—"

Another text. This one read 911. He had to respond.

"You feel like you are on a ship," he said quickly, to get it over with, not at all how he had planned to say it. "I am so sorry, will you please excuse me for a quick moment?"

The client nodded; his boss looked confused. He walked out of the conference room and stopped as soon as he was around the corner and out of sight to call his wife.

"It's about time," she said instead of hello.

"I'm in the meeting," he said, not combatively, he knew better, just so she would understand he didn't have much time. "How's Syd?"

"Cranky," Ellen said, which told Joe right away that her medical condition had not worsened. "We need more of her Advil; we're all out of the liquid and you know she'll take only the liquid. She needs Gatorade or Pedialyte, something like that. Maybe ginger ale, some crackers. We're out of dog food. When are you coming home? It's chaos here. I need you."

Joe realized she was giving him a shopping list. He shut his eyes for a second. He wanted to scream. Ellen was the one who wanted him to take on more projects and now she was pulling him away from the important work and getting in the way of his success to give him an itemized list. It was always something with her. Just this morning she told him she hoped he would take on even more projects. She was thinking they should see about becoming members of the country club near their house. She said everyone was joining, and she didn't want to feel like they were the only ones who couldn't. Plus, she said, it would make Syd's summer.

"How would we look if we don't do it? Or worse, if we can't do it?" she asked him seriously as he was gathering his things for the meeting today. "And what would that do to Sydney's social life? All the other kids belong."

Ellen had followed him around as he was trying to get out the door, saying there was some sort of meet-and-greet next week that they were invited to. She wanted to make sure they could afford it. More than that, she had said, the club checked their financial records so she hoped that would look impressive. When she said this, she looked at him pointedly, like he was 100 percent responsible for their financial good standing, and really, he was. She said she didn't know how much of that information leaked even though of course it was supposed to be kept confidential. She wanted to look good in the neighbors' eyes.

"I hope you're getting more work," she had said, not in the nicest tone. "I heard Brian is earning in the high six figures. You aren't even close."

Her comment came through loud and clear. He wasn't successful enough. He had to do more. But how was he going to take on additional work when she wasn't letting him do the work he already had? And, for a fleeting moment, he wondered why she had to burden him with all of that just before such an important meeting. Couldn't it have waited until later?

Now, as he stood in the corporate-feeling hallway with his phone to his ear and his big client waiting for him to return, he heard the beginning notes of Sydney's cries through the phone and he scolded himself. All the thoughts leading up to that moment weren't wrong, mind you, but now Denial had entered the room. *What is wrong with me?* Joe thought to himself. *My daughter is sick and my wife is taking care of her. What could be more important? She is just doing what is best for Syd and for our home, not to mention the dog. Of course she needs my help.*

The plan had been to finish the presentation and then go out to dinner with the client. Obviously, that wasn't possible now.

"Let me finish up quickly," Joe said. "I'll be home within the hour."

"Fine," Ellen said, like it wasn't quite adequate. Like he was still letting her down somehow, not holding up his end of the bargain.

"Maybe sooner," he added.

"Sooner would be better," Ellen said.

He rushed back into the conference room where the client and his boss were waiting.

"I'm so sorry," he said. "My daughter is sick and I'm needed at home. I'm excited to finish the presentation, but I'm going to have to reschedule dinner."

"I understand," the client said kindly. "I have three daughters."

But the enthusiasm was no longer there, for any of them. Joe finished, the whole time worrying that Ellen was getting more and more angry with every minute that passed before he got home, or worse, that she would text again. And what would that text say? What is more urgent than 911? By the time he said goodbye to his client he felt completely defeated and nervous about what awaited him. He also felt guilty, like he was failing Ellen and, by proxy, failing Sydney somehow by not having the magical power to be in two places at the same time. It felt like a package deal: if he disappointed Ellen then he also disappointed Sydney, and that was just too much to take.

When Joe came in to talk to me the following week, he said he felt that he was letting his family down—clearly Ellen wasn't satisfied, really with anything, it seemed, and he believed it was his fault. I expected that; it is a typical response to this sort of behavior, and it had been a running theme for Joe. But before I had a chance to say too much about that, he said something interesting that made me think for the first time he was moving toward a new point of awareness about what was really going on in his marriage. He was finally in touch with and shared how anxious and burdened he was always feeling.

"Like I am going to be called out at any time," he said. "The texts never stop, they are like rain, falling like drops from the sky one after the other, piercing me on the head, and I can never relax into whatever I'm doing because it's likely I will be interrupted. If it isn't a text about Syd, it's about the roof, or about a leak in the garage, or about important plans we have to make or cancel if the people we are going to see suddenly become problematic in Ellen's eyes. Or it has to do with this stupid application to the country club."

Here was his Denial in play.

"The thing is, each text is important, I mean, it makes sense that Ellen needs my input for these things," he said.

The awareness that had burned so bright at the beginning of what he told me was now fading quickly as he moved toward sharing his Denial with me. And it didn't stop there.

"Really, I shouldn't complain," he said. *"She is just trying to take care of us, to make our life good. She just wants to be the best mother she can be."*

And with those three sentences he wiped out her demands, the constant bombardment of her interrupting whatever he was doing with texts, her relentless devaluing of his work and any success he achieved, his perpetual feeling that whatever he does will never be good enough to meet her approval, and most importantly, no matter how much he does, it will ever be sufficient. A window had opened briefly as he initially voiced his frustration, and then, with Denial's help, it firmly closed again. He is *Missing the Signs* completely, one of Denial's elemental tricks, which happens when you give someone the benefit of the doubt while dealing with lying, controlling, manipulating actions and broken promises. He is giving her the benefit of the doubt and believing that she really has his best interests at heart. This also feeds into his self-esteem because he blames himself for questioning the motives for her exorbitant expectations of him. In other words, he tells himself he should be able to do what she asks of him, that she is not asking for too much.

"Well," I said, to help him reopen that window and begin to confront his Denial, "actually, you can complain. If you are anxious and overloaded all the time because of the never-ending demands that you face, that is a real problem."

"You know, it's always been like this, but it never felt so awful before," he said. "I never realized how intense it was."

"With this in mind, how have you stood it for so long?" I asked.

"You know, she has these incredible moments of normalcy, and it seduces me right back in, until the next time," he said.

I have seen this so many times in my office, I can't even count—a relationship or marriage that develops in such a way that someone ends up having absolutely no space and doesn't feel they can breathe, ever truly relax, or let their guard down. Whether it is texts or calls or arguments, there is always a sense of urgency that must be addressed immediately. So, whenever a fight starts—on your way to bed or as you head out to dinner with friends—your partner wants to continue the argument until it is resolved. If that means staying up all night to talk it out, even if you have an important meeting early the next morning, or being late to meet friends, whatever it is that you have to shift to appease them, doesn't matter in their eyes because their needs always take precedence. Whatever your partner demands leaves you feeling guilty when you don't do what they ask, or do it fast enough. My patients who are on the receiving end of it become fearful that they are going to lose their partner's approval and love and they will do just about anything to prevent that from happening, because it is essential to their self-esteem. With that in mind, they welcome Denial in to help them explain it all away so they don't have to confront what is really going on in their life. Denial allows them to avoid facing their unhappiness.

And, as Joe said, it usually doesn't always feel that way. More often than not, it seems that connecting with this person is the best thing in the world. They are a whirlwind of love and attention, and they can make you feel, at least at first, that you are at the center of the universe. In Joe's case, when they first met, Ellen gave him her undivided focus, which was so different from what he had grown up with. His mother had ignored him, so Ellen's constant warm concern felt like exactly what he was looking for in a partner. Also, Ellen talked about how important it was to her to be a mother, and that really hit home. This type of intense love can be a slippery slope, though, because, on the one hand, it can make you feel special and needed, and, on the other hand, it can also suck you in and eventually drag you down. Ellen wanted to go to every party, introduce him to everyone she knew. They were in college at the time, so it was hard to distinguish the intense socializing as a *Watch-Out Sign* of any sort. Ellen was truly the life of the party, and man, he always said, it was great to be with the life of the party. Everyone wanted to talk to them; they were invited to more events than they could go to.

When you first begin a relationship with someone like this, as the famous song from *Grease* goes, they appear to be "Hopelessly Devoted to You." In reality, though, what that illusion of devotion is going to translate to is the expectation that you become unconditionally devoted to them. Despite the excitement and what seemed like very welcome attention to Joe, there were some *Watch-Out Signs* along the way. One time they went out to lunch and Ellen didn't order anything. Joe asked a few times if she was certain she didn't want any food, and she assured him she was. He was starving, so he happily ordered a hamburger and fries. As soon as it arrived, while he was working the ketchup out of the bottle, she reached over and grabbed the burger, taking huge bite after huge bite. Basically, she helped herself to what was clearly his without asking or apologizing. He was surprised, but Denial helped him explain it away. *I guess she was hungry after all*, he thought. *I'm glad at least she ate something.* A few months later they were at a diner. He was with a friend and ordered a roast beef sandwich. When she arrived to join them, she took the roast beef sandwich out of his hand and told the server to bring him a turkey sandwich instead. His friend shot him a questioning look, while Denial took a seat next to him at the counter and helped him once again turn the objectional behavior into good. He thought, *wow, she must really want me to be healthy since she made a better choice for me. She is so nurturing*, instead of seeing it as the controlling move it really was. Another time Ellen didn't like the shoes he was wearing, so she insisted he buy another pair on the way to their dinner. It all felt exhilarating as they swept into the store arm in arm, like they were the stars of a romantic comedy. He got caught up in it all. In the end, though, he should have seen it as the *Watch-Out Sign* it was: she knew best, his choices were always wrong. With Denial by his side, he saw only the good— that she was so wise—rather than the message that his judgment was so bad.

Not every relationship that moves in this direction starts out that exact way, but they all have something in common—the other person makes them feel all-important and special. Sometimes someone might want to teach you something they know, or they want to go everywhere with you. When this happens, whatever form it takes, your self-esteem skyrockets because you are the center of their world and that feels good. But eventually they want you to spend all your time with them, or all your time doing something for them. This is where they turn that hopeless devotion around on you, shifting the focus from you to them. And here is where it gets tricky. They want you to give up the parts of your life that don't include them. As you do that, you lose yourself without realizing it, because you are trying to please them and you want to be with them, so you start to slowly surrender the things that are important to you. For Joe that surrender happened slowly and surely. With all the work he has taken on to please Ellen, he has literally no time to participate in the weekend baseball league he used to love, not to mention his long-gone Tuesday night bowling club. He doesn't even have a chance to go for a quick run during the weekend anymore because Ellen says she is with Sydney all week long and needs some time to herself. He hasn't been to the monthly cousin get-together he used to enjoy in about a year. He is rarely home during the week, so Ellen makes most of the immediate decisions surrounding Sydney. More often than not, Sydney is asleep by the time he leaves work, so sometimes he goes days without actually seeing her awake. He hasn't seen his friends in months. *Who cares?* Denial says. And Joe agrees. *Really, he is glad to do it if it will keep Ellen from being unhappy and getting upset with him.*

Of course, in any relationship there must be some give and take, which often involves compromise, but what I am describing here is something very different from that. This is what I call a *Lose Yourself Relationship*, in which you become absorbed into the other person's life, their needs become more important than your needs, and your own life and all the activities and details that make it up slowly slip away. This is really the polar opposite of the *Going Nowhere Relationship* I talked about in the last chapter. You are going from having too much space there, to having no space at all here. In some cases that can be literal. In fact, Joe has noticed lately that when he walks out onto the porch to have a sip of coffee, Ellen will follow him and talk about whatever demand she has at the moment. When he takes the dog for a walk, hoping for a few peaceful minutes, she will call with one of her famous lists or to voice her disappointment in something he did or didn't do.

Despite all of this, Joe was not ready to face any concrete possibility of a *Hazard Light*. Instead, he let Denial continue to sidle up to him and help him explain it away, as he would do for the next few months. In this case he told himself, *Ellen is a terrific mother; she is looking out for our child. Ellen is right to need some time to herself, she gives Sydney everything she has, she practically bleeds for that kid. Is it really such a bad thing that she wants us to have friends? Or that she encourages me to work hard and be successful? If it weren't for her, I never would have tried for the beach house project.* With Denial there, he believes it all. For as long as he can.

One day about two months later, Joe came into my office. He didn't look good. He was pale and his eyes looked puffy. He was quiet and told me right away he had considered canceling our session.

"Are you sick?" I asked.

"I thought I was," he said. "I thought I was having a heart attack over the weekend. My heart was going crazy. I couldn't catch my breath. I was sweating a lot. Ellen was busy in the yard with Sydney, so I drove myself to the ER."

"That's dangerous," I said, surprised that Ellen would let him do that and didn't take his health crisis seriously. "If you had passed out or worse during the drive it would have been terrible. I'm glad you made it."

"Well, Ellen didn't think there was anything wrong," he said. "In the end, they said they thought I was having a panic attack. So, I guess she was right."

"Wait a minute," I said. "I don't think this is about being right or wrong. You had a medical emergency. Thank goodness it wasn't anything more. But you can't write off the fact that you had a panic attack that was so bad you had to go to the emergency room. Supposing it really was a heart attack? Her complete dismissal of your physical well-being, and her choice to stay with Sydney instead of putting Sydney in the car and going to the hospital with you is really upsetting."

"Well, yeah, it was, but when I found out it was just a panic attack I started to think I could be stronger, and driving myself to the hospital really wasn't a big deal because it turned out to be nothing in the end anyway," he said.

Good old Denial.

"This reminds me of when you were younger and your mother didn't take your appendicitis seriously," I said to him, referring to one of his major childhood traumas. "It is almost as if you have to be at death's door for you to be taken care of properly. Having your wife go to the hospital with you or show you concern should not be dependent on whether it is life threatening or not. She should have been there for you. Telling yourself Ellen was right is what you had to do as a kid to make sense of your mother's neglect, and you're doing it again. But this is not okay."

Joe gained insight from my input, which was helpful for him to understand how his past experience was impacting his current behavior. But his foot was still on the gas of Denial because Ellen was pushing to go on a fancy vacation soon, and he was right back in the position of trying to do what she wanted and worrying that once again he wasn't going to be good enough to have the money necessary.

"I'm afraid we won't be able to go on that vacation," he confessed. "I took on a whole new project. I asked for a fair amount of money and I got it, they said okay and I was so relieved. When I told Ellen, would you believe she said that it wasn't sufficient, which was just what I was afraid would happen, even though it was so much? She told me to march back in and ask for more."

"Did you?" I asked.

"What choice did I have?" he asked. "I might be a good architect, but I'm a bad businessperson, at least that's what Ellen always tells me, which is why I didn't ask for what the work was worth according to her. I thought I had, hell, I asked for more than I had ever asked for before. But actually with the hotel she has in mind for this trip she is probably right."

"Joe," I said. "Can you hear yourself? Once again, she is devaluing your worth and you are going along with it. The fact that you asked for and received a lot more money than you ever expected is a tremendous statement about how valuable you really are to your company. And rather than feeling good about that you're letting Ellen's negativity once again make you feel like you are the one who's wrong instead of holding on to what you know. She is devaluing you once again and you are accepting it."

He reflected on that and seemed to take it in, and then went on to tell me about what had happened that morning.

"I was taking a shower, and in the middle of it she walked in and opened the door and started talking to me. It was without any warning like in a horror movie," he said.

"What did she tell you was the reason for doing that?" I prompted.

"She wanted to know what time I was coming home for dinner. My shower was ruined, obviously," he said. "I'm standing there, interrupted from my relaxation, and having to answer to her about my schedule. I mean, am I crazy?"

"No, the bathroom is a place for people to have privacy and space to themselves. In fact, it's supposed to be one's personal space. Not only are you not crazy; it is really good that you are recognizing how intrusive that behavior is and how violated you felt."

He was steamed up, not from the shower, but from Ellen's disrespect of his privacy. It translated into his feeling that there was no place that he could go that she didn't think he should be available to her. His instinct was to do everything she asked to please her and keep the peace. But it was getting harder and harder. He had given up everything—his family, his friends, his activities, his time, even his shower had been hijacked—to achieve this high-status life for which he felt that he had to be on a constant treadmill to maintain.

He looked at me and took a deep breath.

"I never thought I would say this, but I feel completely lost in my marriage," he said slowly. "I have no voice, no say. How did I let this happen? How has it gotten to this point? I have no time to breathe, no time for myself at all."

I told him he is not alone. Often people get drawn into relationships with people who seem like the most loving and giving people in the world, and slowly it becomes clear that they are creating a life that suits them, but they have no real consideration for their partner. When this occurs, many people are afraid to speak up for fear that their partner will react in anger and threaten them with abandonment by leaving, so they decide they would rather be in a tough relationship than risk being in no relationship at all.

I shared the important skill *HOLD ON TIGHT* with Joe, through which I encouraged him to recognize the things that are essential to his identity and make him who he is. That can be different for everyone. With Joe, that involved spending time with the people he loves beyond his wife and daughter, and taking some time each week to play baseball and go bowling. For others it might be lunch with a friend, talking to their mother on the phone, playing softball or soccer, doing yoga—whatever it is that makes each person a complete and fulfilled individual. Once Joe is able to do that, he can make better choices that will help him preserve these activities and keep doing them in order to hang onto himself and not feel so lost.

"But she'll never let me do that," he said. "She will never agree to letting me play baseball on Saturday mornings when I can be working or spending time with Syd so she can have time alone."

"She doesn't have to agree," I said. "You are going to have to claim it back. She is causing much guilt in you, and you need to recognize that for what it is. You are not ever going to get Ellen's approval or permission to even just take a short, peaceful shower, not to mention anything else. Her expectation is for you to be unconditionally available all the time, twenty-four hours a day, seven days a week, every minute of the day, and in many cases, you can't even do what she wants fast enough. It is literally impossible to keep up with that. Only you can give yourself the permission to slow down and take the time you need. You aren't being reckless or uncaring, you are just taking the few minutes necessary to finish talking to a client or wash the shampoo out of your hair."

In implementing the *HOLD ON TIGHT* skill, the first thing we talked about was carving out some private time for himself which he called Desk Time. He would come home from work and, after saying hello, either before or after dinner, would take half an hour to himself to decompress. The next thing I suggested was that when Ellen bombards him with a demand or a command, to let her know he plans to do it, but not right away. In other words, lead with a yes, I will do it, and then qualify when—in ten minutes, tomorrow morning, sometime over the weekend.

"Give yourself some breathing space so you are not twisting yourself into knots to be at her beck and call," I said. "For now, until we work on your putting boundaries in place, you can start with one by saying the boss is no longer allowing phones in meetings because it is too disruptive. I understand her anger frightens you, so it is easy to be driven by the desire to do anything you can to avoid her outbursts. I've seen patients go to extremes to shut down their partner's temper, losing themselves in the process. But it is about more than just taking back some of what you've lost. It would help to recognize that the expectations you have of yourself to do everything for her, and immediately when she asks, are unrealistic. As a result, you feel guilty, but it is excessive. Try to handle this feeling by appreciating that her demands are unreasonable, so you can stop trying to accommodate her every whim. We will work on your putting parameters in place for yourself. You want to be able to push through your remorse so that you can begin to give yourself approval instead of only finding self-worth in Ellen's opinion of you, given how negative and critical she is. This way you can stop blaming yourself, and you can get back on a better road of determining what is right for you. Give yourself permission to breathe, rather than letting her run your life."

He promised me he would think about it and said he would report back next week.

I had another patient at the time who was dealing with something similar, but it played out in a different way. Joan met Brent on a dating app more than a year before. They had both been looking for a while, and when they met it seemed like they were each relieved to have found each other—they were both so happy that their search was over. They told each other it was meant to be. Brent wanted to introduce Joan to his family after a week together. With Denial by her side, she didn't see this as any sort of *Watch-Out Sign*, but instead told herself *I'm so excited! Most of the other men I've dated never wanted me to meet their families so this seems really great*, albeit a little early. She loved them right away—his three brothers, his parents, his aunt and uncle, and all the cousins. Soon, they spent every weekend with some combination of Brent's family, and a few weeknights. Joan was an only child and her parents lived two states away, so she welcomed the warm embrace of Brent's big family. Before she knew it, they were taking vacations together. Brent's family had money, so they planned one great getaway after another.

She realized, though, that months were going by, and they barely spent any time alone. They had never been away on their own. When she suggested they take a trip to Vermont—just the two of them—Brent scoffed at the idea.

"Why should we pay for a trip when my parents are happy to?" he asked. "Just tell my mom you want to go to Vermont, and she'll plan it."

Of course, that wasn't the point. And, more than not sharing time alone with Brent, she also hadn't seen her own parents in a long time. When she suggested they take a drive one Saturday to see them, Brent made an excuse about an annual family picnic he didn't want to miss. She knew she had thrown the idea of seeing her parents at him out of nowhere, so she let it go and happily went to the picnic. When she asked a month later, he said it was his aunt and uncle's anniversary dinner, which she was strongly encouraged to attend. Before she knew it, a year had gone by, and she hadn't seen her parents. She also hadn't talked to her friends much.

One sunny day in June, Brent proposed. Joan accepted right away. She couldn't believe it; she was finally going to settle down. When she began to talk about a big wedding, Brent said he preferred a small ceremony at City Hall. And he didn't want to wait. She didn't want to disappoint him, so two weeks later, with his mother and his aunt by their sides, they tied the knot. She didn't even tell her parents until after it was over; she knew they would push for her to do it in another way.

Things were great for a while, until she noticed Brent seemed to be paying strangely close attention to their joint back account. He was always aware of everything she took out and spent. Since he made a lot more money than she did, she felt guilty about that. One day, he asked about a twenty-dollar withdrawal, even though Brent spent a tremendous amount of money on weights and other workout equipment, and he had memberships at three gyms that offered different classes and a pool. Basically, he was indulging himself and spending as much money as he liked for the things he cared about, but if she got a pedicure or wanted to go out to lunch, he got angry. Brent made Joan feel guilty about getting any of the things she wanted for herself. She was so intimidated she stopped trying to make herself happy, while Brent joined a fifth gym, this one with a boxing ring. She wondered if and how this arrangement might be fair, but she didn't question it. Instead, Denial stepped in and helped her explain it all away. Denial said *well of course it is okay, it's his income, he can get anything he wants.*

"Is this working for you?" I asked at one of our sessions after she told me about that. "Is this okay with you?"

At first she said yes, it was, that she felt lucky. She told me she was happy to be married to Brent, that they were thinking about trying for a baby, and she loved his family. But one day she came in and I could tell she was upset.

"What's been going on?" I asked her when she sat down and didn't begin to talk as she usually did.

"It's my dad's birthday next week," she said.

"Oh, happy birthday to your dad," I said. "Is that a bad thing?"

"Well, I told Brent I wanted to go, that I wanted both of us to go, and he said no, just a flat-out no, no excuse, no big family gathering that would get in the way, he just said he didn't feel like it," she said. I could tell she was trying not to cry. "I missed his birthday last year, which was okay since Brent had some big family event or other, but to miss it again, I just don't know what I've gotten myself into."

"Well, why can't you go without him?" I went on to ask her, "And the bigger question is, has visiting your parents stopped being important to you?"

"No," she said surprised. "Not at all."

"Then we need to talk about what you can do so you hold on to something really important to you."

"How?" she asked. "How can I do that? I was excited to go together, to finally introduce my parents to Brent. Can you believe they still haven't met him? But then I realized this is the longest I have ever gone without seeing them—so I did tell Brent that I was going to go with or without him."

I nodded, that seemed like a step in the right direction.

She stopped talking and now there was no question that she was losing the crying battle as her mouth pulled down at the corners and the tears started to flow.

"What did he say?" I prompted.

"He said he didn't think I should spend the money to go," she said. I waited. "He said he would prefer I didn't."

For some, the control their partners exercise over them is so fierce that it borders on emotional abuse. Really, the only things missing here that distinguished it as basic control versus abuse are the absence of verbal and devaluing insults, belittling, and hits to her self-esteem.

I nodded again. She wasn't my only patient who had gone from what seemed to be an intensely loving situation where her partner loved her so much it felt just shy of smothering, to saying something controlling like this. And now, Brent's keeping her on a short leash and not making time to see her parents in over a year culminated in her likely missing her father's birthday.

"What did you say to him?"

"I said okay, I won't go," she said. She was crying hard now. "I mean I don't want to lose him. *And I feel bad, I make so little money and he is generous. We eat well, we have a nice apartment.*"

I shared the skill *HOLD ON TIGHT* with her, explaining how important it is to grasp the things that are core to her, whether it is visiting her parents regularly or celebrating a special occasion with them, or just doing things that she used to do that don't involve Brent's agenda and his family. She looked at me and shook her head.

"But the thing is, I do want to be with Brent; that's what makes me feel secure," she said, pulling herself together, no longer crying. "*I know he loves me, so that's why he doesn't want me to be away from him for the weekend. And as far as the money goes, I get he deserves it. He is always telling me how hard he works so he should be able to buy whatever he wants.*"

By then she had completely stopped buying anything for herself—clothes, spa treatments, small gifts for her friends, which had been one of her signature moves, even lunches out. Denial had allowed her to get to this point as she told herself *Brent makes more money, Brent works hard, Brent deserves whatever he wants.*

"From where I sit, it looks like you have given up many of the things in your life that previously gave you pleasure," I said. "Buying pretty clothes, giving your friends small gifts, getting the weekly pedicure you used to enjoy. All of those activities made you happy and gave you self-esteem, but now they are no longer part of your life, so what that means is you have to rely on Brent completely for your self-esteem and happiness, and he is never going to give you what you need. Really, he is doing the opposite. Coming here for therapy was a really important step on your part to take care of yourself, but even that's hard because you have to appropriate money from other places to afford help."

She had told me she was paying for her sessions by skimming money off the weekly grocery bills, either by pretending certain items weren't available or buying a cheaper version of them.

"This tells me that you know Brent would not support this or think that the money was well spent," I said. "The question is, how can you take care of yourself without having to lie about it?"

She could finally see that this was not a healthy relationship, and she began to realize something was really wrong. Why should she have to hide the fact that she wants support? When she came to see me again, something had changed. She had missed her father's birthday and it finally had an impact. She started to realize how much of herself she had relinquished to please Brent. I reminded her again about the important skill *HOLD ON TIGHT* and that it is a tool she can use to reconnect with the pieces of herself that had been lost along the way in this marriage. Finally, something clicked. She recognized how important staying connected to her parents was, that having therapy for herself was essential, that being able to go shopping and buy herself something new made her feel good. She realized that something had to change between her and Brent.

Coming to see me was really the beginning of her being able to ease her way out of the restrictive relationship and look out for herself. And as she used the *HOLD ON TIGHT* skill, she developed the courage to tell him as well. She even went to visit her parents and had a belated birthday celebration with her father.

"I feel like I have just been blinded by my need for Brent's love or something," she said, "And I'm not going to put up with it anymore. If it means our marriage isn't going to work, then I'll deal with that if I have to, but I can't continue to live like this, always feeling so deprived."

I was so glad Joan had reached this point. Now let's take a look at how Joe is doing. For a while, things with Ellen got worse, even though he kept trying so hard to please her. Eventually, he just couldn't do it anymore.

"I love Sydney so much," he said one day. "I don't want to do this to her but what kind of father am I if I am totally broken, and what kind of husband can I be if I am always feeling miserable?"

I nodded, interested in what he was going to say next.

"When I think about *HOLD ON TIGHT* I realize I have done the exact opposite," he said. "Or, more precisely, that I was holding on tight to the wrong things and letting too many of the things I care about fall to the wayside. And I wasn't happy. I pretended I was, I tried to be, but I wasn't. I told her we have to go for marriage counseling, otherwise we're not going to make it. To be perfectly honest, I am thinking about a separation."

Through the course of our work together, he began to appreciate just how trapped, empty, and ultimately angry he was in his marriage. Since he always avoided fighting with her, he never realized how much anger he experienced and carried around inside him. She seemed like the angry one to him, but once he acknowledged his own feelings, he realized the whole situation was eating him alive. Despite his great attempts to please Ellen and make her happy, he began to realize nothing he did would ever be good enough, no matter how much he gave her. He would never fill the void, and he was always going to walk around feeling inadequate and less than. He realized that in her eyes he was never going to measure up. With this understanding he began to withdraw from her. Using the *HOLD ON TIGHT* skill, he managed to bring back parts of himself. Despite his efforts to try to make the marriage work through counseling, Ellen didn't feel things were that bad and wouldn't continue to go. Subsequently they wound up getting divorced.

All these relationships began with men or women who made my patients feel that they were the world, that they were the best thing on the planet. They each felt so important, valuable, and needed, it was like a drug, impossible to turn away. At the beginning, their self-esteem soared because their new love interest or partner wanted to introduce them to everyone they knew; they wanted them with them always. When they felt they were slowly being folded into that other person's life and their own was fading away, Denial helped them stay by telling them *it was all for the best, they were so lucky, they were loved so much*. They were also afraid to jeopardize the relationship, so they didn't speak up, at least not at first; they just went along. They didn't want to make their partner stop loving them, or worse, decide they really weren't as lovable as they had made them feel. They were deep into a *Lose Yourself Relationship*, and the only way to be happy again, to be fully present and erase the resentment that was building, was to bring themselves back.

For many, coming to therapy was the first step in reclaiming space for themselves. It was a way to take care of themselves again in a place where their partner didn't have a presence. It was the beginning of their figuring out if this relationship was really as awful as it felt, a chance to push Denial aside so they could listen to their real thoughts and have their true feelings without being talked out of them. Very often, people jump into what their partner is thinking, trying to understand and anticipate what is to come so they can be ready to protect themselves from the criticism and blame that they feel has become inevitable. This way, they justify their needs and figure out what they are going to do to defend themselves. To this end, I tell my patients to stay in their own head. What this means is to stop trying to figure out what the other person is going to say so that they can defend themselves against the inevitable attack, but instead to protect themselves by focusing on their own needs and staying in control, whether they like it or not. That will help them have the clarity they need to take the steps that will make them happier so they can hold onto themselves. When they get into the other person's head—when Joe anticipates Ellen's demands and subsequent reactions and Joan imagines what Brent is going to do when she charges fifty dollars to the credit card—that is when they lose themselves. When they stay in their own head it is a way to *HOLD ON TIGHT*.

With that important skill, Joe, Joan, and a number of my other patients were able to hang on to themselves, which is the most important outcome of this scenario. Joe and Joan came to understand that Ellen and Brent respectively were not going to change, and so for their own mental and emotional health, and for their well-being, they eventually decided to end their marriages. Recognizing what was going on was the first step for all of them.

In Chapter Ten, you will see how to put your *HOLD ON TIGHT* skill into practice when dealing with a *Dominator*. But in the next chapter I am going to look at what can happen when you avoid the *Going Nowhere Relationship* as well as the *Lose Yourself Relationship*, but you are not necessarily out of the woods. You may be in a relationship with a Going Somewhere Partner who could be straying from you, and you don't want to miss those signs. Once again, Denial makes it all too easy to ignore the *Watch-Out Signs* and the *Hazard Lights* that can be right in front of you. Come on, let's take a look and make sure that doesn't happen to you.

CHAPTER FOUR

You Told Me You Were Just Friends

THE TWO COUPLES WERE INSTANTLY ATTRACTED TO EACH other. They had kids the same age, were both sporty, loved adventures, and, probably most important, were both looking for friends each partner liked. Little did they know how that would turn out. Simon and Nina moved onto the suburban cul-de-sac just weeks before Trudy and Glenn did, and they still laugh that those were the most boring weeks they have had since they moved onto Beachwood Lane. It hasn't even been a year that they have all lived here, and yet they can't imagine their lives without the other. Their kids are in and out of each other's houses as if it were their own. If someone's parents aren't available, the other set will do. Sometimes the husband from one couple and the wife from the other will go shopping together, or make dinner together, or take all the kids for a walk. *Wow*, they each think, *this is amazing! We are so open. We are so trusting. This feels so right.*

Then, one day Trudy looks out the window and sees her husband Glenn and her friend Nina talking on the street. It is perfectly normal, really; they are watching the kids play as they usually do. Trudy and Simon go to an office each day, but Glenn and Nina work from home, so they are the ones who usually pick up the slack with all the kids, planning arts and crafts projects and baking contests. In fact, Trudy is always pretty proud and amazed by how game her husband is to come up with elaborate ideas to entertain the kids. Nina is constantly talking about how incredible Glenn is, how she's lucky to glom onto his ideas for various activities. It all seems like a win-win situation for everyone. But there is something about the way Glenn is standing out there now, a little closer than Trudy would ever think or dare to stand near Simon, a little more intimate than one might be in the presence of his wife's best friend. *No*, she scolds herself. *I am being completely crazy. They are just friends, the best of friends, and there isn't one single person in this equation of four who would hurt someone else in the group.* She laughs a little to herself as she steps away from the window and goes upstairs to get out of her work clothes before joining everyone outside. The next time they are out socializing, she'll tell them about this funny moment. They will all get a kick out of it. Just as she turns away from the window, she sees Simon approach Glenn and Nina from his house. She turns back to watch, and she thinks she notices that Glenn takes a quick step away from Nina. Or *no, maybe he just tripped a little.* She shakes her head. *What is wrong with me? I am being ridiculous.*

Months go by and they continue this way; there are no boundaries between the families except, of course, the most important boundaries. They take a trip to Nova Scotia together, all eight of them, and they go camping. It is wonderful, lovely, so much fun, except for that one time Glenn and Nina had to go into town together to get the chip in the windshield fixed. It seemed totally natural that they would be the ones to go—Trudy was reading to the kids and Simon was getting the burgers ready for the grill. But then they were gone just a little longer than anyone expected. Trudy got a tiny nagging feeling as an hour became two hours and almost three until Denial joined her once again around the campfire and she thought, *what am I thinking? They did me a huge favor. I didn't want to spend my time out of the woods at some auto repair shop.* And they picked up more wine when they were out, and a huge bag of ice, the one luxury she couldn't live without even in the wilderness. *It makes sense that it would take that long, they said the traffic was terrible, and they were being so thoughtful.*

Trudy didn't mention any of this to me until after one evening when she came upon them in the garage. I wish she had, because I would have helped her see that trusting her instincts in a situation like this is very important. But not only was she not ready to hear that; she didn't want to because the open boundaries of their relationship felt like family. That's why she didn't make it a part of her therapy before that point; if she had, she would have had to admit to herself that she thought something untoward might be going on. On that particular night, though, something happened that she felt she had to mention. Trudy was supposed to work late, but she got to leave earlier than expected. She didn't bother to call home; she wanted to surprise everyone. She knew Glenn and Nina would feed the kids, and she thought Simon would probably join them. Honestly, she didn't think anything of it except that it would be fun to all be together, that she was glad she could join them for the rest of the evening. When she got home, she looked through the empty house for them. Faith, their oldest, came through the garage door on her way to bed, and held the door for her, so, she realized later, it closed only once and Glenn and Nina must have thought it was when Faith went into the house. They didn't expect her to get home from work for a while, she thought later. The garage doors were wide open and the wind was blowing. She could hear the tops of the huge trees rustling overhead. She thought maybe they had had a picnic out there, which they had done before on chilly days and nights. How nice, she thought, as she came in behind them quietly. They were sitting in those colorful folding chairs that old people sit in. She was going to say boo! and scare them. She was ready to pounce and imagined a huge laugh afterward. She was about two feet away when her husband of eight years leaned over and put his mouth on Nina's lips. Trudy screamed, they all jumped; it was almost what she had planned and yet not at all.

"What is happening here?" Trudy asked, backing away and looking pale.

"This is not what you think," Nina said quickly, standing up. Were her hands shaking? She moved toward her, but Trudy took another step back. "Trude, you have to believe me."

"I was just blowing smoke into her mouth," Glenn said, acting like that was a normal thing to do. He was using his "we're all in this together" tone. Trudy recognized it. "We had that one joint, you know, the one we've been meaning to smoke but haven't gotten around to? We were so bored, we needed a pick-me-up. We were sneaking it from the kids. They were driving us crazy. That's why we have the doors wide open even though it's freezing."

Trudy looked around. There was marijuana smoke, she could smell it. She could see the small joint in Glenn's hand. Everything he said seemed to make sense. She nodded. *Okay, maybe,* she thought to herself. And when she told me the story, complete with the details of the rustling trees and the smoke, I could tell she was still trying to believe there was a logical explanation for it all.

It was clear to me that whether Glenn was blowing smoke into Nina's mouth or not, by pretending it was nothing he was blowing smoke up Trudy's ass. And, at least at first, Trudy was letting him. I have seen this in my office too many times to count, and it brings together three of Denial's hallmark moves in one fell swoop. More than anything, Trudy is, of course, *Wishing and Hoping*—deluding herself with fantasy that this is not happening. She has been *Missing the Signs*—giving the benefit of thedoubt so she can continue to believe nothing is going on between Glenn and Nina. And now, as they try to explain it away, she is *Believing What She Is Told*—making the unbelievable believable. Let's take a closer look. There can be so many indications that something is going in one direction down a dark road, but the other partner does not want to see it. They hope beyond hope that they are wrong, that the extended trip to the auto repair really was because of bad traffic or having to make stops at stores, that the body language when they stood near each other was an indication of their friendship and nothing more. They think *he would never betray me, he would never do that to me*, even though it sort of seemed this morning that Glenn did everything in his power to get Nina to go to the store with him instead of Trudy. After which Trudy told herself *she was completely imagining that*. It is so easy to buy into a lie and let Denial convince you to accept what you know in your heart is untrue. It is the perfect example of the adage *love is blind*, making you repeatedly give the person the benefit of the doubt, as they continue to get away with their hurtful behaviors. Based on everything I have seen in the past, I worried about where this might go for Trudy. The most important thing for her to do right now was to begin to pay close attention, and to listen to her gut feelings.

I shared my very important skill of *LOOK IN THE REAR-VIEW MIRROR* with her.

"With that skill in your back pocket you will learn to look at everything around you, especially what you think you are seeing but are not sure about," I said. "So, when you see Glenn standing too close to Nina, don't brush it off. Instead go out there and get a better sense of what's going on. Don't let Denial tell you it's nothing, that they would never hurt you. Because if enough signs point to the fact that they might, you will want to check that out."

"Are you saying Glenn and Nina are having an affair?" she asked me. The look on her face was surprising. She looked truly shocked. She was still far away from acknowledging that possibility.

"I understand how difficult it is to hear those words come out of your own mouth," I said. "And I don't know for sure, but I think it's important to consider it based on everything you've told me, particularly how at ease you are with this complete sharing. In the same way you imagine you are safe because you can't see the car in the next lane, it doesn't mean that you won't be blindsided. In other words, it can be an illusion of security. That's why you always take a second look in the mirror, to make sure you aren't missing anything, and I want you to do that here, too. If you suspect that something is off or detect clues or indicators that things are not right—as it seems you have, at least to some extent—look again and investigate them. Instead of trying to figure out ways to explain away what you are seeing, to try to make sense of them, you want to take your doubts seriously and become open-minded to whatever might be going on, rather than staying in a single lane, so that you can finally look out for yourself."

Trudy listened but I know she was still hanging out with Denial because she wasn't ready to accept the real possibility that her husband was being unfaithful to her. Part of this is because of the trust people put in others, especially those closest to them. For example, Trudy might know without question that she would never betray Glenn. She took a vow to always be loyal and monogamous, to support him in sickness and in health, for the rest of their lives. So, it follows that if she wouldn't break that bond, then how could he? People operate from their own perspective and because they are trustworthy, they assume the other person will be trustworthy as well. Also, there is the concept that she placed her confidence in him, that she basically handed her heart over to him for safekeeping, and that should be the thing that prevails, shouldn't it?

More than that, though, there is what I call the *Trust Factor*, which consists of four expectations that are very difficult to give up even in the face of so many questions. The first is *You Will Be There*, in other words, when you place your faith in someone, especially a life partner, you are making the assumption that they will stand up for you, that they will support you emotionally and physically, and remain by your side through it all. This means they will walk beside you in life, holding you up and making your life fuller. The second part of the *Trust Factor* is the idea that *This Will Last*. With this in mind, there is the sense that a relationship, especially a marriage, is ongoing and will stand the test of time. It is not something that might disappear or go away, or that needs constant checking on. It is just something that exists day in and day out, something that is wholly dependable. The next prong of the *Trust Factor* is the belief that *You Will Be Honest*. In any close relationship there is the idea that people will show their true selves and there is no need to hide who they really are. There is an expectation of honesty, and with that comes the sense that there is no reason to question what someone you trust tells you, even when you have some doubts for one reason or another. It follows, then, that if there was something unusual going on, they would tell you, since they are supposed to be honest, that they wouldn't conceal it. There is also the feeling that they certainly wouldn't deny it when directly confronted. The final part of the *Trust Factor* is the idea that *You Will Protect Me*. This is what makes people feel safe in a relationship, the acceptance that the other person has their back and will always stand up for them if need be. With that concept firmly in place, it is hard to acknowledge the possibility that the person they think will do anything to shield them from the bad things in life could possibly contribute to them or even create or cause those bad things.

I knew all of this was going on to some extent for Trudy, and it was a lot to work through during that first time she brought up what had happened between Glenn and Nina that evening in his garage. Whenever any of the factors of trust are broken it is painful, and the person on the other side is left feeling betrayed and alone, completely unsupported in the world. The possibility that this was going on in her own home with her husband and the woman she thought was her best friend just makes it that much harder to believe and accept. No wonder people welcome Denial with such a robust wave, happy to have help explaining it all away and taking the pain along with it. In addition, in order to recognize the possibility that Glenn might not be who Trudy thought he was, basically what she based her entire emotional life and well-being on, would mean she had to admit that she was wrong and had really misjudged her husband's character. That was quite a bit to take in and get her head around all at once.

When Trudy left my office that day, I encouraged her to continue to *LOOK IN THE REARVIEW MIRROR*, to understand that some things were closer than they appeared, to acknowledge and accept what she was seeing, instead of brushing it under the rug. She promised me she would try.

I had another patient around the same time named Alex who was going through something similar. When he first came to me, his marriage was not what moved him to seek out therapy; from everything he said at that time it was solid and he didn't worry it would be anything but that. Sometimes, though, things can change slowly without people realizing it. About a year ago he arranged with his employer that he would do most of his work from home, having to go into the office for in-person meetings only about twice a month, which is also when he came to see me. Before then we were meeting weekly, but things had stabilized for him, and we thought twice a month would work well.

His working from home initially seemed like something that was going to change his family's life for the better; until that point he and his wife Sheila were both commuting into Manhattan, and spent most of the day a good forty-five-minute train ride away from their young kids, who were in school near their house. When one kid or the other was sick, they always did Rock-Paper-Scissors to decide who would stay home, unless it was very clear that one of them had a meeting or a workday they couldn't miss. It was the worst, though, when one of the kids got sick at school and they would have to scramble to get home to pick him up. More often than not the discussion of who would go would lead to a fight. Now they didn't have to deal with it at all. Alex could do his job but also be completely available if one of their boys needed him, and Sheila could go into the office where she worked in marketing for a new luxury hotel chain and never have to worry about her day being interrupted.

"Do you feel you are giving anything up with this arrangement?" I asked him.

"Not at all," he said confidently.

One day he told me that he worried about Sheila's happiness since now she spent her entire commute alone, while before they were together. But he said he felt it was the best thing for the family overall and would ultimately lead to fewer fights between them. Not long after that, he told me things had improved even more because Sheila discovered that one of her colleagues lived nearby and they began to commute together.

"Problem solved," Alex said, wiping the palms of his hands together as if to say that's done and he can stop worrying. It wasn't clear to me for a few weeks that the colleague Sheila was now commuting with was a man. Soon enough Alex began to talk more about his wife's time with her new traveling partner Fred.

"*It's so great*," Alex said to me, and I could almost imagine Denial sitting next to him on the couch in my office. "*I'm thrilled that her commute isn't boring anymore and she has someone else to talk to.*"

There it all was, the *Trust Factor* coming into play, as well as Denial helping him believe what he needed to believe, that it was completely innocent.

There were a few incidents when the train was late, he told me over the next few sessions, and Sheila and Fred would have dinner at a restaurant together in the city before coming home.

"*Thank goodness she has someone to eat with*," he told me.

Then one day he came in and told me that Sheila seemed a little distant. She always loved snuggling together after the kids went to sleep and lately, she hasn't wanted to do that. He said that she says she's so tired from work that all she wants to do is stretch out and go to sleep. When he offers to go to bed with her, she says no, that he should enjoy his television show.

"I miss being close with her," he told me. "*But I totally get it. She's working on a huge project and she's exhausted. I remember feeling that way after long days in the city.*"

Then one evening there was a big power outage, and the trains weren't running. Sheila called to tell Alex that she might as well just stay in the city. He suggested she hire a car service to bring her home, he didn't want to go two whole days without seeing each other, not to mention the boys wanting to see their mother.

"It's impossible," she told him. "Everyone's trying to get out of the city. There are no available cars, and it would be a fortune anyway. Not worth it."

"Where will you stay?" he asked numbly, because of course he knew.

"At the hotel," she said.

For the first time, he panicked; he just had a feeling something was off.

"We'll drive in," he said. "The boys and I, we'll stay with you. They always love a night at the hotel. They can be a little late for school tomorrow."

"That's crazy," she told him. "The traffic is beyond bad. You won't get here until four in the morning."

And so he stopped pushing, and told himself he *WAS being crazy, she would never, ever cheat on him.* He almost asked about Fred, almost, but doing that would make him sound so petty and immature, and he was above that, *their marriage was above that.* After he said those words in my office he looked at me, wanting to believe it, but also wanting me to agree. Of course, I couldn't. Instead, I wanted him to consider the possibility of what might be going on between Sheila and Fred. In my experience it is the distancing, the fact that Sheila wants to go to bed alone and their usual ritual of snuggling on the couch has stopped, that is the biggest *Watch-Out Sign.*

"Has she ever stayed at the hotel on a work night before?" I asked.

"Never," he said. Then, with Denial's help, *"But this was differ-ent, there had never been a blackout like this before."*

"Have things improved between you when she is home?" I asked. "Is she more present and available?"

"Not really," he said. But then, *"This project is dragging on, they're opening a new hotel in Brooklyn, and it is just taking it out of her."*

Over the next two weeks Denial dug in its heels even more than ever, and Alex explained one thing after another away, her wanting to go in earlier each day (the project!), her missing dinner with the family a few nights a week (the project!), and her ducking out of their weekend morning walks (her exhaustion because of the project!). One day, though, he arrived home with the boys after one of their walks and he thought he could hear her talking and giggling. He smiled at the boys and put his finger to his mouth to tell them to be quiet, he did it playfully like they were playing a game and they complied. He made sure the door didn't slam, he removed his shoes, and he crept quietly along the carpeted hall toward the bedroom where Sheila was sitting up in bed, smiling big, on her phone. As soon as she saw him her smile faded com-pletely and she jerked up, then, it seemed, she thought better of it and tried to resume the posture and facial expression she had had before. He told me that she called "Bye mom," into the phone and hung up. The rest of the day was strained, but she never once let up her story that she had been talking to her mother, and she even peppered their conversation with things her mother had told her. Sheila and her mother had a fairly cold relationship, so this more than anything struck Alex as odd. The next morning he asked if I were available for an emergency phone session.

"What do you think?" he asked me point-blank.

It was time to share my skill of *LOOK IN THE REARVIEW MIRROR* with him. I explained what it was and suggested he take stock of all the incidents he had noticed that didn't feel right or might have seemed unusual, along with anything that might come up in the days ahead, and we would talk about them next week. He agreed.

Now let's check in on Trudy. The next week she came to see me and said she thought things were actually getting better. She had noticed that Glenn was suddenly exercising more, riding his bike most mornings and running on the weekends. He also trimmed what she thought had become an unruly beard, which she had not been shy about telling him, so now it looked really good. She took it all as a sign that he was finally listening to her and wanted to look good for her.

"It makes me happy," she said, just as the thought *uh oh* went through my mind.

Really, I was surprised Denial was able to do that good a job by that point; Trudy was clearly such a smart woman. When a spouse or partner suddenly takes interest in how he or she looks after a period of not seeming to care, it is likely to be more than just middle age creeping up and can, in fact, be a clear *Watch-Out Sign* that he or she is looking outward, away from the marriage, and maybe even *Going Somewhere.*

"And," Trudy said coyly, as if she had something really special to tell me, "he started this thing where he brings me flowers from around the neighborhood. I know it is probably bad that he's picking people's flowers but there are so many everywhere, and he comes home with one perfect flower and presents it to me. *I mean, he's really thinking about me.*"

Uh oh, I thought again.

Of course, spouses can bring flowers or other gifts home or do special things for their significant other with absolutely no ulterior motives, but considering everything else Trudy had told me, this was another big *Watch-Out Sign*. This sort of thing can play out in many different ways. As Glenn seemed to be doing, a spouse might take sudden interest in their appearance, either through exercise or buying new clothes. Suddenly they might change their look, grow a beard, cut off a beard, get breast implants or a breast reduction. Out of nowhere they want to be a better version of themselves and begin to invest time and money in making that happen. Or he or she might be spending an unusually large amount of time on their computer, and when they are questioned might say something along the lines of "you want me to make money, well that's what I'm doing." Also, as Glenn was now doing, they may bring gifts out of nowhere. Or they might come up with a new hobby that takes them out of the house more. With all of these situations, Denial will offer some good explanations: *He must really love me, that's why he wants to look good. He cares about our family so much, he is working overtime. She loves me so much she went out of her way to get me my favorite beer. He took up golf; great, now I have a little more me time.* Another thing can happen that can be a big *Watch-Out Sign*, too. After months or years of arguing about a certain hotspot, something that comes back repeatedly in your relationship, they stop fighting you on it. At first, this might seem great because the friction between you suddenly stops and whatever your bone of contention was appears to have been resolved or have disappeared. You might even think, *wow, they are really working with me, or, they finally agree with me, they have come around to see my point of view.* Often that is not the case at all, however, but simply an indication that the spouse who has stopped pushing back is no longer trying with you because they have resigned themselves to the futility of being understood by you and having their needs met. Instead of getting angry with you, as they used to do, they are acting on their anger in a different way and using it to justify stepping out of the marriage because they feel things are hopeless with you. So instead of its being an indication that things are improving between you, it could be a sign that they are no longer emotionally invested in the marriage.

There are other things to be aware of, too, when trying to determine whether your spouse or partner is in a *Going Somewhere Relationship*. If there are changes in his or her normal routine, for example, maybe your partner always came home before dinner without exception but now he or she is working late a few times a week, or your spouse has always been completely dependable but now they are breaking promises at the last minute, missing your son's soccer games or family dinners because something came up. Or if there is a change in your sex life, either you were not having a lot of sex but now you are because your partner is trying to throw you off track and make you think everything is okay between you, or you were having sex regularly and it starts to diminish. All of these things can be *Watch-Out Signs*. We saw this with Sheila and Alex when Sheila stopped coming home for dinner every night as she usually did, no longer went on their weekend family walks, and removed herself from their cuddle sessions.

Whenever my patients mention things like these, I encourage them to pay attention to everything else that is going on around them. More often than not, people are truly surprised when infidelity occurs and comes to light. And it can happen at any time during a relationship. Statistically speaking, it often comes up during times of change, and when people would not expect it. For example, people have affairs around the time they get engaged, get married, become pregnant, or have a baby—times when you would imagine you would be all in it together, but the significance of the events can create so much anxiety and insecurity that people turn to others to relieve stress and build up their confidence. And of course, they can happen at other times, too.

So, for Trudy, Glenn's sudden interest in his appearance along with his suddenly presenting her with flowers, coupled with the moments with Nina, seemed to be suggesting an affair.

"Trudy, to me this all points to an affair," I finally told her. "I may be jaded but do you really believe that the exact minute you walked into the garage was the only moment Glenn chose to blow smoke into Nina's mouth? And couldn't they have just shared the joint? Why did he have to do it that way?"

Trudy nodded. Her expression was solemn. I expected her to make some excuse, to keep Denial by her side, but this time she didn't.

"Let's break this down," I said. "You've noticed multiple times that Glenn and Nina are together, standing a little too close, doing errands together. You said yourself that Glenn has been working on his appearance. You came upon them with their mouths on each other. If you were watching a movie, what would you think about all of this? Would you think Glenn was innocent?"

"I don't know," she said. I took that as progress. She wasn't there with me yet, but she also wasn't denying it anymore.

"Let me ask you another question," I said. "I know you said he's bringing you flowers, so you're connecting that way, but is he as emotionally available as he usually is or as he used to be? Are you talking as much? Is he present when you are together?"

This stopped her.

"No," she said. "He is always busy, always moving around lately. We rarely sit down and talk. We used to do this thing where we would turn out the lights at night after the kids were asleep and we were in bed and we would each have five minutes straight to talk to tell each other about our days, about what we looked forward to, about what we worried about. Then we would each have five minutes to respond to what the other said, making each other feel better or encouraging whoever had something great going on the next day. Sometimes one of us would fall asleep to the other's soothing voice. Really it was my favorite time of the day. We haven't done that in a long time, maybe almost a year."

I nodded.

"How did it stop?" I asked. "Did you just get too busy?"

She thought for a minute.

"No," she said. "At first, he took longer than usual in the bathroom, and we were both tired, so we said we'd pick it up again tomorrow, but then it happened again and again. And then, I realize now, he started coming to bed and reading with the light on until I was asleep, or, if I had the lights out already, he would turn away from me instead of toward me, saying he was sore from a run or something. It didn't seem like a big deal, each night made sense. I figured he was so tired after being home with the kids all day. But now—"

Her voice trailed off.

"So what do I do?" Trudy asked.

"You talk to him," I said. "Confront him, separate from Nina, this is about you and Glenn, and see what he says."

She told me she would think about it.

Alex, too, had reached a similar place.

"I finally brought it up, I couldn't stand not knowing anymore," Alex said. "I asked about the night at the hotel and also about that call."

"What did she say?" I asked.

"She held up her story," he said. "That she slept alone in the hotel room, she keeps adding all these details, like she didn't sleep well, the air conditioning was too loud, and then that she was talking to her mother, that they are trying to mend their relationship and talk more, share more with each other."

"Do you believe her?" I asked.

"Something else happened," he said. "I had a meeting downtown. Of course, I would always tell her where I was going but I didn't this time, which more than anything told me how worried I am, like something is broken between us. The kids seemed fine, there was no reason to think they would need us during the day, but I had a neighbor on backup just in case. Anyway, after my meeting I walked to the hotel because it's just a few blocks away. I didn't even know if she would be there; it's where the main offices are but she goes to different buildings sometimes. And I basically caught them. They were sitting in the lobby so close I don't think I could have put my hand between them, maintaining the most basic whiff of professionalism, but barely. The energy between them was palpable. Despite everything we've talked about, I was still shocked. I couldn't believe it."

"Did you confront them?"

"Not in the moment," he said. "But when Sheila got home that night I said I had seen them and didn't want to interrupt."

"What did she say?" I asked.

"She said they are just friends," he said. "She won't admit to anything. She said they were just talking, that they had had an exciting meeting and whatever energy I thought I saw was just enthusiasm about plans they had for the new hotel."

Seeing them together in that hotel lobby, sitting close to each other and appearing to be so connected, changed something in Alex. It was at this point, because he was finally breaking through his Denial and no longer believing everything Sheila said, that he was ready to discover the truth. And he did. He became serious about investigating what was going on between them, and it wasn't long before he found what he was looking for.

The next time we talked he told me what happened.

He had had Sheila's email password all along; he had had it for years but never felt a need to use it, or, to be more accurate, didn't want to know, even after he became concerned. But now he felt he had to; he was ready to learn the truth. He logged in and, at first, it seemed like a lot of work emails, a few about an upcoming high school reunion, but nothing more. And then, he found a file marked TRAIN and somehow he knew. He said he was shaking as he clicked the first email, which was written to Sheila from Fred and talked about looking forward to seeing each other on the train. In fact, all the emails in that folder were either from Fred or to him. Each email became increasingly intimate until one that was written on Thursday, in which Sheila said she had never felt so fulfilled sexually. Alex confronted her.

"And do you know what she did?" he asked me. "She told me they were bored on the train so they implemented their own creative writing club, and these emails were exercises in writing, in telling a story through letters. Can you believe it?"

This is a common occurrence after an affair is discovered. The people who have done the betraying often continue to lie to minimize and make it not so terrible, but once the other person knows what is going on they go on the hunt, find more information, and realize they are continuing to be lied to. The infidelity itself is a terrible realization, but not always a deal-breaker. It is the lying that is completely unacceptable and most difficult to get over. What is oftentimes the most distressing to many who experience the shock and the awfulness of infidelity, is that when they finally have proof and are presenting their partner with clear-cut evidence, the partner continues to deny the affair. For many, this feels like irrevocable damage. They have been gaslighted and made to believe they were crazy to feel the way they did. When their partner continues to lie to them, it goes back to the *Trust Factor* and leads them to believe they can't have faith in or trust this person at all. The worst part of it all is that they no longer feel they are safe or protected by them. That is where the real fallout can be.

When dealing with infidelity it is a pick your poison, because once you begin to see the signs that something might be going on, you can take it one of two ways. Either, with Denial by your side, you can choose to ignore the voice in your head and the feeling in your gut so you won't have to deal with the pain right away. In that case, you can continue to avoid it and live with the gnawing suspicion that something is going on, but you constantly have to make it disappear, which is hard work. If that is your choice, then you are continuing to live with Denial. Or you can kick Denial out of your house and deal with it.

If you choose to deal with it, three things can occur after an affair comes to light in one way or another. The first is that the marriage or relationship will end. Sometimes the betrayal was too egregious, and the anger was too intense, that there was no way to repair the damage done. Plus, there can be that lost *Trust*

Factor, which can often be impossible to recover from. But it doesn't always go that way. It sounds counterintuitive, but I have seen it many times. An affair is discovered, a couple goes through a very difficult time, but ultimately decide together, after the affair has ended, that they want to recommit to each other and to their marriage.

Believe it not, for many, an affair can breathe new life into a relationship and make a marriage even better than it was before. For this to happen, the person who betrayed the partner has to take ownership of what they did and commit to doing everything to restore the trust they once shared. They have to be willing to listen to their partner's distress, compromise on issues that they were stalemated in previously, learn how to work through their anger, find new ways to please the other person and show how much they care, and focus on letting their partner know how much they value them. Most importantly, the person who had the affair has to not only convey their apology in words but commit to rebuilding their partner's trust through actions in order to be able to move forward as a couple. This is done by listening to their partner, by being responsive to their partner's needs, by being up-front about their own comings and goings, and by being committed to apologizing for what they did for as long as their partner needs them to so they can finally feel safe and understood. I tell my patients often, there is no shelf life on how long you may need to apologize to let your partner know how bad you feel about what you did and about the intense pain you have caused them. The repeated apology is the key element to getting to a stronger place together, and really can go on for as long as it takes until the person who was betrayed believes you really get it.

The third thing that can happen is that some people never break through their Denial; they allow it to prevail and it becomes the norm of their marriage. In those cases, an affair can be a stabilizing force, serving the purpose of keeping the marriage in place, which can be necessary for many reasons including financial need or a foundation for raising their family.

The bottom line is that in the end, some people recover from a betrayal like this, and some don't. Some even come back stronger than they were before. Trudy and Glenn managed to salvage their marriage, but not before they moved away from Beachwood Lane. It took a lot of work, but Trudy wanted to for the sake of their family. Eventually, Glenn admitted everything, and was careful to tell Trudy as much as she wanted to know but not more, including the fact that he had indeed kissed Nina that night in the garage, something he deeply regretted. Simon and Nina, Trudy told me, didn't make it. They separated once the affair came to light and eventually divorced. Alex and Sheila, too, ended up separating but still have not moved toward a formal divorce. He has not ruled out the possibility that they might work things out together.

Both Trudy and Alex have told me they wished they had seen it and dealt with it sooner, that they feel almost embarrassed that they let Denial into their home for so long and explained all the questionable behavior away. Trudy told me recently that she would never let that happen again; the second she sees a *Watch-Out Sign* she will ask Glenn about it right away. And she will keep a constant eye in her rearview mirror.

Infidelity hits hard when it's happening to you. There is another side of the coin, however, which is when you are the person who is having the affair, and you're dreaming about your future with your lover in real time. One or both of you may be married to other people but at different stages. Maybe you are ready to end your marriage, and the person you are having an affair with swears they are, too, but just needs more time. They string you along with promises and constantly changing timetables. Or you might be single, and your lover is married. They beg you to wait for them, to not date other people; really, they say, they will leave their spouse soon, but it drags on and months and sometimes even years can go by. Or they are clear from the start that they never intend to leave their spouse, and somehow you make that okay because Denial has you believing they will change their minds. In all these cases Denial can help you hold on, to continue to stay locked into *Wishing and Hoping*. So, what do you do? That is a whole other problem that requires another important skill to manage it, which I will talk about in the next chapter. You don't have to give up control of your life and just wait. Instead, you can take charge of the situation and the timeline. Let's see what the secret is to being able to do that.

Chapter Five

I Can Wait—For Us

Kara really thought it would be different this time. For more than two and a half years she and Mac have been meeting at her apartment whenever he can get away. Every time it is the same. First, there is all the back-and-forth about whether Mac can come to see her. Sometimes he can and, often lately, he can't because something came up at home or at work. As Kara waits while her phone tells her he is typing, letting her know whether it will be a go or a big no that day, she holds her breath. She wants to see him so much it hurts.

Once Mac is inside her door, they sit and catch up—there is always so much to talk about that she saved for *right now*. It is a moment she dreams about constantly—one she is always trying to get to. It is a moment that goes by far too fast before they realize their time together is running out and they walk to her bedroom to make love. It is great every time. And then she finds herself thrust back into the lonely world once again or, more accurately, alone in her apartment counting down until the next time. It is what keeps her going when they can't be together. But today she wasn't going to have to hide in her apartment for the love of her life. Today they were going to meet outside on the sidewalk in front of her building, and then they were going to go out to lunch, to her favorite Italian restaurant a few blocks away. She was going to hold his hand the whole way there. And yet, here she is, alone in her apartment, waiting for her still-secret lover.

Mac has been promising for months now that he is going to tell his wife, Jenny, about how unhappy he is in his marriage. He is in a joyless, sexless marriage, and he swears he is going to end it so Kara and he can be together all the time. He has given her target times for this amazing shift in their world order before, and, heartbreakingly, he has had to postpone it each time. After the first year, he was going to tell her, but then Jenny's mother was in the hospital following a small stroke and it wasn't a good time to create turmoil in their house, which Kara understood. Then he promised he would tell her three months later, before her birthday so they could celebrate out in public; it was going to be the best birthday present ever. She didn't want to hide anymore; she wanted their connection to exist outside of her apartment. She longed for their relationship to be real, it was all she wanted, and he knew it. Before he said anything to Jenny though, Mac's son got the lead in the school play and, well, he couldn't tear apart his family before opening night. So, her birthday came and went, and they were still a couple only behind tightly closed and locked doors. And yet, she continued to stick around, *Wishing and Hoping* that one day this will happen, and soon it was six months later.

They set another date, and another obstacle came up. Just before he was going to tell her, Jenny had a questionable mammogram and needed a biopsy, after which they had to wait for the results. Of course, Kara understood that too. *How could she not be understanding? She wasn't a terrible person. She wasn't a selfish person. She didn't want to pile more heartache onto Jenny when her mother was sick or when she was waiting herself to make sure she was healthy. She certainly didn't want to crush Mac's sweet son when he got the part he had been hoping for in the play, she didn't want him to pull the rug out from under him and ruin his happiness. No, they were all plausible reasons for a delay in ending his marriage.* She accepted all of that. And wow did Mac appreciate it. If anything, it made them even closer, more connected. And then last week he had looked her in the eyes, he promised her this was the time, things were calmer, he was going to tell Jenny. And what did Kara do? She *Believed What She Was Told*. Despite everything, despite his track record, she really thought it was going to happen this time. But as she waited eagerly for Mac to knock, she thought *How am I still here? Today was going to be different.*

The plan had first been to meet in her lobby; that felt right symbolically. Then Mac suggested they come together outside where everyone could see them, and she had loved that idea. It was going to be wonderful. She would approach him and just lean into him, in front of everyone who was out there, to close her eyes and have him be the one thing in the world that was holding her up at that moment, to not care for one second who saw them. He told Kara he intended to talk to Jenny the night before. It took all her might to not call him to see how it went, to just wait until today and talk about it in person. She was bursting with anticipation. But as she was waiting out there, watching people come and go and thinking *she will know, and he will know,* she got a text. *Let's do it the usual way—just one more time—will explain* it read. *See you at your place.* So here she is, feeling confused, disappointed, and angry, and, once again, hiding from the rest of the world.

She has her head down when she goes to answer the door after he finally knocks. Maybe she won't sleep with him this time. Maybe she will make him wait. She cracks the door slightly and there he is, grinning and so happy to see her. He reaches his arm out and grabs hers gently. Who is she kidding? She can't resist him. And as they settle down on her couch to talk, their legs intertwined, she thinks: *We are meant to be together. Everything else will fall into place. All I have to do is wait a little while longer.*

When Kara told me about the plan the week before, that Mac was finally going to tell Jenny and they were going to meet in the open, no longer having to worry about who might see them, I was concerned. So many classic elements of Denial were right there in front of us. The boldest one was Kara's *Believing What She Was Told*. Even though Mac had gone back on his promise repeatedly, even though there was no real reason to think this time would be any different, Kara wanted it so badly that with Denial's help she was able to cast all the obvious roadblocks aside and truly believe it was going to happen. She had no doubts; she was counting on it.

"What do you think is different this time?" I asked her. "Has Mac shared anything with you that would indicate that something has changed between him and Jenny, or is he doing something that makes you feel more confident about it this time? Is there reason to believe that he is going to be able to feel less guilty and finally be truthful with his wife?"

"Well," she said thoughtfully, "nothing has come up. I mean, there haven't been any medical emergencies or work difficulties. I don't think anything unusual is planned with their son."

"I understand that," I said. "The real question, though, is has he indicated that even if something does come up with his wife and kids or whatever it might be, that he is now ready to deal with it so it doesn't put off his plans with you? In other words, has he acknowledged that if anything else happened, it wouldn't stop him this time? That he will now handle it differently?"

Of course, I worried he was just paying lip service to Kara, telling her what she wanted to hear, which was *I love you and I'm leaving*, even if there was nothing to support that. I knew it was likely that he was going to continue to disappoint her and string her along. There was every reason to expect that, based on their history. But she couldn't see it yet. She thought each time he postponed it was just bad luck.

"Just what I told you," she said.

The other part of Denial that is at play here for Kara, and that has been at play through all these months of uncertainty, is *Wishing and Hoping*, deluding herself with fantasy that it will be true, that he will do what he said he would do. She was looking ahead to the future when she imagined they would be together forever out in the open, and, instead of facing how hard her time away from him is now; she was allowing herself to pretend that imagined future was her reality, not what was currently right in front of her. And, of course, she was *Missing the Signs* that this was likely to keep happening with Mac. There was always going to be something stopping him from telling Jenny; he had clearly shown her that, but Kara didn't see it that way. She saw each delay as a single moment, an unfortunate but isolated turn of events, not as a clear pattern.

As many times as I have seen affairs play out with my patients, as we talked about in Chapter Four, I have seen this scenario, too. Two people fall in love, but one or both may be unavailable because they might be married to someone else. That is the basic definition of an affair, after all—a sexual relationship between two people, one or both of whom are married to someone else. And while that is true, there are many possible combinations in which people come together to have an affair. Depending on how it all shakes out—one person could be newly single, either through a recent divorce or even having been widowed, making that person far more available than their lover, who is married and may have kids—the two might ultimately want different things or, even if they in theory want the same thing, one might have a much tougher or seemingly impossible road to get there.

Take Kara and Mac. They met at a work conference—they are both in advertising. It was after hours and Kara was wearing a retro T-shirt impressed with the name of her hometown, Mamaroneck. She caught Mac's eye and then he saw her shirt. He also grew up in Mamaroneck. He called out to her, "Hey, I could really use a slice of Sal's right now." She looked up and smiled big—she has a gorgeous smile—and she said, "I'll take one slice of Sicilian and one slice of salad." They both laughed. That was the quintessential order at Sal's Pizza, which anyone from Mamaroneck knows is the best pizza out there. From there they talked about where they went to high school, people they had in common, and the tennis bubble they both loved at Harbor Island, a park on the Long Island Sound. Their connection was a slow burn. They made each other laugh, the way they both talked was familiar, and there was a strong physical pull. Once they were back in New York, she had coffee sent to his office a few times, the same brand of coffee they had been drinking at the conference and one that was locally roasted in Mamaroneck—their little inside joke. At that point Mac was still in so much Denial about what was going on that he invited Kara to a small dinner party at his house and billed her as a friend. She and Jenny actually liked each other, but Kara intentionally didn't let the friendship grow. A few times, she and Mac met for lunch under the pretense of work. She dressed up in a way Jenny had not bothered to for years, it seemed. And she was so interested in him. It was just a matter of time before they were sharing a cab to midtown to go back to work after a lunch one day, and Mac asked if they could go to Kara's place instead.

As with Kara and Mac, an affair can progress and become serious, and one part of that couple begins to push to make it official and be with that person no longer in an affair, but in a fully out-in-the-open relationship. The other person may or may not be ready for that, but certainly doesn't want to lose the relationship, so he or she appeases that person. They will end their marriage soon, they promise, after the family trip they have planned, after their in-laws' sixtieth wedding anniversary party, after their child has a surgery that is planned down the road. The person who wants it, who is asking for it, will say *okay, I can wait*. Denial helps them believe it will happen; all they have to do is be patient. But then their lover reaches that milestone, and the timeline is extended. They say they meant it, they really did, but now something else has come up for them, they just need a little more time to get through this situation or that. But, they say, one day we will be together, one day we will walk through the streets in the middle of the day hand in hand, we will travel together, we will share a home, we won't have to hide anymore. And there it is, that beautifully wrapped package of *Wishing and Hoping* that keeps them stuck in fantasyland. And so, the tug back and forth continues. In general, their relationship is one-sided. With Mac and Kara, she is always available and he isn't. She longs to be with him, and readily accepts the limited time he offers her. Basically, he is offering her a trickling faucet; sometimes it is even completely turned off, and she is constantly trying to get water from it.

As Mac sits with Kara, he explains that he wasn't able to tell Jenny last night as he had planned. But he makes it very clear that it is not an indication of how much he wants to be with Kara—which, he says, is so much, more than anything. He can talk to her about stress at work in a way he can't with Jenny because the pressure is so great to always do a good job. Kara listens, she gives him her full attention because there are no distractions—no kids to attend to or housework to do. When they are together either in person or on the phone, Kara focuses 100 percent on him. Sure, he loves the sex with her, it's like nothing he has ever experienced, but there is much more between them.

"I will tell her," Mac says. "I promise you. But I need to talk to you about something. I want to explain why I had to meet you here again. Jenny found a lump on her neck. I don't know what it is, but she can't get in to see the doctor until Wednesday. She is traumatized by her whole experience with that mammogram and then the biopsy. I just can't add to that stress."

"But everything was fine that time," Kara says. "And it probably will be again. Isn't a lump on your neck usually just a swollen lymph node? Plus, she's going to have to start to deal with some of these things on her own. Soon you won't be there to hold her up anymore."

"I know, I know," Mac says, taking her face gently in his hands and really looking at her. "You're the only one I want to be with, but I made a vow and, while I don't plan to uphold it for much longer, I mean that, I can't do this to her when she might be facing something scary."

"What if it ends up being thyroid cancer or something?" Kara asks. "Then are you going to have to be with her through the treatment, for however many months or years that takes?"

"No, of course not," he says. "Then we would get everything settled and I would tell her. I want to be with you. I think about you all the time."

That softened Kara; at least he won't delay his telling her if she needs treatment. It makes sense to wait to see what they are dealing with. *Okay*, Kara thinks, *it won't be too much longer.* Denial at its best was there in bed with them as she believed him once again.

They spend the rest of the time talking. Mac has been struggling with a particular project at work and Kara helps him break it down; they talk through it step by step. By the time he has to leave, Mac feels better about work and just lighter in general and she can't even remember why she had been mad at him. She smiles to herself while she cleans up the wine glasses they used, thinking *this will be one of the last times we have to meet here.* But that delay of telling Jenny turns into another delay and then another. Every time they are together Kara feels their intense chemistry, and every time she tells herself waiting will be worth it, he loves her, and he will follow through.

The next time she came to see me she talked a lot about the time she wasn't with him, and how hard that had become for her. They managed to find about two or three hours a week to be together, four if they were lucky. More often lately, though, Mac had to cancel just hours before they had a plan to see each other—one time his son got sick, another time a mandatory meeting was called at work. So, she spends most nights alone. But they were texting and on the phone every day, and that was keeping her going. She loved their time together, but she also loved any contact. She told me that early on she had considered dating other people, but that upset him too much and now, of course, she doesn't want to because she knows he is the love of her life, so why would she do that? I knew I had my work cut out for me.

"Kara," I said. "It seems that even though you are so connected throughout the day you still wind up spending a lot of time alone."

"*It's temporary,*" she said. "*It's just until we can be together all the time.*"

"I know that's what you're longing for. How many times, though, has Mac said that but delayed it?" I asked. "Has he shared with you feeling less guilty and stronger to be able to confront his wife and plan to end his marriage?"

It was basically the same question I had asked her before. This time, she looked at me. She wasn't quite ready to go there, I could tell, and I could still hear Denial in her words, but I could also tell she was finally hearing my questions.

"Because it has to be," she said. "I have invested too much time, too much emotional energy in this to have it all be for nothing. Plus, I respect him for not just dropping Jenny like a hot potato when she is dealing with health issues and also prioritizing being a good dad. I respect him for being thoughtful about it. That says so much about what an incredible man Mac is, and that is exactly why I love him so much. It also speaks to the way he will treat me once we are truly together."

"I understand feeling that way," I said. "But does that mean you have to sit around patiently and wait forever? It is important to recognize that this isn't about his timeline, it needs to be about yours. Life is always going to be stepping on toes with kids' birthdays and medical emergencies. It might never be the right time for him. This has to become about when you are no longer comfortably able to tolerate it because he is never going to become comfortable enough to make a move."

"I feel guilty asking him to do something like leave his son," she said.

"You aren't asking him to do that," I said. "You're letting him know that it's his choice if he's really sincere about taking your relationship to the next level."

She wondered if she was asking for too much, if she was being petty to want to share holidays and think of a future together.

"You have a right to want legitimacy," I said.

I shared my important skill of *SET YOUR DATE* with her. This is when you decide how long you are going to be put on hold, basically how long you are prepared to wait for your lover to make the changes they have promised. The goal of this skill is for you to have a sense of control rather than feeling stuck by the other person's timing. It is also when you explain to them what must happen for you to be willing to stay in the relationship as it is while you continue to wait for the change you are expecting. I told Kara she should begin to think about spelling out a timeline, whether it is two months, six months, or even a year, and if Mac hasn't told Jenny by then to consider which option might work best for her at that point. We discussed what those options might be. She could start dating and continue to give him more time, or it might feel impossible to wait any longer and she could decide in order to date other people comfortably she is going to end their relationship. Or she might tell him that if he doesn't talk to Jenny by a certain date, she won't continue to see him. It's important to note that this is not an ultimatum because she is not trying to control him and tell him what to do. Instead, she is actually giving him a choice that he can either tell Jenny by a specified time or he can choose not to and, in either case, she will manage her own behavior and act accordingly. Already she had been waiting well over two and a half years for things to change, but even if she chose to wait another year or more, it was better than forever. By doing this, she is gaining control and making it her plan and her action to be taken instead of Mac's. Along those lines, I suggested she consider what her options are for right now. Because he's married, why does she have to be home and alone indefinitely on the nights he is with his family?

"I know you said you had thought about dating other people in the past but didn't want to risk Mac's anger, but can we talk more about dating?" I asked.

"I just can't do that," she said. "I don't want to. I sleep with him. I mean, I'm committed to him. Plus, he doesn't want me to. The time I mentioned it, because I was mad and I wanted to get a rise out of him, he freaked out. He told me he hated the idea."

"Of course he hates the idea," I said. "He doesn't want to share you, yet it's okay that you share him? Maybe if he thinks he won't have you all to himself, he'll do something about it. I know you don't want to risk his disapproval but if you think about it, it could really be a win-win for you."

"How so?" she asked me.

"Because if you are going out and feeling sexy and attractive to someone else it is going to shift your energy from being at home and feeling abandoned and lonely to feeling wanted and exciting, so it will boost your self-esteem," I said. "And in addition, it may nudge him to step up his plans to deal with his marriage and if not, if you decide he isn't ever going to come through, at least you have started to transfer out of this affair with him and you have the possibility of discovering someone new. Think of it as moving your energy from being disappointed and upset to spending it in a more positive way talking to new people. It doesn't have to be about starting or looking for a new relationship."

I've seen this happen a number of times before. One of my patients is having an affair and is desperate to be with that person all the time. That person is married and wants to be with my patient but hasn't yet begun to separate from his spouse and home life. And why should he, really? He has everything he could possibly want, a home where he sees his kids every day and his wife who, despite working full-time, still subscribed to the traditional notion that it was her job to manage the house, and his lover waiting for him and always available when he is able to sneak out. When my patients have shaken things up a little and begun to date, it hits home for their lover, they feel it, and it can become a catalyst to talk to their wife because now there is the real threat to their affair continuing. It can be looked at in a similar way to when you have an issue with your employer and want a new job. You can either wait until things are firmly over at your current office, and then be left with nothing and begin your job search from scratch, or, while you are still at your current job you can begin the process of seeing what else is out there. But often fear and doubts hold people back from taking the leap and exploring. They may think the person they are having the affair with is the only game in town, that they will never find anyone else or have sex with another person and beginning the process of looking will only serve to prove this. I have had patients tell me that they feel alone and are afraid of pushing their lover away and then being truly alone. While that is understandable, there is much to be gained by trying. If Kara agrees to attempt to begin dating, she will at least have started to put herself out there. And sometimes, when there is another option, when you find someone else you like even a little, your demeanor can shift slightly, maybe you aren't as available, maybe you aren't quite as needy and dependent as you once were, and that could make the other person begin to worry about you in a way they haven't had to before. Interest from and for someone else, no matter how minimal, will likely impact Kara's self-esteem and her sexual esteem because she will see she is attractive to other men. She will come to learn that Mac is not the only man on earth.

I tell my patients they need to take care of themselves, to level the playing field instead of sitting home alone on a Friday night when their lover is having dinner out with his wife and friends. The initial response to my suggestion is some form of what Kara said: they are sleeping with them, they are committed, which, of course, is ironic since the person they are committed to is married to someone else. What they are really saying is that they are exclusive with their lover, but, obviously, that doesn't go both ways. What I tell them in that case, though, is that they don't have to sleep with other people, but they should consider meeting other people. I explained that none of these things were easy, but they would put the ball back in her court so she is calling the shots, and she is no longer just waiting around for Mac to do what works best for him. I assured Kara that I understood how hard this could be to do, but I wanted her to think about it. She promised me she would.

One of my other patients, Tim, is going through this exact same thing in reverse. He is drawn to Sophia, with whom he is having an affair, in a way he has never experienced before. He didn't even know a physical attraction could be so intense. But he is married to Cindy and has been for eight years. The guilt he feels is immense. He tries his best to resist Sophia—every time he leaves her, he tells himself that is it, he won't see her again—and then, despite his efforts to stay out of touch, when she contacts him he simply can't refuse her. It feels like an addiction. Sophia does all the initiating; at least Tim has the strength to uphold his promise to himself that he won't get in touch with her, but she always does and he can't say no.

Tim met Sophia through a work friend. She tagged along to a business lunch one day and Tim could not take his eyes off her. Under the pretense of work—she works in marketing and there was the chance he might need her services for one of his clients—they exchanged information. They danced around each other for a few weeks and then they met at the same place for lunch, still pretending they would talk about business. The restaurant was in a hotel, and before they even ordered they knew they were going to go to a room together. It wasn't until after they made love that Tim told Sophia he was married. She almost laughed at the earnest way he told her. She knew he was married. She was also married, to a quiet man named Paul. She and Paul were on the downswing, she said with surprisingly little emotion. Tim almost didn't want to know what that meant.

Right away Tim made it clear that he wasn't going to leave his wife. He said he had never done anything like this before, and it just wasn't him. Sophia said she understood. She said she, too, hadn't done anything like this before, that the attraction she felt to him was indescribable. When she said those words, he felt butterflies in his stomach; he was thinking something similar. Still, this wasn't him. He didn't want to do this. He didn't want to be a man having an affair. Every time he left Sophia, he would tell her he couldn't do it anymore. But then she was all he could think about. He imagined her naked, he spent a lot of time trying to conjure up her smell, he thought about when they made love. And then she would reach out—she would text or call—and he simply could not say no. They began to meet once a week, and then twice a week, always with Sophia contacting him. At first it seemed that Sophia was fine with that arrangement, but then she started pushing to see him more. She said she wasn't happy in her marriage and wanted out. She said she wanted to make herself more available to him. She wanted him to do the same.

No way, he said. He was married. He knew he couldn't.

"I stood up there in front of my parents and a hundred other people and promised to love and honor Cindy for the rest of my life," he said in my office, not for the first time. "And I meant it. I did. But I didn't know Sophia was out there. I didn't know she existed in the world when I married Cindy. She is like a drug. I feel like I'm powerless to say no to her."

The thing is, his marriage with Cindy is complicated. It is far from perfect. But they do have a nice life together. They have a beautiful lake house in the Poconos. They love to cook and go out to dinner together. Reading next to her on the couch on a Sunday afternoon is one of the most peaceful times of his week. Up until he met Sophia, he literally told her everything. But their sex life is miserable; it is basically nonexistent. It used to be adequate but then weeks started to go by without sex, and now he isn't even sure how long it has been? Months? He hates to think it might be a year since they made love. He has tried many times over the years to tell himself that the sex isn't important, that there is so much good between them that he can live without the sex. But he can't. He thinks about it constantly, especially now that he knows what he is missing. With Sophia, the sex is amazing, fabulous, off the charts, and he knows not only is it something he can't live without, that he shouldn't have to live without, but that he does not want to live without.

This is another familiar pattern I see in some of my patients. They love their wife and value the comfortable life they have built together, but for one reason or another they have not been able to maintain a robust sex life, or sometimes any physical component to their relationship at all. When that happens, they can easily be drawn into an affair if the right person comes along, as was the case for Tim. Sophia is pretty and seems to want to touch him all the time and everywhere. He feels so flattered; he hasn't felt this way in so long. And the things she wants to do! Sometimes he feels as if he is in his own personal porn movie. He can't get enough! When she reaches out it feels a little like a drug dealer enticing him to get his next fix; really, when he thinks about it, it feels a lot like that. But the knowledge that he is doing something wrong is always in the back of his mind, the idea that he is hurting Cindy. He told me that at night sometimes he wishes he could meld them into one woman so he could have the best parts of each of them.

"I know I'm terrible for thinking that," he said to me. "But I'm supposed to be totally honest in here, right?"

"Yes, of course," I told him. "And you're struggling, I can see that."

"The thing is I'm a good person, but I feel bad all the time. When I'm with Sophia I feel like I'm not giving her enough, I'm not making her happy, and she gives me so much happiness I just can't handle that. And when I'm home with Cindy I feel like a cliché of the worst husband in the world. I tell myself that the last time with Sophia will be just that, the last time. And then she calls, or worse she sends a picture," he said. "The guilt is killing me. I feel like I'm trapped in this nightmare."

He went on to say that he imagines leaving Sophia. He talks himself through the exact conversations he will have, but then they are together and it is like fireworks. After that he tells himself *Cindy would be okay without him. She would survive. She would meet another man.* He can't believe he will ever have the chemistry he has with Sophia with anyone else. *So, knowing that, what is the point of trying to make it work with Cindy anymore?* he wonders. For him it is back and forth and back and forth.

"Maybe I should just leave Cindy for Sophia," he said to me.

"It's wonderful that you're experiencing this passion," I said to him. "But that sort of passion doesn't run forever. Eventually that sexual high will burn out and then you will face all the usual issues with Sophia. You have a strong foundation with Cindy. Have you thought about trying to bring some of the passion you feel with Sophia back to your marriage? It might be worth the effort to see if you can make things work with Cindy before you leave that all behind for Sophia."

I told him about the important skill *SET YOUR DATE,* but with him it was going to be used in a different way.

"Think about setting a timeline for yourself to set a date to deal directly with your marriage. Before looking to end it, let Cindy know how unhappy you are and go and get some therapy. Set a date for how long you are willing to invest in and commit to your marriage, particularly your sex life, so things can get better," I said. I let that sit for a minute. "Try to begin to ease yourself away from Sophia. Don't look at the photos she sends you and take some time before responding to her. The guilt you are feeling sounds overwhelming and if you are not able to leave Cindy, you will continue to prolong the turmoil you are feeling."

"But I want to be with Sophia, too," he said. "Maybe I can keep going this way."

"Think about what I said. This is clearly eating you up inside," I said. "And it is likely only going to get harder if Sophia demands more from you."

Tim was able to manage the affair for a while longer, but it was always stressful. They could never meet on weekends because he and Cindy went to the Poconos. Sometimes Sophia would text him there, sending sexy photos, and then that was all he could think about. He had to work extra hard to be present even for the good things he and Cindy still shared. She was starting to wonder what was going on with him. His constant worry didn't help. And then, out of nowhere, Sophia said she couldn't stand it anymore. She said that if he didn't agree to tell Cindy, she was going to tell her husband she was having an affair with Tim. It was at that point that he got scared and took the *SET YOUR DATE* skill seriously.

"Once she said she was going to tell Paul, I knew I couldn't go on like this for much longer," he told me at our next session. "If she tells Paul I could be exposed, it could blow up my marriage. So I decided I am going to talk to Cindy. Not about Sophia, but about seeing if we can fix things between us. I'm going to propose that we get some help together."

I told him I thought that was a great idea. I also told him the sooner he did it the better because it sounded like Sophia was ready to make her move.

It is never easy, juggling all those wants and needs. I had another patient during that time who was recently divorced and having an affair with a man who was married. It turns out he was her boss at work, and it was very exciting when it started because they were able to be together on business trips and during the workday without much trouble at all. They grew close quickly, and, without realizing it was happening, my patient, Genevieve, fell deeply in love with Jordan. Genevieve had a ten-year-old son and a fairly busy life, but she found she wanted to be with Jordan all the time. Jordan, however, was not as available as she would have liked him to be. He had three young girls. He and his wife had been having some trouble, but their home life was a whirlwind, and he loved being with his kids. He told Genevieve that he loved her, more than he had ever loved anyone before, but there was just no way he was going to leave his wife and the life they had built. There was no way he could leave his girls. He told her that he would do everything he could to give them more time together, that he would try to plan even more business trips in the coming months. And he was true to his word. He was able to schedule two- and three-day trips away, which were heavenly. He was great about staying in touch, always responding to Genevieve when she reached out, and sending her cute notes with lots of heart emojis during the day. He made her feel special; somehow, despite everything, he could sometimes make her feel like a priority. If she complained about wanting more time together, he would list all the things he does for her and she would back down, feeling guilty.

When she was sick, he sent her soup. When she fell and twisted her ankle, fearing it was broken, he managed to sneak away from work and meet her at the emergency room. And one month, when she thought she was pregnant, he was even more attentive than usual, never making her feel that he didn't want their baby. When it turned out she wasn't, he mourned along with her. She often thought of how that would have made this time easier, if they could have had their own secret family together while she waited for him to be with her all the time. Most touching to her, though, was the way he interacted with her son, always listening to what he talked about, bringing him a tennis racquet when he expressed interest in the game and a book series—all ten books!—he talked about wanting to read. Even though he was clear about not ever leaving his wife, Genevieve believed with all her heart that once his kids were out of the house he would.

Genevieve missed him and was sad when she couldn't be with Jordan. All she could think about were the little moments people share when they have a home together, cleaning up after dinner, reading in bed next to each other at night, things they never did together because they didn't have a chance to cook together. She truly thought Jordan wanted to share that with her, too. She could feel him fall deeper in love with her every time they were together, so she knew all she had to do was stick it out and eventually he would come around. There it was, the *Wishing and Hoping*. She truly believed that she would be able to change his mind. He was in love with her, that was clear, and he told her that he and his wife hadn't had sex in months. She was certain that if she just waited it out, he would want to be with her full-time, that their relationship would blossom into real time.

"Hasn't he been pretty clear that that isn't going to happen?" I asked when she told me once again how she knew things would work out with the two of them. I could hear Denial in her voice as she told me she had no doubts that it was just a matter of time.

"*He's such a good dad,*" she said. "*He goes to every soccer game, every school concert. He revels in his girls' successes. The fact that he doesn't want to miss that only makes me love and respect him more. And believe me, I can totally understand. I wouldn't want to leave my son. But it won't be forever. Eventually his girls will be in college and then he'll be left alone with his wife who, as far as I can tell, is the ice queen.*"

"That's all true, but that's what keeps him limited in his availability to you," I said. "No matter how much he wants to be with you, the reality of his life means he can't spend more time than he already is, which is what he repeatedly tells you. So how long can you live with feeling deprived of everything you long for?"

"*It won't be that long,*" she said. "*I just have to bide my time. I look at how good he is to me, at what he does for me, for us. I can handle a couple of years until the kids are grown. I can do that. It will be worth it.*"

The next time I saw Genevieve, she was angrier than I had ever seen her. For her birthday a few weeks before, Jordan had given her a beautiful sterling silver necklace with an elegant opal charm at the end. She loved it and wore it constantly. From time to time, she checked Jordan's wife's Facebook page. She was able to do that without actually being her "friend" on Facebook because they had a few mutual but distant friends in common. She looked yesterday and his wife had posted a photo of the same necklace, only hers was gold. Genevieve spent a fair amount of time trying to see which one was more expensive. Her charm was bigger so in the end she decided he spent more money on hers but still, she couldn't shake it. When she asked him, he said what he gave his wife didn't mean anything, but he had to give her something! It had been her birthday, too.

But Genevieve could barely stand it. Why did he have to give her practically the same thing he gave Genevieve? Why did it have to be so nice? I empathized with how that spoiled her feeling she was special and important to him. I went on to explain that in these situations a husband does attempt to appease his guilt by trying to make his wife happy. To help her accept reality, I then added that she is still his wife, and while that is a hard thing to accept given the circumstances, it is the way it is, and Genevieve will have to deal with that. I told her to remind herself that Jordan has to have involvement with his spouse, that he has made it clear that he wants to maintain his home life, and there is no way around it. It is his self-protection. And it isn't as if he hasn't been honest about this with Genevieve from day one. Still, this whole thing triggered her jealousy, which most of the time she could keep in check. Sometimes, though, her fears and doubts would bombard her and she would think, *maybe he really loves his wife, she is so attractive, maybe I'll always just be second best.*

The question I often ask my patients when they find themselves in situations like this is, will this ever become a true relationship or is it more likely that it will remain an affair that eventually burns out, and burns you out because you are *Wishing and Hoping* for something to happen that, in reality, is not likely to happen at all? I didn't think Genevieve was ready for that question yet. What I thought she might be ready for was the idea that she could begin to take matters into her own hands. I shared the skill *SET YOUR DATE* with her. It's a little different here, too, because Jordan was not promising to leave so there was nothing to push back against there, but Genevieve could take more control. She could talk to him about what he would do if she wasn't okay with the idea of hanging around in this role forever. If it came to that, was he willing to lose her? If so, that was something that would be good to know now before she put too much more time into the relationship. Also, she could use it to, at the very least, leverage more time with him if she let him know she might make changes if he wasn't willing to make any sacrifices for her.

"That all feels like a threat," Genevieve said to me. "I trust him completely and would never give him an ultimatum because I want him to trust me, too. I know without question that he has my best interests at heart. I would trust him with my life."

I asked her to tell me more about that because I wanted to hear her reasoning for how he had her best interests at heart while being married to someone else, with no end in sight to that.

"He cares about me," she said. "He loves me. He anticipates my needs. When I'm alone on a Sunday he'll have a deli sandwich delivered to my door. He is thinking about me. He is very loving."

"Yes he is, but only when he can be. What about the fact that his choice to remain married leaves you alone a lot of the time?" I asked. "That sounds like he is looking out for his own best interests, not for yours."

"*He's going to come around*," Genevieve said. "*Just wait and see.*"

However, time went on and nothing changed. So, Genevieve began to consider her options in terms of how she could SET THE DATE. She decided to tell Jordan that she would wait until his youngest daughter went to college, which was two years away, and asked him if he would leave his marriage then. This would help her determine if he was truly never going to leave his wife, or if he was just not leaving while the kids were still home. If the answer was never, if he wasn't prepared to make any move to be with her on a more permanent basis, then maybe ending the relationship was something she was going to have to work toward being able to do.

"What did he say?" I asked.

"For the first time ever, he said he would think about it," she said.

Let's take a look at how Kara is doing. It turned out that the lump in Jenny's neck was nothing to worry about. Once they got that news, she began to push Mac more and more to tell Jenny how unhappy he was. One day, he told her he wanted to be with her for longer than a few hours at a time. He said he would make an excuse to Jenny to get away with Kara for a few days—a made-up work trip or something. That really hit her in the gut—she was tired of excuses. She just wanted to be with him in the open. With that in mind, she began to half-heartedly date, or at least go on a handful of first dates with other men. Mac could not stand that. He became so jealous he could barely contain himself. Her exercising her independence was a catalyst for Mac's finally telling Jenny three months later. Once that was done, he started to work on ending his marriage.

Tim and his wife, Cindy, are also finding their way, although it is not easy. Tim ended things with Sophia and went to therapy to work on improving his sex life with his wife. In his case, he says he wishes he had done that a long time ago. And Genevieve is still waiting. She is enjoying every minute she gets with Jordan, but she knows she will not do this forever. She can see a date on the horizon, when Jordan will eventually give her what she wants, or when she will have to forge a new path. In the meantime, she told me, she might date a little. Who knows who else might be out there?

And Kara? Today she and Mac met on the sidewalk and had lunch at a restaurant. They kissed in front of everyone who walked by. He is now separated from Jenny and moving toward getting divorced. He and Kara have already talked about the possibility that he might move into her apartment one day. Whatever they decide to do, though, today is the best day so far. Today, Kara finally has her day in the sun.

In this chapter we talked about how Mac, Tim, and Jordan all had problems connecting with their wives on different levels. We witnessed how they wound up in an affair because they had so much disconnect in their marriage; either they tried to tell their partner how unhappy they were but ultimately weren't able to, or they wound up feeling defeated and like nothing was ever going to change, which made them vulnerable to the attention of someone else. They found themselves fantasizing about being with that someone else. But what happens in a marriage that gets you to the precipice of this point? More specifically, how did Tim find himself in a sexless marriage with his wife in the first place? Let's take a look.

CHAPTER SIX

Maybe Tomorrow We'll Have Sex?

WHEN TIM AND CINDY GOT MARRIED, THEIR SEX LIFE SEEMED fine to both of them. Neither had had many sexual relationships before, and when they finally began dating, the intimacy they shared felt comfortable. Cindy once even told her sister, "It was nice." They had been friends for a long time before they became romantically involved. They spent many platonic weekends together, going to the movies, playing on the same coed softball team, sharing meals. Cindy really counted on Tim for companionship because it had been hard to get any dating off the ground. When he finally confessed that he had feelings for her beyond their friendship and suggested they give it a shot, she thought, why not?

The first time they had sex it seemed good enough. There were no fireworks, but nobody complained either. Their kissing was slow and steady, never too out-of-control. They undressed side by side, their eyes on each other, but there was no rushing, no urgency. It felt exciting, though, because neither had been close to another person or really been touched beyond a hug here and a kiss on the cheek there among friends for a while. They were both happy to have reached this point. Any acknowledgment of a lack of a great physical connection was superseded by the exhilaration of the newness of their relationship. It was a thrill to have taken this next step together, to bring their friendship to another level, but it was not a barometer of Cindy's sexual desire or their compatibility. That, unfortunately, was lost in the shuffle.

The eagerness of wanting to be in each other's presence was intoxicating for Cindy, so at first it was easy and made sense to be intimate multiple times a week. Naturally, given that, Tim assumed her sexual appetite matched his. He didn't realize that it was just a reflection of the fact that she was happy to be with him. For her, it was much more about the physical closeness and the connection to another human being than it was about the sex. Those first few weeks and months, whenever he initiated, she was happy to go along. She especially liked the time they spent in bed after they made love. They would talk quietly and snuggle, and they would tell each other their secrets, the things that made them who they were. She looked forward to those moments so much, it was worth it to her to get through the sex. Of course, she never told Tim that. In those early days, she just appeared to enjoy it all.

The truth was, though, that even from the beginning their level of desire was different. Tim wanted to make love three to four times a week, even more if Cindy were open to it. She started to wonder if he was always in the mood. Cindy, on the other hand, thought one to two times a week was plenty, and probably even too much for her taste. Sure, she realized, people did it more often at the beginning of a relationship, but that wasn't going to last forever. As months went by and Cindy began to have more excuses, it occurred to Tim that she wasn't in the mood quite as much as she had been, and, really, if he were being honest with himself, not quite often enough for his palate. Even so, they had a lot in common, and they had similar life goals. They thoroughly enjoyed each other's company. At that point neither questioned their decision to come together or considered what their varying styles in the bedroom might mean to their future.

Cindy was sure Tim's sexual enthusiasm would wane the longer they were together. She was counting on it. Her mother had told her a story about a mythical jar of beans—you put a bean in the jar every time you have sex the first year you are together, and if you take out a bean every time you have sex after that you will never empty the jar. In other words, everyone's sex life slowed down. So, they would be fine! Still, that wasn't what Tim was thinking at all. He was fairly certain that the more comfortable Cindy became, the more she would want to be intimate with him. He imagined getting into a routine of having sex most nights of the week. Wasn't that what married people did? All he had to do was give her some time.

Even though she was not the one to typically initiate, every once in a while she would, and he loved it. Those unexpected moments usually came out of nowhere. One night they were watching television and he was zoning out, he wasn't even think-ing about sex, but she must have been because she reached over and began stroking his penis gently. He thought, is this really happening? He was thrilled. He hadn't even planned to try for sex that night. She moved closer to him and began to kiss him and he knew she was all in, they were going to make love. He wondered what had sparked that. Had there been something sexy on the show they were watching? He wanted to remember so he could re-create it. Maybe now things were really going to heat up, he told himself. This was what he had been waiting for! It didn't happen again for months, even though he often hoped it would. In fact, after that, on the nights he initiated it, because it seemed that was the only way he was going to be able to be with his wife, he often thought of that night and it turned him on immediately. Then one night, a few months later, she did it again and, once more, his hope and expectations were fueled.

As time went on, however, she reached out to him sexually less and less, and eventually a year went by and she had not initi-ated at all. Not only that, but she refused his overtures more than she accepted them. She never quite said, "Not tonight, dear, I have a headache," but it really felt like she might as well have. She had to get up early, or she had eaten too much at dinner, or she couldn't get her friend's dying mother out of her mind. It became painfully clear that things were not moving in the direction Tim had hoped, one in which they had sex multiple times a week and it was effortless, no stressful push and pull. Instead, he realized, not only was she not initiating anymore, but much to his distress he was repeatedly encountering a big red stop sign when he made it clear he would like to make love. He was getting more frustrated by the week. Weren't they husband and wife? Wasn't that what spouses were supposed to do? This was not turning out the way he had imagined it at all. He began to wonder whether there was something wrong with him. Didn't Cindy find him attractive anymore? Was she drawn to women? He even wondered if bringing a third person in might help. Did she wish they could be just friends again? Because that was certainly how she was acting. He was completely confounded and desperately trying to make sense of it.

The only silver lining at first was that when Cindy wasn't interested in sex, she would offer to give him oral sex. He figured she might feel tired or even achy from her run that morning and might not want to be touched, but she still cared about his pleasure and about being close to him. It took him some time to realize that that hadn't happened in a while either. It used to be at least twice a month, but now, he wondered, when had been the last time she wanted to do that? Three months ago? Five months ago? Once that thought entered his mind, it was difficult to shake.

It is hard to pinpoint exactly when it became an issue, when Tim would retire for the night and wait and hope Cindy would initiate and, when she didn't, he would reach out and, more often than not, she would turn away instead of turning toward him. Every time, with Denial's help, he would tell himself, *she's working so hard. She's so busy at work. She must just be too tired.* And the next night he would be just as hopeful as he had been the night before. *She knows how important this is to me*, he would think to himself. *Surely, she isn't going to go three nights in a row without wanting to have sex with me.* He was aware that in general things seemed good between them. In the morning Cindy would kiss him at the breakfast table, she would sweep her hand along the small of his back. She smiled and shared stories about her day. She seemed happy. Even so, he would sit there thinking *does she really not know how upset I am? Does she really think I'm okay that we aren't having sex?* Despite the excuses he made almost nightly to himself on her behalf, there was no question that he was feeling excruciatingly rejected, which was very painful to him and his sexual esteem took a hit. Again he wondered, was she not attracted to him? Did she not find him sexy enough? Every rebuff started to feel bigger than it should have because now there was no consolation prize and, he was aware, he was beginning to expect her roadblock. Now when she said no, there was just nothing. Just a big, fat no, though it was always a nice no. Cindy was consistently apologetic, saying she felt bad but she just didn't feel up to it tonight. She assured him it wasn't him; it was her. She stood by her same list of excuses: the pressure of work, her racing mind, being tired or too full after dinner.

Suddenly it had been so long since they had had sex that it was almost hard to imagine how to get back to it. If she had said no the last five times, she had said no the last ten times. Truthfully, he couldn't remember the last time she said yes. Night after night he would either wait for her to do something and she wouldn't, or he would try, she would say no and offer nothing else, and he would lie there smoldering with anger, feeling rejected. Tonight, though, he decided he would give it his all. He had made sexy and flirtatious comments to her all day. He lit candles next to their bed, one of his signals that he was interested in making love. But he wouldn't leave it at that. He would suggest a bath together, something they used to do at the beginning of their relationship.

As he waited for Cindy to finish up downstairs, he was hopeful. He breathed in the rose scent of the candles and waited. Just the smell turned him on, and he looked forward to Cindy's coming to the bedroom. Surely, she will see the signs, he thought, as his wish that she will know how much this means to him kicked in. Denial was right there next to him letting him believe *tonight will be different*. When she came to the door, however, she barely looked at him.

"Oh," she said like she was surprised to see him waiting there like that. How could she be? he wondered. It was Friday night, and they hadn't been together in a long time. He had been hinting about it all day. Also, he had been hoping she would smell the rose candles on her way up the stairs. Tim refused to be deterred. He walked to her, smiling, and took her face in his hand. He leaned in and kissed her gently. She kissed back and he began to relax, he must have misunderstood her initial reaction. He moved his hand down over her breast and she put her hand on his, moving it away.

"I had a really hard day," she said quietly. "I just want to get into bed and read. I'm sorry."

"Come on," he said flirtatiously. "What does a guy have to do around here to get some loving? I miss you."

"I'm right here," she said, leaning in for a hug before walking over to the candles and blowing them out. He watched as she walked into the bathroom and closed the door behind her without another word, leaving him alone and cold. That's it, he thought. I'm not doing this anymore. He decided in that moment that he was no longer going to reach out to Cindy just to have her turn him down. He didn't want to find himself in the position to be rejected again.

As time went on, Tim and Cindy became more and more caught up in their careers, and one or both often got stuck at the office and didn't even make it home before the other was already asleep, or, when they both arrived home late together, before Cindy collapsed into bed making it very clear she didn't have an ounce of energy to do anything else. Soon Cindy began to work toward a promotion, so she was even more absent than she had been before. It was hard for either of them to recall when they last made love. Sex now felt like something that was a part of their past, not like something they still did together.

I have seen this many times with my patients; they have a different level of desire from their spouse and a scenario similar to what is happening in Tim and Cindy's bedroom plays out. When this is the case, it is easy for their sex life to eventually become completely derailed. If one partner says no a lot, it can take a real toll on their sexual bond. When one person is turned down multiple times, it is inevitable that they will get angry and resentful. As a result, they try to take control by retaliating and making their partner feel the way they do. They say I'm going to deprive you like you are doing to me, and they try to withhold. When couples reach this point, two things can happen. They wait, and if and when their partner does finally initiate, they say no out of spite and don't end up having sex even though it is really what they want. Or the other person never initiates and then they are at a *Sexless Standoff.* The anger can begin to smolder under the surface and, with each person staying in their own corner, they might not have sex for a long time. In some cases, months can turn to years.

Another problem that can come between people is the quality of making love. It is common that two people still want to be together but have completely different ideas about what makes sex good. One wants to talk dirty and dress up, while their partner likes to keep it clean and simple. One likes to give and get oral sex, and the other doesn't at all. There is also the question of positions. One partner likes to try different things and change positions when they are making love, but the other person is comfortable only when they are using the missionary position. One of the trickier aspects of telling your partner what pleases you is that they wind up feeling controlled by your preference, and that they have to do it in order for you to enjoy sex. While this can happen with other things, too, it is particularly true with sex. If, for example, you tell your lover you like to hold hands during intercourse, the other person might think they then have to do that and could wind up resenting it.

All of this was going on with Tim and Cindy. They managed to have sex sporadically for the first four or so years of their marriage, but it became more and more difficult and tense. Not only did they have very different levels of sexual desire, but they also had different ideas about what they should do when they managed to make love. Tim liked to spice it up a little, he liked to refer to his penis by a name and he always wanted to give Cindy's vagina a name. That had bothered her from the beginning, but she went along with it at first, or at least she didn't protest, but she always tried to pretend she hadn't heard him. He misinterpreted her complicity for enthusiasm, so he kept it up. It grated on her. How could he not have noticed that she didn't like it? she wondered. It was so clear. She had grown up in a house with two quiet and fairly repressed parents who never talked about sex; they never touched each other in front of their kids, and to be honest, Cindy just felt weird about it all. She had thought there was the chance that would ease up, but it hadn't. All along, Tim thought if he kept at it, she would eventually feel more familiar with it and might not tense up as much when he tried to personify their sexual organs.

"It's just become so stale between us," Tim said one day in my office. It was long before everything happened with Sophia. "I don't know what to do. I am really starting to think it is never going to be comfortable between us like it was at the beginning."

He told me that he was feeling defeated, that he wasn't sure it was worth the effort anymore because Cindy always shut him down these days. Sometimes, the person who is far less interested in sex might see it as a relief that their spouse has backed off and is no longer asking them for physical contact. It might feel to them that they are finally being understood and listened to, that their needs are being considered. But that is really a *Watch-Out Sign* because it indicates that their significant other has given up, he or she is no longer trying, and they may be approaching

the point of no return. At that stage the person who is not interested in sex might feel they have entered a different phase, one
in which things are okay but they are living more like brother
and sister than passionate lovers. They might tell themselves they
don't mind, that they share many other things that will keep
them together. But the truth is, any lull is likely accompanied by
feelings of hurt and rejection for the partner who wants more.
That person's self- and sexual esteem might plummet, and they
may seriously begin to doubt their self-worth. This is when people can become dangerously vulnerable to having an affair. If the
right person comes along, someone who gives them attention and
makes them feel good about themselves, they can decide to stray
from the marriage as Tim did with Sophia. Tim felt so mad at
Cindy he couldn't take it anymore. That is sometimes the first step
in making someone vulnerable to looking outside the marriage
for sex and assurance that they are, in fact, still attractive, as Tim
eventually did. He used the anger he felt toward Cindy to justify
his affair with Sophia. It helped him deal with the guilt he felt
once he and Sophia connected, at least at first. But, as we know
from Chapter Five, he and Cindy were ultimately able to make it
work. So how did they do that? How did they get from point A
to Point B, and, finally, to Point C?

Many people have been there. They find a partner, get married, and things don't go as they had hoped, especially in the sex
department. But instead of dealing with it head-on, they find
themselves *Wishing and Hoping* that their partner will magically
turn into the lover they want them to be. They tell themselves all
sorts of things with Denial standing by their side: *he's busy, she's
stressed with the kids, tomorrow will be different.* It is that hope
that keeps them stuck and then, when it goes on for too long and
nothing changes, the simmering anger and resolution can become
a wall between them.

By this point, Tim was deep into his affair with Sophia, and
the guilt he felt surrounding that had grown considerably and was

immense now. He had come to the conclusion that he wanted more than anything to make things work with Cindy. When Tim expressed his hope to work things out with Cindy, I shared my important skill *LEANING IN RATHER THAN LEANING BACK* with him. This is something that helps you handle your anger straight on, so it doesn't grow so intense it fuels you to act on it by having an affair. Instead of withdrawing and retreating, smoldering, or trying to control the other person, this skill shifts the control to you in terms of what action you can take to deal directly with the problem at hand. With it, you no longer allow so much to go unsaid, as Tim did with Cindy. I encouraged him to stop taking a backseat, waiting for Cindy to come to him and initiate, but rather to manage his disappointment by doing the opposite and being proactive. I explained that taking the lead and reaching out to Cindy again, rather than sitting back and feeling bad about himself, was a healthier option. That way, if Cindy continued to be unresponsive or even reject his overtures, they would have something tangible to address and work through.

"In other words, make the choice to act so you don't continue to feel so hopeless," I said to Tim. "It is all about putting the ball back in your court and exercising control. Instead of lying there and getting more upset and enraged, own your sexual desire and initiate. If Cindy says no, which she might, don't turn the other way in anger but instead deal with it head-on. If she puts the brakes on when you indicate you want to make love, you have to let her know you are upset about it. In addition, it is important to distinguish between whether this is really about timing, if she is truly just tired or stressed on the occasions when she says no, but is open to sex other times, or if she is inhibited and she just doesn't want to have sex at all, in which case you will have to deal with that. Once you make that distinction, you will know what you are facing and can move forward accordingly. If it turns out to be more about the timing than about you, knowing that will help you not take it so personally."

I suggested considering what I call *Scheduled Spontaneity* in which they can plan ahead and look forward to sex at a future date if the immediate timing isn't right. In other words, if Tim reaches out but Cindy says she is not in the mood because she is too tried or stressed, then she needs to take responsibility. Let her choose a time when she thinks she will be more receptive to being sexually intimate and let him know when that will be. That way she has input as well about the landscape of their sexual life, and it is not all about his timing and when he wants it. Hopefully by using that skill they can recapture the good feeling they once shared. Tim was skeptical. He said things often got tense between them now when the mere mention of sex came up. I told him that was common with couples who were going through this, but that addressing the matter rather than stewing over it was going to be much better for their marriage overall.

"It's about not pulling back in anger, but putting yourself out there," I said. "And while it can feel awkward, it's important to hold Cindy accountable. You need to deal directly with her rather than letting your anger block out your sex life. If she doesn't want to make love on Tuesday, then you can agree to do it on Saturday morning when the pressure of the week lets up a little."

"But what do I do if I look forward to it all week and then Saturday morning rolls around and she rejects me again?" he asked.

"That's when you tackle it head-on and talk about it," I said.

"You say that like it's simple," he said. "But what if she just refuses to follow through and when I try, she says no again and won't talk about it?"

"I know this is hard to do," I said. "The reality is you have a problem and it hasn't gone away; it has only gotten worse over time. *Wishing and Hoping* that it is going to get better, and deceiving yourself that it isn't so bad hasn't worked. It's time to confront what is going on, even if it is upsetting to both of you. You can acknowledge that it is difficult. It's the only way to get through your disappointment and be able to look forward to connecting sexually. If she says no again on the date you planned, think of it this way: if you were going to go to dinner with a friend or play racquet ball and they had to cancel with you but offered no explanation or plan to reschedule, wouldn't you pick up the phone and say, hey, what happened? Well, the same goes here. In fact, this is even more significant. If that happens, ask for an explanation, and, if need be, another rain check. Push it forward and come up with another time to be intimate together. Stop making excuses and stewing inwardly about it; put the problem out in the open."

Tim agreed he would try. However, he also knew he did not want to and could not live a life without sex.

Around the same time another patient of mine came to me with a similar problem. Sally was outgoing and energetic; she was beautiful and had a lot of sexual energy. Even so, she found herself in a marriage in which sex was very scarce. She felt trapped in a situation in which she spent a lot of time *Wishing and Hoping* that her husband, Kevin, would turn into a great lover, the sort of man who considered her needs and slowed things down enough that she could find her rhythm and enjoy making love to him. She fantasized about engaging in foreplay, about receiving oral sex, and about touching each other slowly and gently. She tried hinting to him about these things with comments like, "it would be nice to stay in bed longer," because she did not want to tell him she didn't enjoy the sex they shared and risk hurting his feelings by being too specific. Regardless, their sexual encounters were always rushed affairs in which her husband appeared to think only about his own pleasure. Denial allowed her to believe it would change, that surely next time he would pay more attention to her, he would be a more sensual lover. And every time, she was disappointed. It was a cycle that kept her stuck and unhappy.

She had a handle on so many things in her life that when she told me her marriage was bordering on becoming sexless, I was surprised. She explained that the sex she shared with her husband wasn't good. She never felt satisfied. She said it was always too fast, there was no foreplay at all. They didn't even kiss anymore. He would come to bed ready for sex, he didn't even need any help to get an erection, and before she had a chance to feel sexy, he was in full swing. Sometimes she felt a twinge of excitement, but before she could even catch it or settle into that feeling, he was finished and rolling off her, ready to go to sleep, and she was left feeling confused, rushed, disappointed, and lonely. Eventually, she became so frustrated that she tried to take the hinting to the next level by being specific. She told him that she wanted more during their time in bed, maybe he could kiss her neck, perhaps he could touch her breasts, what about a little tender talk? He would always say of course, he wanted that, too. With Denial by her side she would actually Believe What She Was Told and she would think, *next time it is going to be better, next time it is going to be great.* But it never happened. Despite Kevin's reassuring her that she always looked good, she was starting to think that she really wasn't turning him on and was not, in fact, sexy enough for him. This made her feel really inadequate and terrible about herself.

Our "*Sexpectations,*" that is, whatever each person expects from the other when it comes to their sexual life, determine what does and does not happen as well as the anger and disappointment that follows. As we have seen with Tim and Cindy, and now with Sally and Kevin, there are many factors, including how often it happens and what is considered to be good technique. Other factors can come into play, too. There are times when men are quick in bed because they are caught up in their own desire. Other times performance anxiety can be a barrier. However, men can learn how to slow down their pleasure and manage their anxiety to enhance their relationship. Other times, the responsibility of birth control can cast a pall over the bedroom. There might be a dispute about who should be responsible for wearing a condom, or taking a pill, or using a diaphragm. If one partner gets stuck carrying the burden, they might be resentful and think, why should I have to do it? Therefore, they don't, and they stop trying to be intimate. None of these issues mean their sex life has no hope. The important step is to get to the heart of the conflict and figure out what is going on between them. The real question Sally had to answer was whether her husband was in fact a selfish lover, or they could work together to make his technique and her experience better.

Sally and Kevin had two kids and busy lives. In the summer they spent weekends fishing as a family, and in the winter they cross-country skied together. It is exactly the way they fantasized it would be when they were dating. They had joked about having the family of kings, one boy and one girl, and they did. They both supported the other in their work. Everything they had promised to each other was there, except the one thing they had not given enough attention to beforehand—sex. Right from the beginning it had felt like something they *should* be doing. Sally was the one who usually initiated but Kevin always took the hint, at least at first. And it was fine, it felt adequate. Many times, Sally would walk away feeling a little empty and it occurred to her how unfulfilling it was, but each time the concern bubbled up she pushed it back down, thinking, *how important was it in the long run anyway?* She also thought, *it can only get better from here.* That is Denial's contributing factor for a lot of people who find themselves in this situation because it helps them tamp down the alarm bells that might be ringing about why their sexual connection is lacking so much. Denial helps people believe that they can live with it, which allows them to stick around and even marry someone to whom they do not enjoy making love from the start. They might think, it's pretty bad now, but it will improve with time, as we get to know each other. So when Sally and Kevin made love that first year and she just wasn't feeling it, but she loved him and relished the potential of their life together, she told herself *when we are married we will have all the time and privacy in the world to focus on each other's bodies; we will learn what the other likes; Kevin is so kind, of course he will want me to be happy in the bedroom; he is so focused, he will take this up as one of his important causes, I just know it. He will get to know my body; I'll help him explore.* And a tiny, tiny bit of her brain also had the thought, *how important is sex anyway?* Ah, Denial. The truth is, if sex is bad at the beginning of a relationship, it needs to be dealt with then or it is only going to get worse and not, as Denial promises, better. Sally didn't know that yet.

As she walked down the aisle with Kevin waiting at the end for her, she thought ahead to their wedding night and the pressure of sex. And then she relaxed because she knew if she didn't mention it Kevin wouldn't either. She loved him, she couldn't wait to stand beside him, but she was already tired. She would worry about the sex another time. And so, before their marriage had even begun, they were already going down this difficult path. Sally was wrong about one thing, though. Despite that fact that Kevin really didn't want to put much time into sex, he did want to have it. For the first few years of their marriage they developed a routine; he would lean over with puppy eyes, then he would move toward her. She would always think, *maybe it will be different this time.* Before she knew it he was ready to go, and then it was over, and she felt wide awake, confused, and like she needed a shower, instead of feeling sleepy and cozy the way she had just felt before he got the idea in his head. Slowly she began to feel turned off to sex completely because she was always left with the sense of disappointment after experiencing his lack of technique. She avoided being near him the times he would usually look over at her with those eyes. She often waited until he was asleep before coming to bed, or she would stay longer than she had to in one of the kid's rooms after reading books and sometimes just fell asleep there. Over the course of time, since the sex itself was so lackluster and she rarely even came close to an orgasm, she reached the point where she was so repelled by the thought of making love to Kevin that it didn't even feel worth the effort anymore to try to talk to him to make it different.

When Sally backed away and was less available, Kevin became more demanding, which surprised her. Sometimes when she took a long time to get ready for bed or fell asleep reading to one of the kids he would pout when she came to their room. When she wanted to go out to dinner or see a movie, he would begrudge her pleasure and say things like why bother? On the rare occasions she did sleep with him, he was noticeably agreeable and generous. It became clear that having sex meant not only keeping the peace on the home front but also scoring points with her husband, which translated into his treating her well. As a result, she lost even more touch with her own desire because it felt like a chore, like something she had to do, and any sense that it might be something she wanted to do was lost.

"I can't stand sex anymore," she told me one day. "It feels like a demand. Like he wants it when he wants it no matter what I want. And I don't think he even considers how it feels to me. He is a nice man, a good husband, I just think he never learned how to make love to someone the right way. I mean night after night he wants to do it. Even if I don't feel great. Even if I explain it was a really rough day with the kids. The other night my mother was obnoxious on the phone, he could see I was upset and I thought there is no way he is going to try tonight and yet he did."

Here was her Denial, her wishful thinking that he would observe how she was feeling and consider her need for not having sex and accept it by leaving her alone. So often it just doesn't work that way. I told her what I tell all my patients who find themselves in this situation.

"You are not alone; many people end up in a marriage where they are unhappy with their sex life and, as a result, it starts to diminish," I said. "One thing to keep in mind, though, is that sex is an important part of a marriage for the two of you and also for your own health."

I shared the skill of *LEANING IN RATHER THAN LEANING BACK* with her, emphasizing the idea that instead of turning away from Kevin by lingering in the bathroom or spending more time with the kids to avoid having to have sex, she should turn toward him.

"It's important to pay attention to your own sexual desire," I said. "And when you are in the mood you can initiate. That way you won't feel like you are just there for his pleasure and that your needs don't count."

"What if I'm never in the mood?" she asked.

"Start paying attention to your own desire and think back to the beginning when you felt like a team and when you were excited to be building a life together," I said. "Tune into and become aware of your own body and connect that to remembering when he was your ally and not when he was someone you wanted to avoid."

She promised me she would try.

In the meantime, Tim was trying to break away from his affair with Sophia, with whom the sex was like nothing he had ever experienced before, because he wanted to make things work with Cindy. Ultimately, despite the deep physical connection Tim felt to Sophia, he believed he had much more to lose if he ended things with Cindy than if he did with Sophia. He finally told Cindy how he felt, what his thoughts were about their sex life, and, ultimately, that he had strayed from the marriage. The admission of infidelity was like a tidal wave, causing huge ripples in their home. She finally realized what a low point their sex life had reached and the toll it had taken on their marriage. She could see now that the relief she had felt when he stopped asking for sex, thinking he was understanding her wishes, was unbeknownst to her because he had been with another woman. It was a painful revelation to how much damage their sexual differences had taken on their relationship. Tim assured Cindy that he had firmly ended things with Sophia, that he would never see her again, but repairing their marriage was going to take a lot more than that. Through talking and convincing Cindy to join him in therapy, Tim promised he was ready to take responsibility for what he had done. He wanted to do everything possible to fix the broken trust with the hope of rebuilding their intimacy on an emotional and a sexual level. Because he was willing to deal with his betrayal, it helped her begin to heal and see that he really meant what he said and was sincere about the remorse he felt. He reassured her that it was about the sex, that he wasn't in love with another woman, and that helped her to believe in his sincerity in wanting to mend their marriage. Cindy was able to acknowledge that she loved him enough to try to get through the damage the infidelity had caused.

After they reached the point where they both knew they wanted to work on their marriage, and Cindy trusted that Tim meant it, we were able to begin to deal with their sex life. At first, the fact that Tim had not been fulfilled left Cindy feeling that there was something wrong with her because she didn't want to have sex as much as he did. She wondered if she were to blame for some of it. In my office, Cindy admitted that she questioned whether this was her problem since Tim seemed so much more drawn to sex than she was. She just wasn't interested; it felt like a chore, and she realized early on that once she let the process begin she wouldn't be able to stop it until Tim was satisfied. She certainly didn't want to seem like a tease, so she avoided it more and more. She was just so overwhelmed at work that when she got home she wanted to rest. It had nothing to do with Tim really, she loved him and she liked living with him; she just wasn't very interested in sex. She thought for sure he would get the hint and not try so often, but he kept trying, he was so hopeful. And boy, had she felt guilty. There were a lot of days when she also felt pressured, and that was not a good feeling at all. Finally, she admitted that putting names to their sexual organs really turned her off, and when they had engaged in sex, she found herself just waiting with dreaded anticipation for Tim to use one of the names he had come up with for his penis or her vagina. It made her cringe every time and took away any sexual desire she may have had. After she said that she looked down and waited. Clearly that had been difficult for her to admit.

Tim listened to everything Cindy said with quiet interest. After she was finished speaking, he told her he had no idea that was how she had been feeling, He said that was the last thing he wanted. He just felt the urge to have sex much more often than she did, and he was trying to be playful, but he also agreed their sex had been a bit lackluster. He promised he would pay more attention to her, and he would never ever utter those names again. Slowly she was able to trust that Tim was fully invested in their marriage, and this was truly all about being more sexually explorative and bringing excitement into their life. She believed him when he said he wanted it with only her, not with anyone else. Once they got through that and Tim's feelings were firmly established, she was finally able to hear how he felt and what was missing for him sexually, and she agreed she would be more open to his needs, too.

Using the skill *LEANING IN RATHER THAN LEANING BACK*, she learned to proactively talk specifically about what would excite her and turn her on and stop trying to protect his feelings by skirting the situation. As a result, over the course of the next few months, they were both able to talk about their personal preferences and came up with ways to spruce up their sex life. When they were both finally able to pay attention to each other's needs and share what they liked in bed, they recognized that by choosing to want to please each other by following their requests, they were able to sidestep any resentment. In order for it to work, though, it had to be their decision to engage in whatever sexual behaviors their partner preferred. They came to see they were giving each other a gift, a roadmap to their personal sexual pleasures, and they accepted it happily. In other words, they were taking the guesswork out of it for the other person, and they could see it was a win-win for both. Once they were able to do that, they each felt listened to, understood, and cared about, and they both began to have a better experience in bed.

Cindy and Tim decided to spend some time talking and cuddling before sex. This made Cindy feel comfortable, and it prolonged the foreplay she needed to help put her in the right mood. Knowing he wasn't going to say something that turned her off also helped. These adjustments took them away from some of the pressure and seriousness they were feeling and allowed them to relax and remember why they were drawn to each other in the first place. They were even able to laugh about the idea of sex among friends, since that was, of course, how they started out.

"We're friends with benefits," Cindy joked one day in my office.

"The best of friends," Tim added.

Eventually, Cindy let go of some of the inhibitions she still carried with her from when she was younger. Tim finally felt that they were in this together—they were a team in the bedroom.

Sally, too, leaned in and told Kevin about her unhappiness. At first, he was a little defensive, he was so taken off guard. Because she had never mentioned it before, it really surprised him. But when she explained she wanted to make it work, that she wanted him to be happy but she also wanted to be happy, he softened and they were able to talk it through. Their solution was to choose two nights a week when sex was most likely on the table. That way Sally didn't get into bed every night worrying he was going to ask for it and she would have to say no and disappoint him or, worse, do it with him when she really didn't want to. That gave her five nights a week when she could truly relax without any pressure. It also allowed her to prepare for the nights they did plan to have sex—that *Scheduled Spontaneity* that they could look forward to. Sometimes she got a babysitter for the afternoon shift so she wasn't so frazzled by the end of the day, or she decided to order in dinner those nights so she didn't have the extra burden of cooking and cleaning, and she could sneak in a half-hour bubble bath to make her feel relaxed and sexy. They also left room for the possibility that she could say no if the night they chose wasn't a good one, but on those occasions she would offer up another night that week that they could look forward to. It has made all the difference in the world.

If both partners want to remain together, as long as they each have the other's best interests at heart, and are both committed and invested in the relationship, they are usually able to find a compromise that allows for both people's needs. In the next chapter we will look at doing the same thing around different issues—if your partner promises they will change something they do and you wait and wait with Denial by your side, *Wishing and Hoping* and *Believing What You Are Told*, but the behavior remains the same, what can you do to finally bring that much-needed alteration about? Come on, let's find out.

Chapter Seven

I Thought You Said You Would—Or You Wouldn't

WENDY COULD HEAR IT BEFORE ANYONE ELSE, THE SLIGHT uptick in Ricky's tone when he got to his third or fourth drink. It was fairly subtle, but it always made Wendy's stomach begin to churn because she knew what was coming: more drinks, slurred words, eventually an aggressive tone, and after that, who knew? What she did know was that once she heard that slightly higher pitch in his voice there was no going back until he went to sleep for the night and they could start again the next day.

When Wendy and Rick first began dating and then got married the following year, she enjoyed their drinking together. She thought it was so much fun that he would come home from work for what he always called "the cocktail hour," and he would make a show of blending different drinks or opening a new bottle of wine or sharing a beer he had just discovered. She told all her friends how lucky she felt, like she was in a movie or something. Sometimes, if they drank more than usual, he would get a little rough in bed. She didn't mind, though. The truth was, she sort of liked it.

The first time Wendy had any awareness that Ricky might have an actual problem with his drinking was one night over a year into their marriage when she had a bad cold. She had been coming down with it for days but pushed through at work and kept up with their usual nightly drinking routine. She was getting worse though, and thought a break made sense. She was sure Ricky would agree. She suggested they skip their cocktail hour that night and just have some chicken soup and ginger ale. At first, Ricky said sure, that made sense to him; but after a little while he got so antsy, walking back and forth from the dining room to the den, not able to settle down to watch the movie Wendy was looking forward to seeing.

"Hell," he had finally said, making his way over to their makeshift bar. "Just 'cause you don't want to have a cocktail doesn't mean I don't. Am I right?"

She could see him relax as he prepared himself a gin and tonic, and then another, and another. She told herself, *yeah, he's right, just because I feel under the weather doesn't mean he shouldn't still partake in our usual routine.* When, for the first time, she watched him get drunker and drunker while she remained sober, she told herself, *no harm, right? It's not like he has to drive anywhere.* And when they went to bed that night and she was achy and had a stuffy nose and he still insisted on having sex, she told herself, *wow he must really love me if he wants to have sex with me when I look like this! I thought for sure my red nose would turn him off.* Wendy hadn't been drinking the gin and tonics along with Ricky, but she sure had her own shot of Denial that night.

Even so, Wendy couldn't shake the nagging feeling that things were not as she thought they had been, namely two newlyweds innocently enjoying an alcoholic beverage or two every evening. Seeing Ricky's drinking play out while she wasn't having anything at all had really struck her. She noticed that for every glass she had, he had two, sometimes three. She wondered if that was an actual problem, or if it was just normal since he had a good sixty pounds on her. Most nights, when they would share a bottle of wine, she would still be on her first glass by the time he had kicked the rest of the bottle and was already opening a second one. After that, there were times when she would come home from work and suspected Ricky had already been drinking. She could smell liquor on him and that change in the way he spoke came sooner on those days. Eventually, it seemed that became their norm and happened most days. The next time she chose to opt out and not drink, he insisted he wanted to anyway, and then he went on to want to have sloppy sex in bed. She was turned off by his drinking and said she really didn't want to. He couldn't believe she meant it; he was slurring his words by then, and she thought, *he's right, we always have sex at this time.* She decided to stop protesting and just let it play out. It was the first time she really didn't enjoy sex with her husband. She decided she had to talk to him about the drinking.

"Listen," she said the next morning. "I've noticed you've been drinking a lot more lately. Especially last night. Do you know that you were like really messy drunk? I can see a difference between us now that I'm drinking less, and I just want to make sure you're okay because you seem to be drinking more than before."

"I'm okay, babe," he said, taking a huge bite of his granola. "I don't know what you're talking about. I'm not drinking any more than I have all along."

"Really?" she said. *Huh, maybe he hasn't been. Maybe I haven't been paying close attention. Maybe he hasn't been doing it more but last night was just an exception.* With Denial's help she was taking last night's events as an unusual situation and putting them outside their norm instead of within their usual reality.

"Sure babe, I'm okay," he said. "This is not a problem at all for me."

Okay, she thought. *That's a relief.*

They went back to their regular routine and things seemed fine for a while. If Wendy drank along with Ricky, she had no concerns. However, when she didn't join him because, say, she had a big presentation the next morning or wasn't feeling great, she got that nagging feeling again when he kept on drinking. She wondered if he really was like this every night, and she just hadn't seen it because she had been drinking along with him. She just wasn't sure, so she decided to pay attention. She still drank with him, but less, taking a step back so she could get a better view. Suddenly he wasn't as funny as he had been before, and the sex was becoming unappealing most of the time. He smelled like alcohol these days and she couldn't stand it—really, she wanted no part of it. There were no slow, intimate moments between them anymore. It seemed to always be all about him.

She could barely sleep thinking about it, so the next morning she brought it up again.

"Okay, so I drink," he said. "Sue me!"

"Don't be ridiculous," Wendy said. "I'm just trying to make sure you are all right."

"I'm more than all right, babe," he said. "I've already told you that. I can handle it. For goodness sakes, I'm going to work, I'm doing my job, I'm keeping up with all the responsibilities I have. Has my drinking affected any of that? No, it has not. I could stop anytime if I wanted to. You're making a big deal out of nothing."

He's right, she thought as Denial sidled up next to her. *He does do all that. He's working, doing everything, he's never late, he never messes up at work. What is the big deal? He has to have something to help him relax. I'm probably overreacting. It is just a couple of drinks. I guess I'm being overly concerned.*

Wendy wanted to believe him so much that, with Denial's help, she accepted his words and tried not to worry. But that became increasingly difficult. When it happened again, in an effort to avoid another sleepless night, she confronted him on the spot.

"Have you been drinking all this time?" she accused him when he finally came to bed.

"What are you, the police?" he asked her through gritted teeth.

He was clearly drunk and not responding in a rational way. It turned into a bitter disagreement and kept them up late into the night fighting, so she didn't sleep much despite her effort to try for a more restful night. When she told me about the exchange,

I told her that one of the most important aspects of dealing with a partner's drinking is to not talk about it while he or she is actually drinking. It is, in fact, the first step toward putting controls in place.

Certainly, Wendy is not alone in navigating this difficult road. So many of my patients are married or in a committed relationship, and are dealing with one difficult, annoying, or even destructive behavior or other that their partner engages in regularly. Whenever two people live together there is going to be some of that—she doesn't close the door properly, he leaves the thermostat down too low, she has the television on far too loud, he doesn't clean out the sink after doing the dishes, she tells him to wash his hands too much. The list could go on and on. As tough as it can be to take it, some are behaviors people can learn to tolerate over time and accept as a character quirk of their significant other. When the conflicts come up, those behaviors can cause frustration or a flare of anger, but a tolerance can be developed to deal with them. There are other behaviors, however, such as drinking too much or spending too much money—in some cases money the couple doesn't even really have—or having an adult family member such as a sibling or niece or nephew rely on a family member in what might be considered an overly dependent way, that are harder to take. It is important to distinguish between the benign but annoying behaviors and the ones that can be harmful and dangerous to the relationship and possibly to the people involved. In Chapter Six we saw what can happen when people don't come together and talk about trouble with their sex life, but instead deny there is an issue at all. We saw how that can tear apart a marriage and lead one or both partners to the point in which they may be vulnerable and open to having an affair. However, if they are able to unite and focus on each other and the problem at hand, all of that may be avoided. Here, Denial is a way to cope with a partner's behavior that leaves the other feeling unseen and not listened to, uncared for, and, at times, neglected. A prime example of that is Ricky's wanting to and needing to drink even when Wendy was sick, or when she had a big work event the next day and didn't want to feel hung over. He was thinking only of himself, but he was able to twist it around so Wendy thought he was right. As we have seen many times, Denial's job is to help people normalize upsetting bad behaviors.

Many of my patients see these behaviors playing out in front of them in their own home and they tell themselves, *he's a good guy* or *she's so sweet, they don't want to hurt me.* It is what Denial wants you to see and believe. But in most cases like these people could wait forever and their partner's bad behaviors will never change; the only thing that can change is their taking control to do something about it. The hard part is, they don't want to rock the boat or appear to be impatient and demanding. From those small annoying actions that their lover does or doesn't do, to the bigger ones, their expectation is that they should be more understanding and tolerant. Therefore, they accept their partner's lip service that they will start or stop doing what's troublesome. They *Believe What They Are Told.* They trust what their partner says—all the well-intentioned promises to do things differently—rather than recognizing the repeated transgressions. *I just need to give them some time. They said they will stop; I should give them a chance. They don't mean to upset me.* Even worse than that, as we will see with Wendy and Ricky and many of the others, there is often an element of self-blame in which the person on the receiving end of the transgression is told it is their fault and they believe it.

One day Wendy came home from work and Ricky was in the kitchen with a drink. She said hello, and when he answered her the pitch in his voice was already at the heavy drinking level. That was the first time she had experienced that. She now knew enough to not talk about it that night, he was already too far gone, but when she refused to have sex with him, he called her a bitch, something he had never done before. Her first thought was *who is this guy? The man I fell in love with and married would never call me that.* It was in that moment she knew his drinking was way out of hand and that she had to do something about it. Given the work we had done and my guiding her to not talk about his drinking while he was drinking, she now knew to wait until the next morning to talk about it.

"I'm really worried about your drinking so much," she began.

"This again?" he said. She could still smell the alcohol on him from last night.

"Ricky, I'm worried."

Then he told her, "I can stop anytime. I just don't want to."

"Why don't you want to?" she asked.

"Because I enjoy it, and it relaxes me, and I've told you a hundred times I have it under control."

Once again, she accepted what Ricky told her. She certainly didn't want to think he was an alcoholic. Ricky's assurance made her feel better. But that lasted only a week or so. One Friday shortly thereafter, they went out to dinner with another couple. They all ordered cocktails, and then Ricky insisted on a bottle of wine, then another, and then a third. Wendy could see her friends exchanging glances. She guessed they were mostly worried about the bill—it was going to be really expensive—but she was also worried about Ricky. His pitch had reached that high embarrassing level and he was saying fairly inappropriate things. He commented on Wendy's friend's lowcut blouse and something about her husband's hair likely being cut at home because it looked so unprofessional. He also began to talk to the servers more harshly than Wendy would have liked. She was relieved when the dinner was over and they said goodbye. Despite knowing better, she just couldn't wait until the next morning to say something.

"That was awful," Wendy said to Ricky. "Your drinking is out of control."

"If it is out of control, it's because of you," he said.

"How is it because of me?"

"First of all, you are always on me for something, the garbage, my towel, you are constantly complaining. And then you make me spend one of my only free weekend nights with your boring friends. I mean, anyone would have to drink to get through a meal with those people."

Because of her therapy, Wendy knew once again she was heading toward an argument, and so she stopped talking at that point and chose to wait until the morning. But she couldn't sleep. She began to seriously doubt herself and Denial helped wash her resolve firmly away. *Maybe he's right,* she thought in the early hours of the morning. *Maybe I am always picking on him, telling him to take out the garbage or hang his stupid towel. Maybe he does need help to relax—he works hard all day and then he comes home and I'm on him, too. I am probably riding him too much. I should work harder to get off his back and be more understanding. And he's right about my friends. I love CeCe but her husband is bit of a dud. Maybe I should just see her alone at lunch and not make Ricky come along.*

She started to feel really bad about herself. Was she actually an awful and demanding wife who didn't do nearly enough to make her husband's life easier and better? Was she making it worse? Ricky was working hard all day at the office, why couldn't she be more supportive and leave him alone? Or do more herself so she didn't have to bug him to do it? Would it kill her to put his towel back on the hook? That would take like two seconds each day. Plus, she was starting to wonder if she were to blame for all of it. She had been all in for the cocktail hours until very recently. She had even bought the cart they used as their makeshift bar at an antique store downtown for Ricky's birthday.

"Maybe you could limit your drinking to one or two drinks," she said at breakfast the next morning. They had been silent, but she felt she had to do something. He looked up from his scrambled eggs.

"I'll make a deal with you," he said. "You back off and don't bug me so much, and I'll try to drink less."

"Sure," she said, thinking this shouldn't fall entirely on him. "I can do that."

It was a Wednesday morning, so Wendy thought, great, we'll have two nights of his cutting back and see how it goes. She went to work feeling good, completely *Believing What She Was Told*. She imagined a quiet night with hot chocolate and mini marshmallows, maybe a little slow sex that wasn't fueled by alcohol; they hadn't done that in a long time. They talked a little during the day and all seemed fine. When she arrived home at the usual time Ricky was sitting in the kitchen with a gin and tonic in his hand. She knew immediately that she was going to be in for a tough night, but she also knew bringing it up now would do no good, he was already too deep into the liquor. She waited until the next morning.

"Hey," Wendy said slowly when Ricky finally made his way into the kitchen for breakfast. "I thought we were going to take a break last night."

"What?" he asked. "I thought that was a joke, babe. Plus, what are you? My mother?"

"Come on, Ricky," she said. "I don't like this. I'm thinking you have a real problem here."

"You think I have a real problem?" he asked, and the look in his eyes was nasty. "I think you have the problem. You're the one who is trying to control me. You stress me out. Can you just let up a little? Everything doesn't have to be perfect."

She took a step back. *Maybe he's right*, she thought; *I do try to control him, even right now I am trying to control him. I always want everything to be just so. Why can't I be more accepting?*

"I'm sorry," she said. "You're right."

Once again, she waffled. In that instance she bought into his Denial, accepted that she was being unreasonable and demanding, and placed the responsibly on herself instead of on him, where it belonged, and holding him to it. She decided she would back off, try to stop being so controlling, and maybe things would lighten up. She told me all about this when she came for her next session.

"I couldn't really see it before," she said to me. "I was blaming him, but I think a lot of his drinking is really caused by my demands, because of what I'm doing. In addition to his work being so stressful, I just add to that, and he feels he needs to drink a lot every day."

"How do you think you add to his stress?" I asked.

"You know, I always want the apartment to look good and he's not neat, leaving his wet towel on the bed, leaving tons of food in the bottom of the sink when he does the dishes, stuff like that," she said. "He never takes the garbage out. It just gets higher and higher and sometimes I feel like I'm going to scream. I guess, when it's gotten really bad, I ask him in an angry voice if I am the only human in our home who is capable of taking out the garbage. I feel bad about that now. Also, I don't think he likes my friends very much and I push to spend time with them sometimes. I think he's bored and annoyed when we see them."

"And you think each of those things combined has led him to have to drink to excess so he can tolerate it?" I asked. "That those things are so bad he has to self-medicate with alcohol?"

"I guess so," she said. "Yeah."

"I understand why you have been made to feel that way," I said. "You've built a relationship on which you listen to each other and trust what the other person says. That's exactly what you're doing here. But the truth is, that is what Ricky wants you to believe. If he is drinking as much as you think he is, and if his behavior is becoming more erratic and belligerent, I think this is a much bigger problem than the towels you mentioned wanting to be straight or the garbage not being taken out. This is not your fault. You are not responsible for his drinking. He is blaming you to make you feel guilty. He wants you to believe if you handled things better, or, as he puts it, if you were less controlling, that he wouldn't drink. But none of that is true."

I shared my important skill *THREAD THE NEEDLE*, through which I encouraged Wendy to put all the words, the promises, and the intentions together with the actions and behaviors she actually sees so that she can make it a tool to use to manage the behavior that is threatening to tear her marriage apart. I explained that she has to pay close attention to his drinking behavior—when he starts to drink, how much he continues to drink—and really ask herself whether she did anything to trigger his needing three drinks instead of one glass of wine at dinner. Since he told her he is drinking because of her, she has to clearly see if that is true, if he actually takes a drink in reaction to something she said or did. When she comes home to find him already drinking, for example, and they haven't even interacted yet, how is she responsible for that? Or, if she simply greets him with a hello and asks how his day was, and before she knows it he's annoyed because she can't see he's stressed and has to walk right to the bar, she will realize that she had nothing to do with that choice. Sometimes the person drinking will begin to complain out of nowhere—this dinner is cold, you are late, why didn't you answer the phone when I called today?—and she has to be aware that that can be part of the pattern, but she still is not to blame for any of it, especially his drinking because of the things he mentioned. Eventually she will see that what he is saying about why and when he drinks is completely separate from her, that it has nothing to do with her. He is drinking because he wants or needs to do it. Up until that point her Denial has matched his. She believed him when he said he didn't have a problem, and when he told her he could handle it. She accepted it again when he said he could stop anytime if he wanted to, and then when he blamed her for it. Now, though, with the skill *THREAD THE NEEDLE*, she will be able to move away from Denial and what she is being told, to instead realizing that what Ricky is saying and what he is doing (along with why he is doing it) are two very different things.

"What is happening right now is intolerable," I said. "And it might only get harder if you aren't able to get some control soon. When you're living with someone who has an alcohol problem you can fall into a pattern of trying to keep them happy and not upset them. You can become codependent on each other as you try to maintain some level of peace in your home. What's important for you to start to see with this skill is that Ricky's drinking is separate from you."

"I really think you are making too big a deal out of this," she said. "I don't know why I even brought it up in here." Once again, her Denial was still in place.

"Just think about what I said," I told her.

She said she would but reiterated that she thought I was wrong. Ricky may drink a lot, but he wasn't an alcoholic. She believed him when he said he could stop anytime if he wanted to.

These difficulties can arise with different family members, too. We see it often with spouses or romantic partners, but it can also be the case with siblings and other relatives. I had another patient who had a completely different issue, but a similar situation. Amy was struggling with the demands of her brother Ron. He was the baby of the family and had always had a hard time finding his way in the world. Their father was no longer alive, and their mother lived about three hundred miles away in an adult community moving toward needing more nursing care, although she was completely clear-headed. Amy and Ron had another sibling, a sister named Josephine, who lived across the country and was not the best about keeping in touch.

Ron calls Amy regularly and wants to talk about his health problems, of which he has many—asthma, bad knees, acid reflux—and his conflicts at work, which also seem to be never-ending. He likes to tell her how he is managing them or not, depending on the week, and she listens because she feels sorry for him. She knows he has nobody else to turn to. But her kids need her to help them with their homework and to just be generally present for them, and on the nights when he calls, that usually all falls to the wayside. He also stops by out of nowhere to talk. He can't stand his boss, and he always has one unbelievable story after another. Sometimes she is just putting dinner on the table when he rings the bell, and she'll tell her family to go ahead and eat without her. She'll end up missing the great stories of the day—what her son did in music class or what her daughter did in math class, whatever it might be—and even though her husband dutifully repeats it to her when they are going to sleep, it isn't the same. She wants to hear her kids tell their stories in their own words. She feels torn in a million directions. Ron never had an easy time making friends and Amy just doesn't want him to feel alone in the world. She wants to be a good sister, and, to her, that means being there for Ron when he needs her, which is often. Once, before their mother went into the nursing home, she asked Amy to be extra aware of his needs. She said her biggest fear is that he would become so despondent that he would get depressed again, and she wanted to avoid that. That happened once when he was in his twenties, and it was awful. So now Amy carries the responsibility of being a good sister and also of being a good daughter by making sure her brother is functioning so she doesn't let her mother down.

The other day, Amy, her husband, and their kids were all ready to walk out the door to take a nice fall hike when Ron appeared at their door with yet one more crisis. Apparently, he lost his temper with his boss and now he was afraid he would get fired. He was very upset, and he had to talk to her right away. He was a clearly a nervous wreck, pacing back and forth on their front porch.

"Come on, Mom," her daughter said, pulling on Amy's wrist.

She looked pleadingly at her husband. What should she do? And then she thought how lucky she was to have the family she has. Of course, she didn't want to miss this walk, but there would be more. Ron, on the other hand, had nobody else to turn to for support.

"You guys go," she said. She saw her daughter's face crumble. "I'm going to hang out with Uncle Ron for a little while."

Amy's husband later told her that their daughter was upset and cried afterward. She never really cheered up and none of them enjoyed the hike. It felt like a chore to get through instead of the great family outing it was supposed to be.

"Something has to change," her husband said. "We're just as important as he is."

"I know," she said. "But we're so lucky. He isn't as lucky. I owe him this."

She felt she had to do everything he asked her to do. Every time she imagined saying no, or telling Ron she would call him back later or that she didn't quite have two hours to talk today, she was afraid of his anger and wracked with guilt. How could she not be a good sister to him? What would her mother say? What if this was the time he felt so alone in the world that he went over the edge? She would never forgive herself. Once, when she was in grad school, he came to talk to her in a panic and she tried to put limits in place with Ron. She told him she had a final that afternoon and would call him later. It turned out he lost his job that day, but she didn't know that. He didn't talk to her for three months. What if that happened again, if she turned him away after something really bad had happened? With their mother so far away she just couldn't take the chance. No, she told herself, she was doing the right thing.

Last Thursday they were backing out of their driveway to go to her daughter's birthday party at the local bowling alley when Ron pulled in next to them.

"No!!!" her daughter screamed.

Amy felt her stomach knot up. She looked at him in the car next to them. He looked pale with dark circles under his eyes. There was no way she could say no to him. She rolled down the window and he did the same.

"Come to the party with us," she suggested. He had been invited but he thought he had to work. Something must have happened with his boss. "We'll find a quiet place to talk there."

"I just don't want to be around people," he said. "I have a lot to tell you."

"But," Amy tried to protest.

"Please, Sis," he said. "I need you."

"I can't do this anymore," she said to him. "I'm missing these precious moments."

"Sis, I promise, I won't do this for a while after this, but something happened. It was a really bad day."

He had promised before that he would try to be less needy, that he just had to get through this one hurdle, that he would do a better job next time, be more independent. Sometimes a week would go by, sometimes even more, but it never lasted long. He always got back into the same difficult and demanding pattern. Sometimes when things were beginning to go downhill again, their mother would call Amy and tell her to be ready to step in and help him, maybe she should even get the guest room ready just in case. Amy lived in fear of that just in case—how much more needy could be get? Did her mother think Ron might move in with them one day? Even so, each time Ron promised he would improve, Amy would say, "Let's see if he can do it, let's give him a chance." And then he would end up on the phone for hours or at their door.

"I always tell him there are better ways to do it," she told me recently. "Like he could just text to see if I can talk, or we could talk for a shorter amount of time. Or he could come with us wherever we are going and we could talk there. But, you know, I am asking him to behave like I would and clearly his problems far exceed mine, so I guess I can't even imagine what he is going through."

"He is a grown man," I reminded her. "You are not responsible for him."

"Well, I am," she said. "I mean my mother thinks I am, and there is nobody else to do it. If something happened, if he got depressed again or he stopped talking to me, I would never get over it."

"It sounds like it is taking a toll on your family life," I said.

"What choice do I have?"

"You do have a choice," I said.

I shared the skill of *THREAD THE NEEDLE* with her, through which she would be able to be clear on and sort out her guilt around not being a good enough sister and what that really means. In other words, it would help her see exactly what he is doing and come to recognize a chronic history of needing to be supported and not being emotionally able to take care of himself. I asked Amy what she does when she feels down. She said she talks to her husband sometimes, or she goes for a long walk by herself to think things through.

"Those are all normal responses," I said. "What Ron is looking for from you is too much. You shouldn't be expected to take it all on."

"But I worry about my mother," she said.

"I know," I said. "She worries about him, I get that, but she is not helping you. Really, she has allowed a forcefield to develop that is making you the one who is absorbing the weight of his trouble, but it comes at an expense. You are missing being with your kids. You missed your daughter's birthday party. How much more are you going to lose out on?"

There was no disputing that. She said she would try to *THREAD THE NEEDLE.*

Another one of my patients was also dealing with a bad behavior that was getting harder to live with. Nathan was beginning to think his wife, Ingrid, was not being completely honest with him about their finances and the money she was spending, although he couldn't quite put his finger on it. He was away on business a lot, and she kept everything running in their house and with their elderly parents when he was out of town. If a pipe burst, she called the plumber and it was fixed before he even realized there had been a problem. If his mother got sick, she took her to the doctor immediately. If their daughter needed a ride to a faraway soccer tournament or a dance recital, Ingrid got her there without a complaint. He was grateful for all of that. While he knew she was spending money, he was clueless to what extent. He felt they had to be more of a team and work together, but he didn't get the sense that was happening.

In reality, what was happening was that Ingrid's mother had never stopped helping her out; she still paid for a lot of her daughter's expenses. Because of that, Nathan didn't see some of the bills. He was aware when she gave them some money at the holidays and on their birthdays, but he didn't know she was also giving Ingrid money separately and regularly. He kept telling himself *things were fine, she knew what she was doing*. Lately, though, he had noticed an abundance of jewelry, shoes, and handbags, none of which Ingrid needed. When she started to take over the closet in the hall, he felt he had to say something.

She told him it was costume jewelry and not worth a lot, or the shoes were old, he just hadn't seen them before, and his Denial, along with his guilt for accusing her of something, would settle in. *Oh, for God's sake*, he would think. *I'm away so often, of course I don't know all her shoes. She's probably had them forever. What made me think they were new? And the jewelry couldn't possibly be real, a stone like that would cost a fortune. Why am I making such a big issue out of it?*

Still, he would often see four or five packages arrive once or twice a week and he acknowledged that seemed like a lot of stuff. Of course, there were details he didn't know yet, so he wasn't seeing the full picture—that was, until last week when he ran into his neighbor Lou and that picture began to come into focus a bit more.

"Hey Nate, I'm glad I ran into you," Lou said. "Have you been getting all those packages? They were piling up at my door."

"What packages?" Nathan asked.

"I'm not sure," Lou said. "We've been getting your packages. They have Ingrid's name on them. Sometimes they are out the door right away, I thought maybe there was a mix-up, but these last weeks they have been hanging around. I just want to make sure you know they are there."

"Thanks so much," Nathan said, getting a sinking feeling.

Nathan told me Lou went on to explain that for the last month or so Ingrid had been having a bunch of her packages sent to their house.

"Maybe I'm really missing something," he said. "Is it possible she is deceiving me? I mean, we were already getting a lot and it sounds like there are a fair amount at the neighbor's waiting to be picked up. Her explanation made sense to me, that her shoes weren't new and everything else. Do you think she was lying to me though? Is she spending more than I thought?"

"Did you confront her?" I asked.

"I did," he said. "She told me the neighbors had it wrong. That since she was away from the house taking care of her mother, she didn't want the packages to get stolen so she asked Hali, Lou's wife, if the delivery people could try them if nobody answered at our house. She said it was no big deal."

"Do you believe her?" I asked.

"Well, it makes sense," he said. It could make sense if it was just that, but it was, in reality, another facet of a bigger picture that was going on behind the scenes that he still didn't know about, namely that Ingrid's mother was paying for a lot of what she was buying, and that Ingrid had a separate bank account through which she was hiding much of it.

I shared the skill of *THREAD THE NEEDLE* with him, suggesting he take everything Ingrid said and did and look at that next to the facts. In other words, despite what she is saying, she is still buying a lot, they are accruing more credit card debt than usual, and their closets are bursting at the seams. She is telling him one thing but clearly doing something else. Given this reality, how does this add up to her being responsible and not spending too much?

The next time Nathan talked to Ingrid, she told him he didn't need to worry.

"I have this totally under control," she told him. "If you want, I'll cut back a little."

"So are you, I don't even know what to call it, overshopping?" Nathan asked her.

"Overshopping? What, did you just make that up?" she asked. "I assure you I am not overshopping. But, if it bothers you, I will shop even less than I am now."

He shared this exchange with me the next time I saw him.

"When people have a shopping problem or any like this that involves a form of excess, they will have an explanation for everything," I said. "That seems to be what is going on with Ingrid, but from what you're telling me her behavior is continuing."

"That's just it, I'm not sure it is," he said. His response reminded me of when Wendy thought I was overreacting about Ricky's drinking at first. There is a common sense of having to defend a loved one no matter what they are or are not doing. "I wonder if there is some misunderstanding. Our credit card bill was smaller this month even though Lou said they had a pile of our packages at their house. Maybe she is slowing down. Maybe she's still buying things, but each thing is less expensive?"

"Ask her about it," I suggested. "And keep in mind the skill of *THREAD THE NEEDLE*. In fact, write down on paper what you are seeing and what you know to be true in terms of her spending habits and the bills that you are dealing with, so that you can contrast that against what she wants you to believe."

He nodded.

"And consider talking to her about the enormity of the financial strain she is creating," I added. "It is going to be really important to figure out a budget and ask her to do the same so that you have a sense of your resources and what you can afford."

He looked at me as if to say that was much easier said than done, but he said he would try.

Meanwhile things were getting worse with Wendy and Ricky. He was drinking more and more, especially on Friday and Saturday nights. They would settle down to watch a movie and he would be asleep in a matter of minutes, leaving Wendy alone and barely able to hear the dialogue because he was snoring so loudly. In addition, he regularly picked fights with her—complaints that would come out of nowhere: the stove wasn't clean, the lasagna noodles weren't properly cooked, she spent too much time on the phone with her friends. She felt constantly blamed. And yet she would always be surprised. She would approach each night and each weekend as if it were going to be different. She would think, *we are going to have a nice night or a great day* and before she knew it, he would be attacking her for something and she would be on the defensive. It was often even worse when they went out for dinner or to a bar. He would have one drink after another and become belligerent and insult her, and each time she was shocked when it happened.

"How come we can't get along?" she asked me. "Sometimes I don't think I can live this way anymore, and then I remember how much I love him. I am never going to feel this way about anyone else, I just know that. But—"

"But what?" I prompted.

"But sometimes I think maybe I'd be better off without him," she said.

"Have you told him that?" I asked.

"Only when I'm really angry, not when he would ever think I actually meant it," she said.

"What is his response?"

"That he'll stop drinking," she said. "That he doesn't want to lose me."

"None of this is easy," I said. "A lot of people drink and they drink excessively—they may even be an alcoholic—but it doesn't mean you don't love them. You have to figure out what you can live with—sometimes people have to leave, sometimes they can find a way to put limits in place that make staying possible."

"What sort of limits?" she asked. I could tell she was interested.

"Well, you mentioned how unpleasant the sex can be when he has been drinking," I said. "So you could let him know that if he is drinking and you smell it on him, it is a turnoff and you don't want to be with him intimately. Be prepared for him to turn that around on you, though. He might say your withholding sex is leading him to drink, but stand firm and let him know that is not the case. He isn't drinking because you won't make love to him, the truth is you won't make love to him because he is drinking."

Wendy nodded.

"The message you want to give him is that you love him, you want to be with him, but there are certain things you can't tolerate," I said to her. "His drinking excessively is one of them. Being together intimately when he's been drinking is another."

"Now really isn't a good time to make a big wave," she said. "He is up for an important promotion, and I just don't want to put pressure on him more than I already have."

Her fear was holding her back.

"Wendy, I understand, but the truth is there's always going to be something stressful going on; do you think you can stop making excuses for him?" I asked.

She looked down. I think in that moment she knew I was right. I took it as a good sign and reminded her of the skill THREAD THE NEEDLE and encouraged her to consider putting boundaries in place.

When I saw her a week later, she seemed lighter and maybe even relieved.

"I talked to Ricky," she said. "I told him I love him and I do want to be with him, but I don't want to have sex with him when he's been drinking a lot. I shared that he smelled like alcohol and sometimes was rougher than usual. If he wanted to be with me and could limit his drinking, I was all in. But when he was drunk, it killed my desire. He was quiet, I don't know if he was sulking or not, but he didn't push back."

"That's great," I told her. "You are finally taking care of yourself, speaking your truth, and not being in a situation with him sexually where you are compromising your own feelings. You are now *THREADING THE NEEDLE.*"

She continued that she could see that she was not responsible for his drinking, which was a huge relief for her and helped her alleviate a tremendous amount of the guilt she was carrying. She was clear that she was going to hold on to the declaration of love that she could be with Ricky when he wasn't drunk, and not on the other nights. While he continues to drink, and on occasion excessively, the nights that he wanted to be with her he curtailed his drinking enough that she was able to be with him intimately. Thus far they have been able to walk that fine line and they are making it work.

The next time I saw Amy she told me that Ron had come to her office one day saying he needed to talk. This time he was late for his rent and needed to borrow some money. She had a big meeting, and the clients were already waiting in the conference room. She told him he couldn't stay and at first he seemed shocked, she said, and then he got angry. She explained about her meeting and said she would be so happy to meet him for lunch in two hours. He walked away saying no thank you, he would handle it on his own. As soon as he left she doubted her choice. *What was I thinking? He needed me. What if he does something bad? It will be all my fault. What would mom say if she knew I turned him away when he came to me for help?*

"Let's talk about that," I said. "You were at work, doing your job and he came to you to say he needed to talk. He wasn't in physical distress, what he wanted to talk about could certainly wait, and you simply said you needed a few hours because you had an important meeting and you could see him soon. Does any of that sounds unreasonable to you?"

"I don't think so," she said.

"Is it unreasonable to ask you to risk your job?"

"Well, yes," she said.

Again, by using the skill of *THREAD THE NEEDLE* she was finally able to see that her brother's demands were completely untenable and she was at risk of damaging her life both personally and professionally if she tried to appease him every time he asked for the help he wanted. Slowly, she was able to see that if he refused to speak to her or accept her requests to talk later or for a shorter amount of time, she wasn't responsible for what he did. She was offering more than she needed to; if he couldn't see that it was really his problem and not hers.

At my next session with Nathan, he had finally understood the magnitude of what was going on with Ingrid, and that it was, in fact, much worse than he thought. He told me he asked Ingrid about the lower credit card bill. She said she had opened another one in her maiden name to keep the first one down.

"She said it like it was a good thing," he said, exasperated.

"That's her Denial," I said. "She is probably lying to herself about what is going on."

I see it often. People continue to deny the flagrant reality. Ricky says he isn't drinking too much and, if he is, it's Wendy's fault for pushing him so much. Ron says this time he has a handle on things; he will get it together. Ingrid says she isn't overbuying and that she is managing their credit card debt by taking out another credit card. Once my patients are able to *THREAD THE NEEDLE* and confront all these bad behaviors and hold their loved ones to the reality of what is really happening, then what they say eventually has to line up with what they do. With that in hand, Wendy, Amy, and Nathan were able to begin to let go of the guilt they carried because they felt they were not living up to the expectations they placed on themselves to support their loved ones and keep their lives running smoothly. Once they were able to do that, they could take control and make a plan that worked for them. It was a prime example of Denial letting other people's actions affect the expectations people have of themselves, and letting distorted information get in the way of what they know in their heart to be true.

Thus far, we've been dealing with the expectations people place on themselves to "be there" for the people they love—be a good enough wife, be a good enough husband, be a good enough sister. In the next section of the book we are going to look at how other people's Denial impacts their expectations of you to "be there" for them and leads to the demands they make of you. We've all sat around the dinner table when an aunt has said something she completely believes that you know to be 100 percent false. How do you handle it? Is it possible to continue to have a relationship with her or any other family member who has such disparate beliefs? Let's start by looking at the differences people have with their loved ones, their uncle, their daughter-in-law, anyone who has a different point of view or set of beliefs. It always seems in that moment that either you are right and they are wrong or you are wrong and they are right—but is there another possibility? I'll tell you all about it in the next chapter.

PART II

CHAPTER EIGHT

Are You for Real?

EVER SINCE GINGER VISITED HER SON HANK, HIS WIFE SADIE, and her adorable grandson Connor for his fourth birthday, she couldn't sleep. She had had concerns about Sadie from the beginning. She was always so loosey-goosey, never taking the time to properly dress up and always breezily arriving late to whatever dinner or event they had planned. Even on her own wedding day she had them all wondering if she would make it on time. She did, which Ginger was glad about, but now, well, it isn't that she thinks she is necessarily a bad wife, it's just that Ginger can't for the life of her comprehend why Sadie goes about things the way she does.

Connor's arrival has just made it all worse. There didn't seem to be any rules or schedules, even though everyone knew babies and toddlers needed both. Ginger had her boys on strict schedules from the time they were six weeks old, and they had thrived. She also had very clear rules and, because of that, they always knew how to act. Sadie, on the other hand, was following a method that involved letting the child lead. When Ginger had a moment alone with Hank, she would mention how strange she found it and he would always nod and agree with her. When she realized that Connor was still breast feeding at age three and a half, or when she witnessed Sadie's letting Connor choose what he wanted for lunch and, when he chose chocolate cake, she gave it to him,

Ginger would make private side remarks to Hank, and he would subtly indicate that he saw her point. She imagined he would file away her comments and then work behind the scenes taking care of things, knowing that his mother was always right.

One day Hank off-handedly mentioned that Connor was still asleep in their bed, and he didn't want to disturb him by going in to get a piece of paper Ginger had asked about.

"Connor is sleeping with you?" Ginger inquired. There was so much wrong with that in her eyes, she didn't even know where to begin.

"Oh," Hank said, realizing his mistake. He was trying to share less personal information with his mother, whom he thought was too opinionated. "Yeah, it's just a phase."

"Well, I know you know better than that," Ginger said confidently. "Children need their own space. Connor needs to learn how to calm down on his own."

"Sure, of course they do, and of course he does. Who doesn't know that?" Hank said.

Good, Ginger thought to herself. *That's great, he already knows that what I'm telling him is correct.* This goes on with many of my patients. She was so invested in holding on to her role of importance in his life that her Denial completely blocked her ability to see he was being sarcastic and dismissing what she was saying.

The day she arrived in San Francisco for the birthday celebration they took a nice walk to the playground. She hadn't visited in more than six months, and it was a pleasure to see her grandson. Connor seemed like such a big boy, walking most of the way on his own, speaking in full sentences. She had just assumed he was potty trained. Her boys had all been well potty trained by age two and a half. At one point Connor said he needed new pants, and Sadie lifted him up and put him on the bench. Ginger guessed he meant he had an accident or had sat in a puddle. What he meant, she realized, was that he needed a new diaper. She was shocked. She had to keep the words *no way* from escaping her lips in front of Sadie. How in the world could Hank allow this? She had been so clear with him about how she felt about these more progressive ways of childrearing.

She watched as Sadie reached into the backpack for a diaper that looked huge. She didn't even know they made kids' diapers that big. She looked away for a second, wasn't anyone embarrassed here? When she looked back Connor was very upset and began to kick, trying to prevent Sadie from changing the diaper. Really, it seemed, he could have done it himself. The whole scene just felt off to Ginger, like he was crying out for help. Clearly, he needed his parents' firm support, not this wishy-washy freedom. It bothered her so much she began to have trouble falling asleep. She knew this sort of thing could lead to Connor's being overly dependent later in life. The next time she saw Hank, she broached the subject with him.

"Aren't you concerned about Connor still being in diapers at this point in time?" she asked, fully expecting him to agree.

"I don't know why you're concerned about it," he said. "What's the big deal?"

Ginger realized in that moment that he didn't really understand the issue. *He's just mixed up about it*, she thought. Sadie and Connor approached them at that time, so she had to stop the conversation. But she would bring it up again later. *Once I explain it better, he'll will get it. He always listens to me in the end.*

Again, Ginger's Denial is so in place that she is clueless to the notion that he's not mixed up at all but is rejecting her input. She was also completely oblivious to how judgmental her comments sounded. I see this often with my patients and they can fall on both sides of this equation. They can, like Ginger, find it impossible to comprehend and accept that one of their family members is behaving the way they are or believing what they believe. The frustration and judgment they feel in light of that other person's actions can be overwhelming, and often it is just a matter of time before it comes out in one way or another. The flip side is that some of my patients find themselves on the receiving end of those judgments and it seems ludicrous to them that their family member could be so unreasonable and closed-minded. The bottom line is that it can be a challenge to deal with family and friends who have conflicting opinions about everything from childrearing to politics to how to manage the pandemic. When these differences come to light, they can cause a tremendous amount of tension, and even, in the case of mask- and vaccine-resistant family members, be detrimental to others' health.

When things get really bad, rifts can form that, in a variety of cases, lead to people becoming estranged from each other. In those situations, grandparents and grandchildren might be kept from seeing each other, brothers and sisters might stop talking, a niece might turn her back on her beloved aunt whom she always knew was whacky but has now taken it a step too far, and parents and adult children can find themselves in a standoff that neither knows how to end. It's what I call a *Cold War*, where people live out their anger by using it to keep a distance between them. When that happens, the resentment becomes more important to them than the relationship itself, and it is used to justify the split they initiate and uphold. Along with that comes a whole lot of heartache, love that isn't expressed, occasions that are missed, memories that are never created, and too many milestones that aren't shared.

When Ginger came to talk to me after her trip to celebrate Connor's birthday, she was so upset about Sadie and what Ginger thought of as her lack of good parenting skills that she wasn't thinking about this bigger picture and what could be lost. Instead, she was focused only on what she truly believed was helping Connor.

"I called Hank last night," she told me. "I'm going to do an intervention."

Before I had a chance to say anything, she explained that her friend Janet had a similar situation with a granddaughter, not around toilet training but around thumb sucking far past what she thought was the acceptable age. Janet told her how she called her daughter and son-in-law and said that she was coming that weekend to talk to them about something. They were so concerned, later they told her they worried she might be sick, that they agreed to have her come. Once she got there, she sat them down and shared her concerns. She told Ginger it worked. They began to put some bitter herb on their daughter's thumb that day. She stopped sucking her thumb within weeks. Using her friend's advice, Ginger felt both supported and justified in confronting Hank and Sadie.

Her Denial was front and center when Ginger said to me, "Hank and I are very close. He's reasonable. He'll see my point. He always does."

"What did you say to him?" I asked, attempting to get a better picture.

"Well, it didn't feel right to trick him and say I had something to talk about and not what it was," she said, which I was glad to hear. "So, I told him what I felt, that Connor is way too old to still be in diapers."

"What was his response?"

"He mostly just listened. We were on Zoom so I could see he nodded a lot as I was talking. He said he would look into it," Ginger said. "He definitely knew what I was talking about. I'm going to speak to him later and we'll solidify the plans. By the time I see you next week all will be well."

I told her I looked forward to hearing about it, although I worried. Scenarios like that can become complicated and wrought with frustration and tension.

I had another patient who was on the other end of this sort of judgment. We were deep into the pandemic and my patient Cliff had done everything to keep his family and himself safe. He wore a mask whenever he was inside any place that wasn't his home, he had gotten vaccinated, and he had held off on socializing beyond saying hello to his neighbors outside, always remaining at least six feet away from them. Everyone in his immediate family was on board with the same procedures. It was the rest of his family—his parents and his brother—who weren't, and they simply couldn't understand why he was making the choices he was making. They rarely wore masks, refused to get vaccinated, and basically did the opposite of social distancing. They went to parties, gathered in groups, and ate dinner indoors, believing that they had to live their lives. Considering all of that, Cliff felt it was putting him, his wife, and his kids at risk whenever he considered seeing the rest of his family. He couldn't comprehend why they didn't take precautions or support and respect the fact that he did.

"They are COVID deniers," he said to me during one particularly frustrating week. "It's like we are living in two completely different worlds. The way they think is confounding to me. I send them article after article, and nothing sinks in for them."

"I'm glad you recognize them as denying COVID," I said. "People use Denial when they don't want to deal with something that would necessitate a change or involve a loss, whether it is a relationship or a lifestyle. If they can make the virus disappear, then they can go about living their regular lives."

"But it is so stupid, and dangerous," he said. "I can't stand it and it will never make sense to me."

"Well think of it like this: Denial keeps you in the dark. And when you are in the dark, you don't see the facts. If you don't have the facts to go on, then you remain uninformed, which can leave you ignorant," I said to him. "The real question, though, is how you can go about taking care of yourself and your family without having to make sense of your parents' and your brother's thinking or keep trying to get them to change their ways."

"I wish it were that simple," Cliff said. "But the holidays are coming up and, when I said we would sit it out this year, they made me feel so guilty. My brother Billy called and basically said Mom and Dad are getting old; we should all be together while we can. But that is my point exactly! They are getting old. They have to be careful. When I said that, though, Billy said they are going to get depressed if they don't see me. Plus, Billy is having a rough go of it and I'm getting a similar message from my parents. Billy's wife left him about six months ago. This is his first holiday without her. I feel terrible about that, but if we all get sick or worse, it just isn't going to be worth it taking the chance right now. I mean, we are a very close family. I *want* to see them. I just want them to get vaccinated and agree to wear masks inside."

"None of them are vaccinated?" I asked.

"Nope," he said. "My parents think it is too much government involvement and my brother thinks it is going to change his DNA makeup. I have sent them so many news stories that explain exactly why those things aren't true, but I don't even know if they read them. The other day I called Billy to tell him to turn on CNN, they were having a really informative discussion about it all, dispelling myths, but he just said he didn't have time to watch and that that was not his trusted news source."

It is never easy to have such completely opposing views within a close family. What often happens is that each believes they are right and the other is wrong, and they spend a lot of time trying to convince the other of what they think is unquestionably true. I understood why Cliff was trying so hard to bring them around to his way of thinking; he felt his health, and really his life, depended on it if he was actually going to see them. The problem was, it was not likely that he was ever going to get through to them and he was going to keep hitting a wall as long as he tried.

"And get this," Cliff continued. "It's my brother's fiftieth birthday and my parents want to take him out for a fancy dinner, indoors I might add. They want to surprise him, since he's been so down lately after his wife asked for a separation. So, they've asked me to babysit for my brother's two kids—who, in their own defense, are too young to be vaccinated—and my parents have said that if I don't, I am solely responsible for ruining the much-needed birthday celebration. They make it seem like there is something wrong with me if I would even consider not doing it."

"What did you tell them?" I asked.

"I said no at first," Cliff said. "And this whole exchange is with my parents, not my brother, because he doesn't even know about it. They will not let it go. They think I am being selfish and ridiculous, and that in this case I should make an exception to my usual way of dealing with things."

"Are there any measures you can put in place?" I asked. "Maybe you can have an outdoor babysitting session, or, if they have a garage, maybe you can hang out there and leave the door open. You can insist that you all wear masks."

"I appreciate your optimism and hope that my extended family members might do the right thing, but let me tell you what happened last week. My brother called in a panic. His car had broken down and he had to get to his daughter's school before it closed—it was his day. He begged me to come get him and what was I going to say? I mean, I'm not a monster. So, I said I'd be right there but please have your mask on when I get you. I thought he had agreed. Well, when I got there he didn't have a mask on. I put down the passenger-side window before unlocking the door and said, 'hey, please put on your mask.' He looked at me and said, 'I thought you were joking, brother.' I told him I wasn't and to put it on. He said he didn't have one with him. We actually had a moment where we looked at each other, waiting for the other to make a move. I backed down, I unlocked the door and he got in and all I could do was hope he didn't have COVID. Obviously, I kept my mask on the whole time. What was I going to do? Leave him on the side of the road? Or worse, leave my niece at daycare wondering where her dad was when she is already upset about her mother not being there every day anymore?"

"It sounds like you felt so pressured that you weren't able to think of any options," I said. "For example, suggesting having your brother call an Uber to go pick his daughter up, or calling your parents and having them go pick her up because they are not concerned about safety protocol. So, as a result, you felt that you no choice but to get him yourself."

The real question he was grappling with was how to handle his relationships with the people he loved who have completely different belief systems and, as far as he was concerned, opposite views of reality. How could he sidestep being polarized when their approach to the pandemic couldn't have been more different, and find a common ground where they could both be comfortable? Was there a way to address it and find some satisfaction so he didn't feel so pushed and judged that it could lead to breaking his connection to his family members? Could he deal with what seems like an impossible situation so that he doesn't wind up feeling helpless, with no choice but to go along and compromise his own well-being? Most important, could he reach a point where he accepted that they were never going to change, they were not going to hear him, and with that in mind still find a way to meet in the middle and maintain their close relationships?

In many ways Ginger was dealing with similar questions. There was no doubt that she loved her son Hank, her grandson Connor, and even her daughter-in-law Sadie. After all, she made her son happy and she had given Ginger the thing she wanted most in the world, a grandchild. But it was hard for her to focus on that when she had so many doubts about the way Sadie was raising Connor. Ginger was traditional and rule-based; she believed babies and children needed guidance and stability, that they did better when they knew what to expect and when their parents led the way. As far as Ginger could tell, Sadie wasn't doing any of that but was letting her four-year-old son make all the decisions. A child was not capable of making good decisions. Everyone knew that. Most important, though, her Denial sat firmly next to her belief that her relationship with Hank was what it always had been; that she still took priority as his mother in terms of what she shared with him. She has not yet fully acknowledged that he is now married and his wife, Sadie, stands in the top spot as far as importance goes if there are ever sides to be taken. This is true whether you are married or living with someone. Often a parent can't see it when their adult child isn't in alignment with them. That lack of awareness is what leads people to these impasses. Someone's parent behaves on the premise that they still have the inside track the same way they did when their child was growing up and even to the point when he or she was a single adult—whether it is voicing their opinion, visiting at the drop of a hat, or demanding that their grown child spend holidays with them—they have not shifted along with the reality of the new dynamic, which is now that their spouse comes before everyone else. It is a difficult change for a parent to realize their adult child has a connection that takes precedence over the one they share and have shared all that child's life. It can take a while before the parent is able to see that the boundaries their son or daughter support are different now.

As promised, Ginger called Hank a few hours after our session. She didn't think anything of the fact that she had booked her flight without even checking to make sure the days she chose worked for them.

"Hi, Ma," he said when she called.

"Hi, Hank, how are things going there?"

"Fine," he said. "We're all fine."

Honestly, she wasn't so sure about that, but she would have her chance to talk about it in person soon.

"I'm all set to come," she said. "I arrive on the eighth, and I'll be there for three days."

Hank didn't say anything. Seconds ticked by and Ginger waited, assuming he was distracted by Connor or something going on in his house.

"Hank?" she finally asked.

"Mom, you can't just tell me when you're coming, we have plans," Hank said. "I'm sorry but that chunk of time doesn't work for us."

"But it's set," she said. "I did nonrefundable."

"Well, you shouldn't have," Hank said.

"I have important things to discuss with you," Ginger said.

"I can't talk now," Hank said. "Listen, I have to go."

Ginger held the phone in her hand for a few beats before looking to make sure he had ended the call. *He must have been busy,* Ginger thought to herself. *I got him at a bad time; he would never hang up on me. I'll call again tomorrow, when Connor is in preschool and the house is quiet. Then he'll be able to focus better and he'll listen. He'll see how important my visit will be for all of them.*

Ginger slept fine that night, and waited until 9:30 to call Hank again, giving them plenty of time to get Connor settled and make sure Sadie was already at her office. She knew that getting Hank alone was key. Maybe he was so noncommittal last night because Sadie was within earshot. Maybe he needed time to break it to her.

"Hey, Ma," he said. "Did you cancel?"

"Cancel?" she asked, surprised by his suggestion. "No, I'm still coming. I wanted to talk more about it. I figured you just needed time to think about it, maybe talk it through with Sadie."

"Are you kidding me right now?" Hank said. "I didn't need time to think about it and I didn't talk to Sadie. Your visit isn't going to work. Cancel your flight. I don't want to talk about this or, frankly, anything with you right now. And by the way, keep your opinions to yourself." And he hung up.

Wow, Ginger thought, *I must have really gotten him at a bad time at work. He would never intentionally hang up on me. I know he knows I'm right.*

Things only got worse. Ginger continued to run the clear red lights that Hank put in front of her. Her Denial kept her from seeing the possibility that he meant what he said. No matter what his response was, she returned to the fact that he needed her and always welcomed what she had to say. In the end she didn't go, thinking Hank needed more time and that she would reschedule soon. The flight had been exceedingly cheap, so she didn't feel like she lost much at all. The morning of our next session she reached out to them about a completely separate topic. They had a summer trip planned to the beach, and she was just checking in to see if they had any questions about the dates or the accommodations.

When she came in to see me, she looked down. I remembered that when she had left the week before she was sure that by the time she saw me again she would have visited her son's family and all would be corrected in her eyes.

"How are you?" I asked. "How did it go?"

"I just don't get it," she said. "Hank keeps saying he doesn't want to talk about it. But he has always been open to what I have to say. And I know he can't possibly agree with what Sadie's doing. She must be controlling him. This isn't like him. My theory is that he doesn't want to make waves with her. She is so volatile. But honestly, he can't be listening to what she says. He knows better. I'm sure he doesn't mean it. I haven't gone to see them yet. He asked me not to, which is so confusing to me. I know he'll come around."

"I can see how it can be confusing to you since things have not gone as you expected them to," I said, seeing Ginger's Denial about where Hank was coming from in relation to her criticism of Sadie even more clearly now.

"The worst part is that I rented a big house at the Jersey Shore for the whole family this summer. We plan to be there for my sixtieth birthday in late June. But when I wrote to them this morning about it, they wrote back and said they might not be able to come, that they didn't want to deal with the judgment and scrutiny I was putting on them. I told them I wasn't judging; I was just looking out for my grandson. And really, what does one thing even have to do with the other?"

"Oh my, this situation has really spiraled out of control," I said.

"I just need to catch him at the right time," she said. "Hank is such a good son. He has always respected and welcomed my opinion. It feels like Sadie is brainwashing him or something. She has turned him against me. Why would he be listening to her? I'm his mother. He can't really think he knows more than I do."

"Of course you are his mother," I said. "And you always will be. But think back to when you first got married. Didn't things shift a little for you then? Didn't your husband and the new family you were creating together become your focus in terms of how you made decisions and where your priorities were?"

Ginger's eyes lit up as she thought back to the beginning of her own marriage.

"I do remember that," she said. "In fact, it wasn't until my husband got a little mad at me for always running to my mother that I changed the way I did things a little. But it took a long time. I'm not ready for it with Hank."

"You might have to be," I said. "Even though it is not easy."

On the heels of this, Ginger was basically offering unwanted advice in a rather aggressive manner, and I wanted to help her see that that was not necessarily a good way to reach anyone, not to mention a daughter-in-law who might already be on the defensive.

I shared the skill of *KNOW WHEN TO HOLD THEM, KNOW WHEN TO FOLD THEM* with her.

"With this you will learn when and how to use empathy to know if it is possible to have an open-minded conversation that can lead to a middle or common ground, or even a truce to just agree to disagree," I explained.

I have shared this skill with many of my patients. It can come in handy when dealing with differences of opinion as Ginger is with her daughter-in-law, or with political arguments that might separate a family, and also with navigating the pandemic or any national health crisis. It is useful when someone has or is the recipient of a judgmental stance about anything from career choices, marriage partners, having a baby or not, how you raise him or her when they arrive, political beliefs, and if you do or don't wear a mask to stop the spread of a deadly virus.

"I want you to think about what you can and can't accept," I said. "Think about what you can live with and what you can't. Is it more important to you to have your grandson in your life despite the fact that you don't like Sadie's methods, including her potty-training procedure, or are your feelings so strong that those things are deal breakers if Sadie and Hank won't agree to change their ways?"

"I wasn't thinking of it that way," she said. "Of course, it isn't a deal breaker, I'm just trying to help them."

"It seems reasonable that you would see it that way," I said. "But have they asked you for help?"

"Well," Ginger said, "I guess not."

"A good rule of thumb is that unsolicited advice is usually unwelcome. Stop telling them what they should do. I can appreciate that it's really hard to hold back from sharing your opinion, especially when it has always been easy to do with Hank. But telling people that you think they are wrong is generally not the best way to reach them. It will lead them to shut down and tune out whatever you are saying. Rather than an intervention, as you called it, where you are trying to stop them from doing something, try to have a talk that is open, with a give and take. You want to use the conversation so that you are setting up the possibility that they will ask you what you would do in this situation. The real goal is to create a situation in which you can naturally offer your opinion, instead of forcing it upon them. That way there is a better chance of it being received and not rejected."

"I wouldn't even know how to begin something like that," Ginger said.

"You can start by asking Sadie why she chooses to do things the way she does. Do you know anything about her own upbringing? In the end it might come back to that, either she had too much structure and she is trying to do it another way, or maybe her parents did it this way, too, and it is all she knows. Whatever the case, knowing where she is coming from might help you accept her choices better. Unless Sadie or Hank says something to you indicating they just can't change another diaper and implying that they would welcome your input about that subject, my suggestion to you is to tread much more lightly. The bottom line is never offer guidance unless it is asked for."

Ginger nodded.

"You know that isn't my style," she said, smiling. "I've always been direct. It has always worked well for me."

"I know how strongly you feel about these issues, and I can see how sometimes being direct is a positive," I said. "In this situation, though, there might be a better way. Consider the skill and let's see how things are next week."

She agreed that she would.

When Cliff came to see me the next time, he said he got a respite that he never would have asked for on the night be was supposed to babysit for his brother's kids. His brother got sick and ended up with a bad (but not too bad) case of COVID. They canceled their plans and Cliff was off the hook for the moment.

"He's feeling better," Cliff said. "Which is great. But now he thinks my precautions have been even more unnecessary since he says it was really no big deal. More than ever he doesn't get why I'm changing my whole life to avoid this virus. I told him he was very lucky, that many people are not as lucky as he was, and really, he has no idea yet if he is going to have any of those awful long-haul issues they talk about. I know if I just keep trying I can reach him. I just have to find the right article or the right sad story. He is a smart man. I just have to keep looking."

Despite Cliff's Denial, it was clear to me that neither was going to budge. Even though Cliff had the science and statistics on his side, Billy and their parents just weren't open to it and had their own set of explanations and facts. Either way, Cliff was just going to continue to get nowhere with them as he tried to explain why he was being so careful. I shared the skill *KNOW WHEN TO HOLD THEM, KNOW WHEN TO FOLD THEM* with Cliff. In his case, this meant using empathy to consider where his parents and brother were coming from to try to understand why they believed what they did and, with that in mind, attempt to find a way to come together despite the differences between them so they can hold each other up instead of tear each other down.

Rather than coming in hot and telling them they are wrong, as Cliff was doing and in the similar way Ginger was proceeding with Hank and Sadie, ask questions and explore the different points of view. I think of it as taking action steps toward the mutual goal of maintaining your relationship. The first step is recognizing that you have a difference of opinion. The second step is accepting that, which is not easy to do. The final step is coming up with a plan about how to deal with it. In Cliff's case that meant no longer trying to convince his parents and brother that they were wrong and that his way was the right way, accepting that they are in Denial about the virus so that they can continue to live their lives the way they want to, recognizing his own Denial that he can actually change their minds, and finally, deciding what he can and can't do to remain comfortable. He used the skill of *KNOW WHEN TO HOLD THEM, KNOW WHEN TO FOLD THEM* and decided he would hold onto his policy to see them only outside without a mask, and inside only if they wore a mask—no exceptions. He also settled on what he would let go of, which was trying to convince them to do things his way, and to stop feeling guilty if they asked him to do something he knew was wrong for him. He also told them that if they did decide to get vaccinated, he would rethink that policy. The choice really becomes either finding a way to meet halfway so you sustain the relationship or standing firm and risking losing people he loves. Luckily, nobody in Cliff's family wanted to lose the other so they agreed that they would never see eye to eye on this one, and they would accept each person's conditions for the duration of the pandemic.

When Ginger came to see me again, this was exactly what she had to decide between. Ever since she had proposed the intervention, most communication with her son's family had ceased. Usually, they would all talk on a Sunday, passing the phone around so Ginger could say hi to Hank, then Sadie, and then her beloved Connor. But last Sunday she called as she always did, thinking surely they could move beyond this, and Hank had answered. He said he couldn't talk, which he never did unless there was really something going on at the moment. Ginger told me she got a sinking feeling. She asked to speak to Connor. She loved her weekly conversations with him and looked forward to them. He spoke in a very serious voice, saying things like, "Grandma, you have no idea how hard preschool is these days," and "I eat an orange every morning to keep me sunny." She would often repeat these amazing nuggets of conversation to Janet and her other friends on their morning walk the next day, and she would carry them with her until the next time, smiling when she thought of them. This week, though, Hank said Connor, too, was unavailable. She couldn't help but wonder what amazing thoughts she was going to miss hearing.

I have seen situations like this when a parent or in-law comes on too strong and actually pushes their children away. I've also seen people lose their family and grandchildren that way. And almost every time, it could have been avoided. I told her that.

"I certainly don't want that to happen," Ginger said firmly.

"No, of course you don't," I said. "The thing to keep in mind, though, is that there can be a breaking point, if you lose sight of what is most important."

She took a deep breath.

"What is most important to me is Connor," she said. "Having him in my life."

"Yes, but you can't get to Connor without the blessing of his parents," I reminded her.

"They are all important," she conceded. "So, what do I do?"

"Use the skill I shared with you. I think already you've determined that the good outweighs the bad, that time with Connor and your weekly conversations when he shares his funny ideas about life are more valuable than telling Sadie how to be a good parent. The goal is to try to understand what their reason is for doing it the way they do. Ask questions. Avoid telling them what they are doing wrong, and instead inquire about the things that worry you."

"Is it too late?" Ginger asked. "I mean what do I do now to get them back?"

"I think first make it clear that you acknowledge that Hank and Sadie are now a team, and if you have any concerns you will go to both of them, not just Hank," I said. "But more than that, you can tell them you can see now that you approached this all wrong. Explain that you don't want to do an intervention after all, that you regret suggesting that. And hopefully you can open a dialogue so you each have a chance to explain where you are coming from without accusing the other of making a bad decision."

Ginger could finally see what she had to lose, and, with the skill *KNOW WHEN TO HOLD THEM, KNOW WHEN TO FOLD THEM* she was able to decide to let go of this particular beef in order to be able to preserve a connection to the people she loved most in the world.

The next week when she came to see me, she seemed lighter than she had in a while.

"We did a family Zoom call," she said. "After our last session I sent an email to Hank and Sadie together so Sadie doesn't think I'm talking behind her back again. I apologized. I explained that when I raised Hank and his brothers things were different, so I have my own view of the way children should be raised but, of course, there are many ways to do it. I told them that it was true that I had worried Connor didn't have enough structure, and I worried about his not being toilet trained yet, but no matter, if they're okay with it, they're his parents. He was the sweetest and smartest and funniest boy in the universe. There is nobody who deserves more credit for that than Sadie and Hank, so obviously they are doing something right. When we finally talked, I shared the things he has said to me recently about preschool and having an orange every morning. At least that was something we could all laugh about together. And then Connor came on and he is just the loveliest boy. He said, 'Grandma, I missed you. Where have you been?'"

"I'm so glad to hear this," I told her. "It sounds like you were able to shift your priorities, which is terrific. Good for you. What changed? Why do you think it's working? What are you doing differently?"

"I hold my tongue when I'm about to make a judgmental comment when they are doing something that I disapprove of or doesn't make sense to me. I realized that it is much more important to have a relationship with my grandson than to voice my opinion about the proper way to potty train. I have to say it is really hard not to get angry and tell them how wrong I think they are at times, but since they aren't asking, I'm not offering. I think I will now know when to hold them, what to hold onto, and when to fold them, what to let go of and walk away from."

"That's really great," I said.

"My goal now is to get them to come to the shore for my birthday," she told me. "Potty trained or not, I don't care, I just want them there. And I'm very hopeful that it will work out."

Let's check in and see how Cliff is doing. Despite his family's coming together and Cliff's saying what he would and would not do during this time, there was one particularly dark day after Cliff's brother recovered when his parents wanted him to come care for him. He was much better, but had had a slight setback and was still weak, and he wasn't able to get himself food. With his wife no longer there, it all seemed particularly bleak. Really, they just didn't want him to be alone. Everyone was busy that day, and they called on Cliff. It was the worst possible situation, to be in Billy's home after he had been sick. Twice Cliff got in the car to head to his brother's and twice he pulled back into the garage and got out. How could he say no to his brother when he was in such distress? Following on the heels of that question was the next one, how could he put himself and his wife and kids at risk? Unlike the time he was so upset when Billy asked him to come get him when his car broke down that he couldn't think straight, he took a deep breath and remained calm, clear, and able to come up with alternatives. He went inside his house and called Billy. He told him he just couldn't come over. He would have a burger and fries delivered from their favorite pub and ginger ale, Gatorade, and Tylenol delivered through a convenience store app. He offered to do a Zoom call to keep him company. At our next session Cliff repeated the conversation to me.

"I waited for him to say something; I know he thought I was going to come," he said. "I felt like this was it, I was really doing it. I was drawing a firm line in the sand. So then I asked if there was anything else he needed before I confirmed the order. He was quiet for a few seconds and then he said *how about some peanut M&Ms?* I said sure and he said, '*thanks man.*' I knew from his tone he meant it. It was really great."

Cliff came to accept that this is his family, this is what they will continue to believe and do, and he is not going to change that. Of course, he worries about their own safety because they are still unvaccinated and don't wear masks most of the time, so he continues to send them articles—he can't help himself—but he doesn't expect to change their minds anymore. He knows that is very unlikely. He no longer tells them what to do. He knows now that he can only make decisions for himself about how he will handle the pandemic; he can't control his brother or his parents. As a result, he finally feels able to say no in the name of his own health. There are still times when they push back and claim they need him this one time, and he has come to expect and accept that. But he still says no and works hard to find other ways to assist them when they need something that doesn't involve seeing them in person and putting himself in jeopardy. He visits them on the front yard and will drive over and talk to them from a safe distance, so too much time doesn't go by without simply being in each other's presence. But when they say *come on, please just come inside* he says *no* and they accept it. He constantly reminds them that this is temporary and that they will reassess as things change with the virus. He will throw in a jab to say the sooner everyone is vaccinated the better it will be, and they hear him, but they don't do anything about it. When the topic comes up, he will acknowledge that it is their decision, but that he won't be able to come inside their house unless they get vaccinated. They are making a choice and Cliff is making an opposing choice, and they are still one big happy family.

The essence, when possible, is to reach a point where you can respect each other's differences and learn to accept them even if you are unable to agree with them. The greater goal is to preserve family ties. Luckily both Ginger and Cliff have been able to do that.

Demands like the ones Cliff's parents and brother made on him are not unusual. In his case, they were tied to navigating the pandemic and that is what caused the tension. I have other patients who also find the demands put on them by family members and close friends to be impossible to live up to, although they do their best. In those cases, it is not so much around a differing belief system that they clash but simply that they can never do enough. In the next chapter you will learn how to deal with the demands made upon you by your children, your spouse, your parents—especially aging—your siblings, a neighbor, really, the list is endless, so you can set realistic boundaries. I promise, you will thank me.

CHAPTER NINE

You're Driving Me Crazy

EILEEN WENT THROUGH EACH RACK AT MACY'S LOOKING FOR A green shirt. There were about ten other things she should be doing at that moment, including making dinner for her family and sending a proposal to her boss, but her mother was freaking out because she needed a green shirt now. She couldn't get out herself because of the snow, so she had enlisted Eileen's help. Eileen was moving so fast, trying to get this done, that she worried she might miss something and actually prolong the process. She slowed down to take it all in. Blue, yellow, red, black, no green. Why in the world did it have to be green? She walked to the next rack and the next, watching the clock move from her family's dinner time and beyond, hoping her boss would understand the delay. Finally, she landed on a green shirt. She pulled it out, looked it over. Perfect. She quickly called her mother.

"I got one," she said when her mother answered. "I'll drop it off on my way home."

"Great," her mother said. "But I'm about to have dinner, and *Jeopardy* is on, plus I just got JoJo to quiet down."

JoJo was her dog. Eileen took a deep breath.

"I thought you needed it for tonight," Eileen said. "You said it was urgent."

"I need it for tomorrow night," her mother said, like it was all the same.

"Well, I wish I'd known," Eileen said. "I could have done it tomorrow."

"So, can you come later? You know how JoJo bothers me during dinner when he's awake," her mother continued. "Can you bring it over after?"

Eileen hesitated. That was not convenient, but she could make it work. She would go home first, make sure everyone had eaten, send the proposal, and then head to her mother's once everything was cleaned up. That made sense. She knew her mother had a hard time with the dog at dinner time. *Plus*, she thought, *she's lonely. She is probably using all of this as an excuse to see me later, the quietest time of her day. Really, it's the least I can do.*

At 8:50 she called her mother.

"I'm heading over now," she said, the green shirt in her hand.

"Great," her mother said.

When she got there, she could see her mother's driveway wasn't shoveled at all, even though she usually hired a kid from the neighborhood to do it. She got out of the car and carried the shirt to her door. As soon as she rang the bell, the dog went crazy.

"Come around to the back," her mother called through the door.

Eileen trudged around to the back, which was equally snowy with the thinnest layer of ice developing on top. Her mother met her at the door with the dog on his leash in one hand and a shovel in the other. She raised her eyebrows as if to say *which do you want to do first?* Eileen handed the shirt over to her. Her mother leaned the shovel against the wall and grabbed it with her right hand, not even glancing at it, and tossed it onto the table inside the door without a word. She had told Eileen earlier that she needed it for a themed book club dinner. She grabbed the shovel again and held it at the ready.

"Mom, don't you usually ask one of the kids down the street to shovel?"

"Yes, but since you're here, I need you to do it because he couldn't come," she said.

"Why didn't you tell me? I could have maybe gotten somebody else," Eileen said.

"Oh, what's the big deal?" her mother asked.

Once again Eileen took a deep breath. Her mother had been living alone for two years now, ever since her father died. The winter was always harder for all these reasons, Eileen reminded herself. Her guilt started to creep in. *It isn't like this is something that happens all the time. It's an exception. She's always alone. I'll just do it.*

"Let me take the dog first," she said. She liked JoJo. His mother said he was a mix of a Yorkshire Terrier and a Poodle, but Eileen thought she was just guessing. She was grateful her mother had the dog's company. They walked slowly around, trying not to slip, the dog clearly desperate to have a chance to relieve himself. Once she got back to the house, she began the long task of shoveling and salting the walkways and the driveway. By the time she got home it was two hours later, her husband was worried, and the kids were fast asleep.

"We missed you," her husband said, as he met her at the door. Eileen had been absent for almost the entire evening.

"Tell me about it," she said in annoyance. "I thought it was a quick drop off and it turned into shoveling her entire driveway. I'm exhausted."

She went right to bed and was asleep within minutes. The next morning before the alarm went off, the phone rang.

"It's too icy for me to walk JoJo," her mother said. "You must not have salted enough. You have to come over and walk him."

"But I have to get the kids to school," Eileen said, thinking ahead. "And if it's icy it's going to take extra time to clean off the car and everything else."

Disregarding her, her mother said, "Well he has to go out. He can't walk himself. Do you want me to break my leg?"

"Mom, you are not going to break your leg," Eileen said. "You walk JoJo every day."

"Not when there's ice," her mother said.

They were quiet for a few seconds, but long enough for Eileen to start to feel guilty again.

"You're upsetting me," her mother said. "I thought I could count on you. Don't you love me?"

"Mom, don't be ridiculous," Eileen said. "Of course I do."

"Then why can't you help me when I need you to?" her mother asked.

"Okay," she said. "I'll be right there."

Again, to deal with the guilt, Eileen told herself *she's right, it could be dangerous. She is getting up there in years, she has no one else, it's got to be me. Maybe I can see about a dogwalker for the rest of the winter—*

This is a common occurrence for many of my patients; in fact, I would say this is one of the situations I hear about often—dealing with the impossible expectations family members and sometimes friends place on them, and the burdened responsibility they feel in the name of pleasing their loved ones and keeping the peace. The problem is, they lose much of themselves in doing so, and it is literally never enough. Eileen gets the shirt her mother needs for a social gathering, takes it to her at her mother's preferred time, but none of that seems to even register with her mother as far as what she is doing for her. Instead, her mother assumes she will walk her dog and shovel her walk and driveway, even though Eileen has her own family to attend to. No "thank you" is uttered. Instead, first thing the next morning she gets another call—this time, somehow, it is Eileen's fault because she didn't salt the area enough—at least that's what her mother believes. Going to her mother's again will mean either making the kids late for school or putting more pressure on her husband to take them when he is already stretched to the limit. Clearly her mother is not thinking of any of that, she is thinking only of herself, and when she throws in the threat of a possible injury if she does it herself, as well as a question of Eileen's love for her, Eileen feels she has no choice but to go. It can play out differently for other people: maybe an older parent wants to be in constant touch through calling or texting; an aunt expects a weekly visit; an adult daughter anticipates that her mother will take care of her kids whenever she needs her to and with no warning; or many other scenarios. In many of these instances, my patients try "to be there" for that person, but no matter what they do, it is never enough. The person will always focus on what they did not do, as Eileen's mother did with the salting, rather than what they did—which was find the shirt, walk the dog, and shovel the driveway—and they will continue to ask for more. The worst part of all, though, is that there is never any appreciation or gratitude.

Eileen couldn't believe it. From the way her mother had described it, she expected her driveway and walkways to be iced up. But when she got there, they looked fine.

Eileen worked to tamp down the anger she was feeling by reminding herself: *She's alone. She's probably scared that if something happened to her there would be no one to help her, and if things got really bad, who would take care of JoJo?*

"Fine, I'll take him for a walk," she said.

"Here," she said, handing over his leash. "And remember, this is his long walk, at least a half hour."

In an annoyed voice she said, "Mom, I don't have a half hour. I wasn't able to make the kids' lunches yet because I rushed over here, so I still have to do that and get them to school. I have two work calls before noon. I just don't have that much time."

"Oh please, the kids will be fine," her mother said. "They are more resilient than you ever give them credit for. Just let them buy lunch today."

Eileen looked at her incredulously. She didn't say a word but grabbed the dog's leash and began to walk away, saying to herself, *Oh God, what's the big deal? If this is what it takes to keep her calm, I'll just do it. Why am I making an issue out of it?*

The next time I saw Eileen she was focused on how burdened she felt and how plagued she was by her relationship with her mother. She was struggling with the tremendous anger she felt at her mother's unrelenting demands and the guilt she experienced when she considered pushing back because she felt so underappreciated. We talked about her trying to get a handle on what were reasonable requests on her mother's part and what was over the line so she could begin to sort out when it made sense and worked for her to say yes, and when she would have to begin to start putting limits in place and say no.

In addition to the requests about the dog and the shoveling, there were daily phone calls to check in and listen to her mother's litany of complaints, which were maddening and time consuming to hear. Any time she would attempt to hang up, her mother would say something along the lines of, "I am eighty-four years old, who else can I tell this to? This could be my last phone call, for all I know."

"It's so stressful," Eileen said to me. "My mother never once says thank you for anything"

"I understand," I said. "It is extremely upsetting. There is no acknowledgment or gratitude for how devoted you are and how hard you work to keep her happy and feeling loved. You do everything you can to be a good daughter, and all you ever hear about is how you fall short and miss the mark."

"Everyone goes through this in one way or another when their parents get older," she said, trying to brush it off. "I sound so selfish not wanting to help her."

"On the contrary, you don't sound selfish at all, you sound selfless," I said. "You want to help her to such a degree that you are losing yourself in the mix."

"Sometimes I feel like I could paint my mother's house, take the dog for a week, make her dinner for a month, and there would still be more to do," she said.

"That's because it's true, you're starting to get it," I said. "Your mother's expectations are completely unreasonable, and it is actually impossible for you to ever meet them."

When my patients are experiencing this, they often feel they have to do the right thing and say yes to their loved one because they feel responsible for their well-being. They believe they must drop everything at any time and always be available. However, they are in Denial to how oblivious to them their family member is being. Even when they feel pushed and exasperated, they find the idea of saying no to be hard to grasp. And, as is the case with Eileen's mother, often these family members or demanding friends are oblivious to and deny the fact that the people they are asking to do things for them have legitimate needs that are important. They never acknowledge or respect them. When Eileen's mother asked her to come first thing in the morning, she didn't even consider the strain it could put on her family. They never recognize the other person's need because it interferes with getting their own needs met. So, instead, in the same way Cliff's family denied COVID in Chapter Eight, they make it disappear.

The goal was to help Eileen see her mother realistically to help her get past her own Denial of her mother's Denial of her needs on any level. By doing this, she would be able to anticipate how her mother was going to act, and not get so hurt, angry, and guilt-ridden, but instead could plan to put effective limits in place to look out for herself.

Another patient of mine named Hope was going through a similar predicament with her sister Maureen, who never thought twice of leaning on Hope when she needed help. Whether it was to come over and take care of her baby, take their mother to the doctor, or babysit for her toddler, there seemed to be no end to what Maureen expected Hope to do for her, and, of course, no recognition of what any of it might cost Hope in terms of time or sacrifice. In other words, Maureen saw her sister as someone who was there to help her life run more smoothly, but it didn't matter to her how much havoc that might wreak on Hope.

The other day, for example, they were all planning to meet at their parents' house in Westchester for dinner. Hope had a root canal that afternoon and was still numb from the Novocain and had a headache. She was parked on the Upper West Side, where her dentist was, and thought Maureen could either walk or take an Uber or cab to meet her. As she walked out of the dentist's office, Hope sent Maureen a text.

Meet me at the corner of Eighty-Ninth and Broadway. We'll go to the garage from there.

Hope assumed Maureen was already on her way and was just waiting for the message to tell her exactly where to meet. Hope waited, the numbness starting to wear off, eager to get in the car and to her parents' house before its effect was totally gone. Her phone rang.

"Hey, can you come get me? I'm at Bloomingdale's," Maureen said, like it was no big deal.

"On Lexington?" Hope asked, incredulously.

"Yeah," Maureen said unapologetically. "I have really heavy bags."

Hope couldn't believe that Maureen was so unaware of the fact that she had just been at the dentist and was uncomfortable. Hope had told her about the root canal this morning.

"Come on, Maureen, I'm in pain," Hope said. "Please just get in a cab."

"You know this is my one day out without the kids," Maureen said. "Can't you come get me? I did a lot of shopping."

Hope knew Maureen had gotten a babysitter so she could spend the day shopping, and her husband was going to meet all of them at the house with their kids. But she was free, unencumbered by the kids. She could easily get in a cab.

"No way," Hope said. "My mouth is starting to throb, and that is in so many wrong directions I can't even tell you. Plus, the traffic is terrible at this hour. It could take me an hour to get to you."

"Don't be ridiculous," Maureen said. "I'm like thirty blocks away. It will take ten minutes."

"And across town," Hope said, exasperated, but already she felt her resolve fading. She could spend the next half hour arguing, her gums aching more and more, or she could just get in the car and pick up her sister. *It's true she never gets out. I'll just go do it. This is her one day out of the house and away from the kids*, Hope told herself. *I don't want to make it a bad day.*

"Fine, I'll be there as soon as I can," Hope said, completely disregarding her own pain.

"Text when you get here," Maureen said, like she knew Hope would say yes all along.

Hope recounted the incident to me, saying that the drive to her sister more than doubled the time in the car for her.

"Boy, it just never ends with my sister," Hope said. "She is completely oblivious to the fact that going to pick her up is an extra hour on my end. She doesn't even care that I was at the dentist and not feeling great. But even though it doesn't seem fair, I still feel guilty."

"You're right," I said. "It's not fair. That's what you have to hold onto so you can begin to even things out for yourself, because Maureen is never going to make it fair or work in your favor. Her Denial is the equivalent of having what I would call *Legal Emotional Blindness*. She simply can't see your emotional needs. Maureen is in the dark when it comes to your reality. It is you who need to see the light and stop trying to enlighten her."

I shared with her the same thing I said to Eileen: that it is hard to accept that a loved one would be so uncaring and completely tuned out to her well-being. She, in fact, is actually in Denial about Maureen's self-absorbed Denial of her needs. With that in mind, she can begin to move beyond it so that she is no longer surprised when Maureen acts this way and asks for one thing after another with no regard to how it will affect her.

"Maureen is aware only of what she personally wants and needs, and often you are her path to get there," I said. "As a result, she is never going to see or understand your concerns because they interfere with hers. This is distressing because you want her to see you and acknowledge you, and respect that you're a person, too. In addition, you want her to consider you and appreciate what you do for her and give her, but she can only focus on what you don't do for her. It is as if her head is in the clouds. All she knows is what she wants from you, and if you refuse her, you're letting her down and disappointing her, no matter the reason."

Maureen's demanding that Hope go out of her way and pick her up even though she had just had a root canal was a perfect example of this, and I told her that.

"It's like there's a hole in the boat," I continued. "You can't empty it because as soon as you bail water, it pours in again. No matter how hard you try, you can't keep the boat afloat because you can never bail enough water, and the same is true for how much you give Maureen. You say yes over and over, but it is never enough; you are furiously trying to keep up with the water gushing into the hole and eventually you are going to sink with the boat."

"I hadn't thought of it that way," Hope said. "That makes a lot of sense."

When Eileen came to my office for our next session, she told me about her mother's wanting to take her to lunch and then go shopping at the last minute, which would have meant canceling plans with her friend.

"I would love to do that, Mom," she said. "But I can't today. I already have a lunch date. Can we go tomorrow? Or Wednesday?"

"What plans are so important?" her mother said. "I'm your mother. Who could be more important than that? I haven't been out of the house all weekend. I'm going stir crazy. I literally haven't seen another soul. Plus, I'm busy the rest of the week. It has to be today."

"I've had this lunch planned for over a month," Eileen said.

Her mother was silent. *Maybe I can reschedule that lunch for later this week,* Eileen thought, going back to the familiar pattern of feeling guilty. *She said she was alone all weekend. She needs me more than my friend does. Plus, it's better than getting the cold shoulder from Mom.*

"Okay, Mom, I'll see what I can do," she said, giving in again.

"Great," her mother said, having known Eileen would capitulate. "Pick me up at noon."

"My friend understood, but still," Eileen said to me during our session. "It was like I had to, or I would not only feel guilty but I would face my mother's wrath. She decided she wanted to go to lunch with me and that was it; I am totally at her disposal."

"Look, I know it's hard to deal with your mother's being angry with you when you are already going above and beyond the call of duty," I said. "Think of it this way—you are both on a seesaw, but your mother is up in the air and you are on the bottom. It's uplifting for your mother, and she is taking you for a ride to support her. But this leaves you doing all the heavy lifting and always being stuck on the bottom. It's essential to start to balance things out."

"I love that analogy," Eileen said. "That's helpful. I can really see that."

I shared the important skill *USE WHAT YOU KNOW* with her, which would help her begin to set the realistic expectations for herself that we talked about at a previous session, whereby she would now have the tools to distinguish between over-the-top and never-ending demands and those that are reasonable. The goal is to see the total picture more clearly, everything that is asked of her as well as everything that she does and does not do—in her case that she tried so hard to meet all of her mother's demands and no matter what she did, her mother wanted more and never once considered how it would all affect her. By doing this, Eileen will be able to shift the overwhelming responsibility she felt toward her mother and learn to set limits, so she no longer found herself trying to meet impossible and continuous demands. By realizing that she is already doing a lot, she can finally stop jumping through hoops to win her mother's approval. This will put an end to her always feeling that she is falling short and feeling guilty, and understanding that whatever she does, her mother will ask her to do more. In fact, the harder she tries, the more her mother will demand because she is constantly testing her to prove her love.

"In other words," I said. "Consider everything that is going on, how much your mother is asking of you, how much you are doing, and, equally important in this equation, how much your mother does for you to reciprocate what you do for her. You will see it adds up to a very lopsided situation that is, in fact, unsustainable."

I explained the steps to take to be able to do this. The first is to accept that you can't alter or control the other person; you are never going to be able to change your mother's mind. The second is to stop trying to explain or justify and defend yourself and what you did or didn't do, because when you do that your mother will only refute what you are saying and blame you.

"It comes down to what I call *Demander's Denial*," I explained. "It's important for you to see that you won't be able to ever change your mother's expectations of you, no matter what you do. But you can change the expectations you have of her and thereby alter how you behave toward her. Doing this takes the sting out of her behavior, so she is no longer a bee that hurts you but rather a fly that is just annoying. The rule of thumb is that there is no reasoning with unreasonable people."

"Hmmm," she said. I could see she was thinking about it but couldn't quite determine how to get from what she was doing now to saying no sometimes. "I know what she is going to say. She is going to say that I don't care about her, that I'm neglecting her, that she is all alone and now she will be even more alone, and why am I being so mean? Just when I think I might say no, she pulls out the one thing that is indisputable, she says, 'I'm your mother,' like that makes everything okay and gives her the right to ask anything of me."

"I know; you are not alone in hearing that," I said. "But let's just talk about this. Do you think you are being mean or neglectful in any way?"

She thought about it and said, "No, I don't."

"Well, this is the reality that you have to hold onto," I said. "The true picture is that you love your mother completely, but she is asking too much of you, running you ragged, and you just can't keep it up. Eventually, you are going to be so exhausted that you aren't going to be able to take care of anyone. Think of it this way: if you are on a plane and there's an emergency, you aren't going to be able to help anyone, including yourself, if you don't put your own oxygen mask on first. It is the same thing here. By putting limits in place, you are protecting yourself and giving yourself breathing room so you can be there for the other person without feeling suffocated."

Eileen said she would give it some serious thought.

The "I'm your mother" or "I'm your father" or even, "I'm your sister" declaration plays out for many of my patients like it is a ticket to ask for anything and everything they want. I also see this type of scenario a lot between friends where one carries the burden of demands because the other person thinks they have more time because their job might not be as demanding or they are single and not dealing with the pressure of a family. Whatever the case, they expect unconditional time and caretaking.

My patient Lauren was dealing with this. She had been friends with Tiffany for well over a decade. They met in college, and now Tiffany had a husband and a young baby, and Lauren was still single, working at a consulting job, and hoping to find the right life partner soon. Ever since they graduated, they have taken an annual long weekend away together, and they agreed they wanted to keep that up even though their lives were busier now. Their friendship was always a little one-sided, with Tiffany calling most of the shots. It wasn't so obvious when their biggest question was who would pick up the take-out food (Lauren) or who would buy the beer for the party (Lauren, again). Over the years, though, it has become much more exaggerated and, while Lauren is committed to the friendship, she feels increasingly frustrated by the demands Tiffany puts on her with very little giving back.

Last month they took their annual trip and decided to go to Disney World. Tiffany sent Lauren a list of the places she wanted to go, which hotels were acceptable, and which parks she wanted to visit which days.

"Hey," Lauren said to Tiffany. "Why did you send me this? I thought we could do this together."

"Come on," Tiff said. "You are so good at it. In another life I think you should have been a travel agent. Plus, you've got more time than I do."

So, Lauren did it all. She bought right into Tiffany's demands, which led her to deny what she knew was right: that they should share the task. Instead, she told herself: *Tiffany is busy, she has a baby, I want to be a good friend.* She booked the airline tickets, chose a hotel, got park tickets, and made dinner reservations. One night when they were in Disney Springs, after seeing a show that Lauren had researched and booked, they walked out into the warm Florida air.

"Where's dinner tonight?" Tiffany asked, as if it was all on Lauren.

"I don't know," Lauren said. "This is the one night I didn't make a plan. I figured we could walk around and choose a place."

Tiffany glanced at the packed walkways.

"Really?" she said in an annoyed tone. "You can't *not* have a reservation in Disney. We'll wait for hours. How could you do that?"

Lauren was taken aback. For this one reservation she hadn't made she had made fifteen, maybe even twenty detailed arrangements for their trip. She had done everything, and yet Tiffany hadn't even thanked her. In fact, Tiffany had accepted it all as her due, shrugging and complying when Lauren asked her to Venmo half of the money to her as if even that were an imposition. She just hadn't had the energy to pin down one last night and thought, how crowded could it be on a Tuesday? The answer was, very crowded. They went from restaurant to restaurant, being told it would be a ninety-minute wait, or a two-hour wait, or longer. Up to that point everything had run smoothly. They had had a good time.

"You know, you could have helped with the reservations," Lauren said. "You never even really asked what I was planning, you just expected it to get done. This is my vacation, too."

"You're kidding me, right?" Tiffany said. "I was counting on you. This sucks. I can't believe you let this happen. I'm going back to the hotel."

When Lauren came to see me a week later, she said that moment stuck with her for the rest of the trip. It was a pattern with them: Lauren did everything, made all the plans, stopped what she was doing when Tiffany had to vent or when she needed something, but when Lauren asked her to understand that she had messed up that one night, or the one time she asked if they could switch their plans at home from a Thursday to a Friday because Lauren had met a possibly nice person on the dating app Hinge and that was when he was free, Tiffany just wouldn't budge. And yet, even though this happened often between them, Lauren found herself constantly surprised by Tiff's negative responses. She told me about some of this at one of our sessions, and then immediately swooped in to defend Tiffany.

"I think once she gets over the hump of having a young baby, she will be more giving," she said. "I have to cut her some slack."

"Was she more giving before she had the baby?" I asked.

"Well, not exactly," Lauren said. "But I did mess up the Disney thing."

"Okay, so you made a mistake, but do you think it warranted her being so hostile and nasty to you?" I asked.

"No," she said. "Absolutely not."

"I agree," I said. "Therefore, if you are going to maintain your friendship, you have to avoid these kinds of clashes and the expectation that you are going to handle everything."

I shared the skill *USE WHAT YOU KNOW* with Lauren, too. I encouraged her to think about putting limits in place so she not only stopped taking on the brunt of the work organizing what they did together, but also so she didn't feel so responsible when things went downhill, or when Tiffany proclaimed they went wrong.

"This was supposed to be a fun trip for you and yet you did the lion's share of the planning, so in many ways it turned into a burden," I said. "Not only was she not appreciative for what you did, but she wound up being mad at you for the one thing you didn't do. It doesn't have to be that way. Have you told her next time you would like to share more of the planning since she seems to have specific preferences?"

"I have," Lauren said. "But the thing is I have more time, and Tiffany knows it. She tells me that often. She expects me to do it all. The other day when I couldn't talk to her when her baby Lance was sleeping—it was the middle of the day and I had a work meeting—but she was upset with her husband and wanted to vent, I told her I could call her in an hour, but she said Lance would be up by then and that I wasn't being good friend. Honestly, the whole thing—first it made me mad, then it made me feel bad."

"The question there is, does her lack of consideration for you feel like she is being a good friend?" I asked.

"I don't know," she said honestly.

As our session came to an end, I asked her to think about that.

Let's take a look at how Eileen is doing. She was handling things a bit better until her mother's birthday rolled around. This year she was turning eighty-five and kept announcing how important this birthday was, so the pressure to get it right was overwhelming. Eileen planned a surprise lunch with her mother's three best friends and a future weekend away that she wanted to give as a gift that her mother could look forward to. She fully expected her mother to be really pleased.

A few weeks before the big day, Eileen sat in my office visibly tense.

"My mother wants her birthday to be festive with a capital F," Eileen said "I have memories of her birthday when I was a kid: it was never good enough. My father would work hard, buy her a watch, or plan a dinner, and by the end of the day they would always be fighting—why did you choose the Italian place for my birthday? We go there once a week—it isn't special. Or, where did you buy that watch? And when it turned out that someone had been selling watches in my father's office lobby my mother freaked—you can't even go to a store for my birthday present? So now, my father isn't here anymore, and it's up to me to make her birthday great. Plus, she is going to be eighty-five. That's a big birthday and last night she said, 'You know, this might be my last birthday.' I mean, how do I deal with that? I can't stop thinking about it."

"That sounds difficult," I said. "What are you going to do for her?"

"Well, I invited three of her best friends to her house for a surprise lunch. I'm going to make her the tomato and goat cheese quiche she loves for lunch, get her favorite bread, and I made a handmade card with a special birthday poem that I wrote in it that I plan to bring to the lunch and read in front of everyone."

"Wow," I said. "That sounds like a fabulous celebration."

"I hope so," Eileen said. "I really do. Oh, and as a gift I'm giving her a weekend away to the college she went to. I'm thinking of setting up a private tour, and maybe getting in to see her dorm—it's still there. To let her know I'm planning this I am going to give her a blanket with the name of her alma mater on it. What do you think?"

"I think that's incredibly thoughtful and loving," I said.

"I hope my mother sees it that way," Eileen said. "I think she'll really like it."

On the night before her mother's birthday Eileen went over everything, obsessing about the details, and it all seemed great to her. All she wanted to do was make her mother happy because it was a big milestone. Despite the intense strain she shouldered, she believed it was worth it. *I'm glad she's still alive*, she thought to herself. *I feel sorry for her since her world has gotten smaller over the years.*

When I saw her the following week, I asked how it went.

"I thought it had gone well," Eileen said slowly, rubbing her forehead with her hand. "I picked up all her friends, and the food was great. Everyone talked and laughed and couldn't get over the poem I had written. One friend, Bessy, brought a poster she had made with old pictures. Her other friend, Johanna, brought a playlist of their favorite songs. She said her son helped her make it and I could tell my mother liked the fact that other people were chipping in to make her birthday great. We were together all afternoon. I drove everyone home. When I came back to spend the rest of the day with my mother, she was quiet. I thought maybe she was sad that her time with her friends was over. So, I said, 'Mom, what's wrong?' She looked right at me and said, 'you didn't send me my birthday cards, they usually arrive in the mail the day of my birthday.' I was incredulous. The fact that I took the time to write the poem, read it to her in front of her friends, and they got to hear all the love I had for her, and her only comment was I didn't get the cards you usually send through the mail?"

"What a disappointment," I said. "It appears that no matter what you did or what you could have done she still would have found something to complain about."

In the same way Maureen didn't see Hope's needs, it sounded like Eileen's mother, at least historically, couldn't see the things Eileen was doing, or the things her husband had done all those years for her; she could only see what wasn't done. It is also similar to how Tiffany couldn't see all that Lauren had done for their Disney trip, what she got stuck on was the one reservation she didn't make. Eileen and I had talked about this before—how her mother was impossible to please no matter how hard she tried.

"*USE WHAT YOU KNOW*," I said to her. "You spent weeks planning her birthday. You were thoughtful and kind. You spent money, you were creative, you showed your love five different ways. There is a lot you did for her to be thankful for."

Eileen looked at me and nodded. It was hard to dispute the facts.

Things had not gotten easier for Hope when dealing with her sister Maureen; if anything they were more out of control. Not only did Maureen constantly ask Hope for help, but lately she had also been expecting Hope to pick up all the slack with their mother, who had a knee problem and had been to multiple doctors in the last month. The first few appointments were no big deal and Hope was happy to take her, but the third and fourth were during important work meetings, so Hope asked if Maureen could do it. She hired a babysitter when she got her haircut or to play tennis, it didn't seem like an unreasonable request.

"You want me to have a babysitter come stay with the kids so I can take mom to the doctor?" Maureen asked. "You can take her without having to have someone come to your home to take care of the people you are responsible for. It makes sense that you would do it."

"I have work meetings both times," Hope said. "It would take a lot of rearranging."

"So rearrange them," Maureen said. "That will be far easier."

For you, Hope wanted to say but didn't. Even though she ended up doing it because of her usual guilt and the added concern that her mother would find out neither of her daughters was jumping at the chance to take her to her fourth medical appointment, Hope sensed she couldn't keep this up indefinitely.

"You are not alone," I assured her. "A lot of the patients I work with are grappling with the exact feelings you have. Here is a skill that works and can help you—*USE WHAT YOU KNOW*. In other words, consider everything that is going on, how much Maureen is asking of you, how much you are doing, how much Maureen does for you. If you use what you know, you can start to balance things for yourself. Maureen isn't going to do that; she thinks it's her right to ask you to do anything for her or anything that will make her life easier, and if you continue to do what she asks out of guilt in an effort to please her, the imbalance will be ever-present."

"I love her and at times I do feel sorry for her, that's why I try so hard," Hope said. "I don't want her to doubt my love for her."

"The hard thing to accept is she always will doubt it," I said. "Any time you don't give her what she wants, in her eyes you will not be a good sister. It's important that you get that. She simply is unaware that she is making your life consistently harder as you attempt to accomplish what she asks of you. The takeaway for you is knowing that how much you love and care for her does not equate to how much you do for her, despite that being her belief. The goal of *USING WHAT YOU KNOW* is to see it all clearly and acknowledge that you could bend over backward every single day for her, and it is never, ever going to be enough. Her requests are not going to stop coming; it is always about proving that you care. With that in mind, you have to find a way to protect yourself. It is necessary to say no sometimes and put limits in place."

"But what can I say no to?" she asked.

"You have to decide which demands are too much for you and feel like a sacrifice. From what you've said it sounds like the ones that interfere with your already scheduled plans and work meetings are excessive and are the ones you need to consider saying no to. So, for example, getting your mother to the doctor. If you know your schedule you can let your sister know you can take mom to the doctor this week but not the following week, and if Maureen isn't able to do it when you are busy, you can make alternate plans or reschedule her appointment. Inform your sister what is going to work for you, so essentially you are saying yes to less and not turning her down. You are scaling it back and therefore holding onto the control."

"That sounds hard," she said.

"It is," I agreed. "But it is doable. As you start to deal with your guilt, you will build up your emotional muscle and realize you feel better; that will give you the strength to continue to do it and get stronger over time."

Hope said that made a lot of sense to her.

The essence of dealing with loved ones who are driving you crazy is getting through your Denial of their Denial of your needs because they are so self-absorbed. The problem is that everyone looks for permission from their significant other to do what they want to do, but they will never get it. Being able to see them for who they are is what can help you feel freer from guilt. The reality is that Eileen's mother is never going to tell Eileen she is satisfied, Maureen is never going to tell Hope to take a day off from helping her, and Tiffany is never going to tolerate Lauren's not being available to her for any reason. My patients, however, still try to be validated in order to feel okay about taking care of themselves. As I mentioned, the first step in breaking the cycle is to understand what is happening—that they will never get the approval they are seeking and their loved ones will continue to raise the bar. The second step is to embrace the skill *USE WHAT YOU KNOW* by remembering everything you have done and do for them against the backdrop of all their hurtful words and behaviors. This way you take the element of surprise out of it, which breaks through your Denial. Once you expect their reaction to whatever you do or don't do, you become aware and break out of Denial. Then you can change your expectations of them, so when they are critical or blaming of you, you are not wounded by it because you saw it coming. You are no longer shocked by what they say and caught off guard as if it is the first time it ever happened. By using this skill, you can start to predict their negative behavior, which enables you to prepare for it. This way you learn to respond rather than react to them, so that you can handle them in the moment as well as in future interactions. Eliminating the element of surprise is a game changer because it diminishes Denial.

I think of it as getting yourself off the playing field where you are squarely in the action and able to be blindsided, tackled, and hurt at any time. Instead, you move yourself to the bleachers, where you are a spectator. This way you can clearly observe what's happening and are no longer in danger of getting injured. You have been longing for their understanding as a measure of how much they love and care about you. Being able to do this will give you the emotional separation you need so you don't get upset and feel bad about yourself when you are putting limits in place around their demands. Developing your ability to observe what is going on emancipates you, so instead of being stunned each time and feeling like a deer in headlights, you can see the foul play taking place, blow the whistle, and figure out what the right next step is.

Your new approach may upset them, make them angry, and even cause them to lash out at you. But the fact is, they are always getting angry at you for something anyway, regardless of how much you do, because they will always ask for more. As we saw repeatedly with all three of my patients, they will attack you for the one thing you didn't do, while never thanking you for the multitude of things you did do. You can never win. With this in mind, you might as well take care of yourself. Using limits, you can choose what to do and when to do it, so you consider yourself—they won't and don't. You can say, "yeah, I can do that but not today," or, "let me think about it," giving yourself some time and space to decide. You don't have to immediately agree; you can take time. And if, when you hesitate, they say, "forget it, then," you can accept it and say, "okay, fine." Lead with what you can and will do and put your limit on it; this way you know you are helping them in a reasonable way. You are doing something, just not everything. Eileen, Hope, and Lauren have all been able to do this, and they have all managed to reduce the distress in their life and maintain the relationships with the people they love no matter how demanding they might be. They can now see their loved ones more realistically and know what to expect from them. They were able to put limits in place around how much they now give. They took control of their own behavior and accepted that they will never have their mother's or sister's or friend's understanding. In other words, they gave themselves permission, without needing the approval of their loved one, to set limits and change their actions, and had the confidence to know they were doing all they could.

The other goal is to hold onto your own reality. This means learning to expect the blame and criticism from them so you don't take it personally, and not expecting appreciation, a thank you, or gratitude so you are not discouraged by the absence of it. When Eileen's mother tells her she isn't doing enough, isn't thoughtful enough, Eileen knows that is simply not true. When Maureen tells Hope she isn't being a good aunt or a good sister, Hope now knows better than that. And when Tiffany claims Lauren doesn't care about her because she is not willing to miss a meeting to talk to her, she knows she is still a good friend, and does plenty to show it. One of the things I tell my patients is that even when you are able to do this and accept this knowledge about your loved one, it is understandable that you may feel sad or disappointed that, in the end, your relative or friend can't relate to you in the way you want them to. However, finally seeing through your own Denial helps you navigate the relationship, so you stop feeling weighed down by tremendous anger and guilt.

In this chapter we have talked about the demanding mother, sister, and friend, but what happens when you have the *Dominator Spouse* who is always blaming you and controlling you? What can you do when that demanding person is not outside the house, but inside? In Chapter Three we met Joe and Joan, each dealing with an overbearing spouse. Let's look at how they learned the skills they needed to deal with their anger and guilt, putting limits in place to be able to ultimately end the destructive relationship. It was a long road, but let's see how they finally did it.

CHAPTER TEN

Why Are You Always So Angry?

AUDREY'S MOTHER WAS DYING, AND THE LAST THING IN THE world she wanted to do was have sex with her husband, Nate. But the guilt she felt because of that was overwhelming her.

"This is torture," she said to me during one of our sessions. "I have to be there for my mother, but I feel like I'm a terrible wife because I don't want to have sex."

"Is that what you really believe?" I asked.

"Well, yes, I mean Nate must be right," she said. "That's what he tells me all the time: I don't care about him, I'm not supportive, I'm selfish, I should be able to take care of my mother and keep him happy, too."

My immediate thought was that she was not alone in feeling wrongfully culpable when living with a controlling spouse and shouldering all the anguish that went along with that. I also knew, in light of what she had just said, that we had a lot of work ahead of us.

Audrey had talked about her mother's illness often over the years. She was old and had been sick for months. She had had a bout with ovarian cancer years ago, which she recovered from, and now she was just so weak she couldn't perform normal tasks any longer and was fading more each day. From what Audrey said, nobody could quite put a name to it, just natural decline, old age. Audrey often commented that she thought she should be handling this better. Really, she acknowledged, these last years had been an unexpected gift, but she just couldn't quite rally. Nate didn't say anything about how quiet she had been—she wondered if he even noticed—but most nights when they got into bed he reached over in his usual way to initiate sex. Up to this point in their marriage he expected to have sex with her multiple times a week; he had established that early on. She knew that and was not happy about it. She also believed there must be times in a marriage when something else was going on and they could take a break from their normal routine. She had talked to him about it, but he simply wouldn't accept it. He said one thing had nothing to do with the other.

Just last night it happened again, and it had been a particularly bad day with her mother. There had been a split second when it took her mother a few beats too long to recognize her, and she couldn't get the moment out of her mind.

"Can we just talk a little tonight?" she said to Nate when they were settled in bed, the covers firmly pulled up to her chin in what she hoped would be a clear sign that she wasn't interested in any physical connection.

"Sure, hon," he said, reaching out for her. "After sex. I've been thinking about you all day."

Usually, she gave in to him; it just wasn't worth the fight. *He loves me*, she would think to herself. *One of the reasons he married me is because I turn him on, and now I can't exactly ask him to turn that off. He works so hard; he deserves to relax at the end of the night.* She would be able to close her eyes and will the image of her mother away for the minutes it took to satisfy her husband. She didn't enjoy it, but it was far better than the spiral of guilt she felt if she didn't do it.

Last night she did what she usually did. She closed her eyes and tried not to picture her mother struggling to find her daughter's name in her muddled brain as Nate climbed on top of her and started to kiss her. All she could see was her mother fumbling, her face blank, and, instead of being able to push it away, she wondered, what will happen tomorrow? And the next day? How bad is this going to get? Might there be a time when she forgets me completely?

Nate was already into it. He was moving on top of her, his mouth on her forehead and then her ears. How long could this possibly take? She thought to herself as the seconds ticked by. *You can do it*, she silently coached herself. *Keep going*. But almost without willing it to, her arm shot up between them and pushed him away.

"Nate," she said. "I'm really upset about something that happened with my mother today. I'm just not in the mood. Can we save this for tomorrow?"

He pulled back and looked at her with what she could only describe as confusion and anger.

"What the hell, Audrey," he said. "You could have told me sooner. Before I started."

She thought to herself, *is he kidding? Like it would have made a difference! I know from the past it doesn't matter. He doesn't care.*

"Come on," he said, softening. "I'll help you get your mind off of it."

"I don't want to," she said more forcefully, rolling out from under him and sitting up. "I'm still too disturbed by what's going on with my mother."

"Your mother is all you talk about," he said, accepting her rejection and sitting up. He cleared his throat and stood, heading into the bathroom. She relaxed, thinking he understood. When he came back out, she assumed he had taken care of his sexual urge himself, which she was fine with. He stood over her.

"Give me a date for how long this is going to continue. If it's too long you know I would have a good case to divorce you," he said.

Audrey froze. She couldn't believe he had said that. Was that even a possibility? She knew it was important to keep up a good sex life. When they got married their priest had offered a few tidbits of advice. The first was, "When you have a family one day, it is going to feel like you are each carrying 90 percent of the burden. You are. So don't think the other is doing less; that will just get you into trouble." The second piece of guidance he gave them was, "Once you are married, don't say no to your spouse's yearnings too often; the other person will go elsewhere." She took it all very seriously, despite how uninterested she was. But this was different. She wasn't just randomly not having sex. She was dealing with the profound reality of losing her mother.

This was really the breaking point, and while it hadn't always been this acute, it had been a long time coming. When they first committed to each other, Nate wanted to have sex at least a few times a week, more if possible, and almost always Audrey would do it because she was afraid of his intense reaction if she said no. Saying yes to avoid his anger was easier. She learned that early. A headache or a sore throat did not count in Nate's book as reasons not to have sex with your husband. Really, nothing did. She began to notice a correlation between their sex life and his mood and generosity. Additionally, he started to question how she spent her time, and pitted himself against everything she did. If she called a friend, he would ask why she would do that when it was time she could have spent with him, the same if she sat quietly and enjoyed her coffee, or wanted to rest alone and read a novel. She began to wonder about all her choices because he had her on edge with them. She found herself consumed with guilt, thinking things like *I really must be a bad wife, I can't keep him content for five minutes. I am always leaving him wanting something.* Her constant doubts based on what he told her—you're no artist, you have no taste, you didn't even decorate the house—eroded her self-esteem. When the kids got older and she considered taking an art class since she loved it so much in college, he told her she was being selfish, thinking only of herself, and she should be available to the kids. She immediately thought, *he's right, what was I thinking? Here I go again. I must be the worst mother in the world. My family deserves better, I should be home after school for them,* and threw away the application for the class.

Not long into their marriage, Nate took control of the money and paid a lot of attention to the budget and Audrey's spending. Audrey worked at a nonprofit that raised money to build hospitals for children in developing countries. It was something she felt passionately about and when they first got together Nate had loved that about her. She made very little money of her own, which Nate insisted she put into their bigger pot of money, and she was very happy to do it, but now he held the fact that she brought in such a minimal amount over her head. Mostly she understood. *It's almost all his money,* she thought. *He should be in charge. He provides nicely for me and the kids. We're never hungry.* The connection she made earlier between giving him sex and his benevolence became especially apparent around the money. When she said yes to sex, he would ease up and stop berating her about spending too much or treating herself to something and they would avoid many possible arguments, but the minute she said no he was all over her for being so extravagant and indulgent. In that way, sex between them felt transactional, you give me this and I'll give you that. The few times when she hadn't given in to sex for one reason or another, things did not go well. He would carry on about how she was going to drive them financially broke, made issues, and refused all her requests for anything, for the kids and for herself.

"You know our budget," he said. "Let's leave it at that."

"I get it, and it usually works," she said. "But it feels constraining to think there is no wiggle room ever."

"Well, there isn't," he said to her. "If you keep pushing, I could take you off my life insurance policy."

She was stung and began, for the first time, to wonder if this was normal. She had no idea how they had gotten to this point. *How did it get this bad?* she thought. Their initial connection had been fine, and he seemed like a really nice and easygoing guy. At first, when they were dating and had to make a decision about where to eat or what to watch, he went with the flow and let her choose most of the time. She never imagined that she would wind up going to the mat with him over every single issue. This goes on with many of my patients: at first things seem easy and before they know it they are disagreeing about anything from where they will live to when to start a family to how many kids to have. If you are with someone who is controlling, these decisions will turn into bargaining chips. So instead of working it out by compromising, it becomes about what you owe them if they allow anything to work in your favor. On top of that, they will never forget: I did this for you and now you have to do this for me. In their eyes, you are basically in a perpetual state of paying them back.

Despite the way Nate presented himself to Audrey at the beginning, after they got married he slowly, over time, began to control many aspects of her life. This was the backdrop leading up to the difficult months when her mother's health rapidly declined. In the weeks ahead she tried not to say no to sex, even though she wanted to. She was terrified he would leave her or, as the priest warned, go elsewhere. *Of course he is going to leave me if I disappoint him,* she thought. *I am not upholding my end of the bargain. I can't bear the fact that I am always letting him down.*

I have seen this with many of my patients, including Joe and Joan. And it is similar to what we just talked about in Chapter Nine, although these cases are even harder because the controlling person is inside your house. You can't get away from them. It is a clear wiping out of your needs, of denying that they even exist, and focusing only on their own needs. They are completely self-absorbed—your mother is dying? It doesn't even register. Instead, it is all about Nate's physical needs. You want more money? How dare you ask for that? Or in Joe's case it is all about what Ellen needs, help with their daughter, good status in the community, and there is absolutely no regard for how her demands negatively affect him—distracting him at work or taking away the last bit of fun he used to have. In Joan's case it was also around money, and wanting to see her parents, which Brent completely devalued. They are all living with the *Dominator*, and in each case they are in Denial of their partner's Denial of their needs. Audrey thinks *he's right, why should he suffer just because my mother is sick?* And Joe thinks, *she has every right to ask me for these things, I would be a terrible father if I didn't give them to her*, and Joan thinks, *Brent is right, he makes more money than I do, he should call the shots.* Control around money is common, as we have seen it play out with Audrey and Nate, too.

These thoughts echo what I hear repeatedly from anyone living with the *Dominator*, who blames them for not giving them what he or she wants. My patients live in fear of unleashing their partner's anger, and then having their own reaction where they lose control and lash out. The crushing guilt that follows is because they think they should and could do better. They think it is all their fault, that if they did the right thing, whatever that might be, they could avoid the conflict. They are constantly trying to control the *Dominator* in their own way by striving for perfection. The thing is, as we saw in Chapter Nine, they could do everything the *Dominator* wants and it still wouldn't be enough; there is no such thing as getting it right with them. They exercise control to get them to do things their way. It often works for a while; the person who is being controlled explains it away with Denial's help. But the impact of the *Dominator's* unrelenting stream of verbal assaults and threats takes a huge toll on their self-esteem, as we saw it do for Joe and Joan, and now for Audrey.

Dominators are expert at manipulation, which spikes your self-doubt. The hallmark of a *Dominator* is that they twist your words, they make you feel inadequate, they blame you, they get you on the ropes defending and explaining yourself, trying to prove how much you do, how much you did, and how hard you try, hoping that they will see and appreciate you and change the way they treat you. The tricky part is that they always snare you by referencing one small kernel of truth that perpetuates your uncertainty. The *Dominator* uses their anger to keep you in line. You never know when the explosion is coming, or when they will give you the silent treatment. Both are intolerable. If you try to confront them, they will turn it around on you. They aim a steady onslaught of criticism at you. When you do react in anger and lash out, they attack you even more. Your guilt makes you think *I'm no angel* and then they make you think your angry reaction is the problem, not their dominating behavior. They know your Achilles' heel and how to use it to make you feel you are selfish, fat, sexually inadequate, greedy, or stupid for not trusting them or for doubting them. They bombard you with a steady stream of cutdowns, telling you that you're useless, worthless, and that nobody else would want you. Somehow, though, they make you think you are the one who is unloving and unsupportive. To top that off, they don't respect you or any requests you might have. If you ask them not to take your car keys or to leave the leftovers you're saving for lunch the next day, they constantly ignore your requests around your belongings and help themselves to what they want from you on every level, so you feel violated and out of control. If you push back, they paint you as the selfish one. They build a story like Swiss cheese; there are so many holes in it they are able to make you believe you are lacking, they prey on your self-esteem, they make you think that if you gave more and did more it would make them happy. They do a character assassination on you all the time. They are the orchestra leader striking up the symphony to play the violins. People live in dread and intimidation in the path of the *Dominator's* anger. Their words are so scorching it is like having acid thrown in your face. They berate you, which leads to your beating yourself up. You lose face, you lose yourself, and you will do anything to avoid it.

And then, when they have pushed you too far and you can finally see the light, they become loving and kind and seduce you back in, saying or doing one nice thing to keep you in place—until the next time.

This is why Audrey, Joe, and Joan suffered and stressed for so long, doubting their own feelings and choices. It is why the person living with a *Dominator* gives in repeatedly, letting it get to the point when Audrey is terrified Nate will leave her if she doesn't do what he says. She is acutely aware that she is losing her mother; she can't lose her husband, too. Then she will really be all alone. In Chapter Three we saw how Joe's work suffered when Ellen sent relentless texts, and he canceled all the things he did for himself because Ellen said he had to spend that time with their daughter to give her the break she needed. We also saw how Joan ended up missing precious time with her parents, culminating in being absent from her dad's big birthday celebration. It was when they all began to realize exactly what and how much they were losing that things started to change, that they could break through their Denial.

But Audrey was still not quite there. During our session, she filled me in on the sexual demands and the threats to take her off the insurance policy or even leave her if she didn't give him what he wanted.

"It surprises me every time," she said.

"That's because being surprised is the signature of Denial because reality is blocked out so you never see it coming and you are always caught off guard."

"Yes," she said. "I imagine he will be reasonable—who wouldn't feel sorry for someone whose mother is dying? But then I realize it's hard on him, too. I mean, is this normal?"

"Are you asking me if I've seen this before with other patients or if this is normal behavior?" I asked.

"Both," she said.

"I have seen this many times before," I said. "And it is not healthy behavior. You don't have to live this way. I would like to go back to something you just said—that it's hard on him, too. Is he close to your mother?"

"I mean, he's nice enough to her," she said. "But no, I wouldn't say he is close to her."

"So, when you say this is hard on him, too, what do you mean exactly?"

"Oh, I mean that I'm not myself," she said. "I'm not fully present. And that's hard for him."

"There are always going to be times in a long marriage when one person can't be 100 percent there, if you have a sick or dying relative, or a huge project at work, there has to be room for some give and take," I said.

"Well, there isn't," she said. "Not in my marriage. There's no room at all."

"That doesn't seem reasonable, and the biggest issue is how guilty you wind up feeling," I said. "It is tormenting you, and that keeps you invested in repeatedly trying to please him. You dread his anger so you decide to just give in and have sex when he wants it even though you would rather avoid it at all costs, because it's easier than dealing with him having a tantrum and threatening to leave you."

She looked at me and nodded.

"That's exactly it," she said.

"Guilt is like being stuck in the spin cycle of the dryer. You go around and around in it until it burns you up," I said.

"And," I continued, "from what you're saying you are negating your own anger because you can't find a place for it. You have a right to be angry. He denies your needs completely. He shows you no consideration or empathy for what you are going through. But to avoid your anger you push it down and you get headaches. Instead, I would like to see you use your anger to advocate for yourself and speak up. Doing that effectively is not the equivalent of actually arguing or fighting. What it means is using it as fuel, first to decide and change what you are willing to accept. Next, to make a clear statement of what you are going to do and how you are going to handle yourself in certain situations when upsetting behavior takes place. Those become the limits you put in place in order to take care of yourself. In other words, use the energy of your anger to stand up for and hold onto what is important to you. This all sets up and leads me to the useful skill I want to share with you. I call it *ADDRESS YOUR DISTRESS*."

Audrey looked very interested.

"By putting this into practice you will work toward not making excuses for Nate and no longer giving in when you don't want to. You will recognize and own your anger and other feelings that keep coming up. You will figure out what you need to do differently and then you can make a direct, clear, positive statement about what you will tolerate in the future and what you will do in the event things are unbearable. This way you will have more control over your own behavior because you won't be reacting but instead will be following through with what you said you would do," I said.

"I like the idea of that, but it seems impossible," she said. "On the one hand, he gets so mad at me and makes these really big statements, like it's over between us if I don't do whatever it is, and that is terrifying. I don't even want to give air to that flame by saying no. And on the other hand, I get why he does it most of the time—he didn't marry me so I could be a sad sack. He wants what he wants. I feel like I'm a terrible wife."

"That's the problem," I said. "That is exactly how he wants you to feel. You are buying into his belief system and suspending your own; that's how you lose yourself. Our goal is for you to hold onto your truth and your reality."

She agreed that she would think about it.

The bottom line is that you simply can't control a controlling person. The only one who can change is you, that's what you want

217

to change; you want to be done justifying your needs and why you do what you do. To do this, stick to the facts, don't explain yourself, validate your own needs, and take them seriously, knowing you deserve to have them met, whether that means spending time with friends or your older parents, taking walks, taking an art class, playing on a recreational soccer league, or anything else. Acknowledge what is important to you and know it is realistic to have those choices in your life. Stop the verbal abuse. You can say, "I want to hear what you have to say but if you call me names or use a hostile tone, I am going to end the conversation either by hanging up the phone or by walking out of the room. I'm not going to tolerate being spoken to this way anymore." With the skill *ADDRESS YOUR DISTRESS* you will finally break free from your victim role and find the courage to trust your gut and hold onto your truth.

Using this skill had worked well for both Joe and Joan as they tried to get out of their oppressive situations and eventually out of their marriages. As I mentioned, Ellen texted Joe relentlessly. She was completely self-absorbed and oblivious to his needs. She texted day and night, when he was in an important meeting, out to lunch, even at the doctor's office. There was no place he could be where she wouldn't contact him. Every single time it was under the veil of an emergency, usually surrounding their daughter. In the end it felt like he was sacrificing just to keep her calm, although, just like the people in Chapter Nine, Eileen's mother, Hope's sister, and Lauren's friend, no matter what he did Ellen was never going to be satisfied. Still, until something changed for him it was all about relinquishing and giving up what he had to her.

Finally, Joe saw how important it was to begin to set limits. The first thing he did in Chapter Three was learn to *HOLD ON TIGHT* to what was relevant to who he was. As we talked about, that meant grabbing back some of the things that were important to him. Next, we talked about the skill *ADDRESS YOUR*

DISTRESS. For him, that meant acknowledging the impossible task of keeping up with the texts and carving out space for himself where Ellen couldn't find him. The texts were too many and each one was too long. He would have to literally stop what he was doing at work to read them, which was disruptive. So, the limit he eventually set in place was that he told her unless it was a true crisis with the children with an SOS at the top, he refused to read them. He deleted all the rest. That was hard for him to do because he had bought into her perception all this time that if he didn't write back to everything right away that meant he was a bad and neglectful father. Over time using the skill, he minimized the texts he read, and it was tremendously freeing for him. As far as carving out space, he put a lock on the bathroom door so Ellen could no longer just walk in on him whenever she wanted. By *ADDRESS-ING HIS DISTRESS*, he stopped making excuses for her that had allowed her to continue her controlling behavior. It also meant he was no longer going to tolerate the emotionally hurtful interactions that had become almost constant between them.

Another key element that goes along with the controlling behavior is that it is infused with a sense of urgency. We HAVE to talk about this right now. You MUST answer my text immediately. They always need you to deal with them NOW; there is no room for you to do anything else. That dominated the relationship, so whenever a conflict arose it would preempt anything else that was going on at the moment. If Joe and Ellen had a disagreement, they might end up staying awake all night because she refused to let him go to sleep until it was resolved. If Joe was working on an important project at home but he didn't behave just as Ellen wanted or expected him to, it could turn into a fight that would take over, leaving no room for him to finish his work. The same was true for Joan and Brent. There were times when they would be on their way to a dinner or to meet friends, and if Joan mentioned she had spent money on something Brent didn't know about, or that she hoped to visit her parents, he would explode, forcing them to cancel whatever plans they had so they could deal with it.

In the end, Joe put a lot of effort into building himself back up and attempting to repair the rift between him and Ellen before he ultimately decided to file for a divorce. In his case, *ADDRESSING HIS DISTRESS* meant putting limits around Ellen's texting and calling, decreasing the sense of urgency he felt that surrounded each interaction, and stopping the tirades of blame and criticism by walking away or ending the conversations. It was a very long and arduous process for him.

The next time Audrey came to see me things had gotten worse. Her mother had died, and she was having a hard time accepting that. Nate saw it as finally a return to normalcy and expected her to jump right back into having sex like they used to without any discussion or interruption.

"Your mother's gone," she told me he said. "You can focus on me again."

Now, though, he was also negating other things in her life. He couldn't understand why she cared so much about the children's hospitals being built in developing countries with the money the nonprofit for which she worked raised, and, she told me, he said she was wasting her time. He told her she didn't do anything, she just wrote thank-you notes to donors.

"Who did you think you are? A philanthropist? A five-year-old could do that," he said to her. "Hey, I have an idea. Maybe one of the sick kids can do it."

She felt more belittled than ever.

"The sex was something different," she said to me. "I mean, I didn't like having to do it if I didn't want to. It felt like a job or a duty or something, but he was always clear about his strong sex drive, so I sort of got that. I figured if I did what he wanted he would eventually change somehow. But he never did. And now he is being really mean."

"The thing is," I said, "his being mean, as you call it, is his anger and his way of cutting down your self-esteem so you feel insecure and keep doing what he wants. It is classic *Dominator* behavior. To this point, your feeling okay about yourself has been based on pleasing him."

"You know all along he has been threatening to leave me or take me off his insurance and I believed he might. But can he do that?" she said. "It didn't occur to me to question him. You know, I never questioned my parents, I just accepted what they said, and I've done the same thing with Nate. The fear stopped me every time."

"Why don't you check it out," I said. "One of the best ways to protect yourself is to get the facts from a lawyer rather than take his word for it because his word is not trustworthy."

"How many things has this man told me that were not true but that he made me believe?" she asked. It was one of the most eye-opening things she had said, and I wanted to let it sit for a few seconds before I responded. This was exactly it. This was her finally understanding that his Denial of her needs was impossible for her to see because she was in her own Denial about it. He declared and made her believe many things that were not true. Her Denial allowed that to happen. But now, well, now she understood. She was no longer completely blinded by Denial.

"Too many," I said. "But the fact that you realize you have been lying to yourself will mean you can start to recognize it now."

"I can't pretend to not know anymore what I now know," she said, and I thought, I would like to put that on a T-shirt, because that is exactly what it means to break through Denial.

"I'm proud of you," I said.

So much of the reason people let this go on for so long is that they are driven by the desire to appease the other person; they think that in doing so it will all somehow be okay. Once you begin to *ADDRESS YOUR DISTRESS*, you can see it more clearly and start to put important and specific limits in place. One step is to stop playing out the usual conversation in your head as you expect it to happen between the two of you. Continuing to do that is toxic. When you get in their head to figure out what they are going to say, and try to defend your needs, you lose yourself and your clarity. Doing that is like having *Emotional Acid Reflux*; you keep repeating the conversation in your head the way you wish it could go. You get caught in a loop—the same way you do if you are allergic to onions and peppers, or any food that upsets your system and keeps repeating on you. The aim is to stop listening to the *Dominator*'s voice and start listening to your own.

You want to focus on what you are going to say, regardless of what they come back at you with. You are not looking for them to get it; what matters is that you get it and you are now going to inform them as to what you are going to do and how you are going to handle yourself. You are no longer explaining yourself to gain their understanding. Instead, you are speaking your truth so you can handle yourself in relation to the other person, but it is important to make sure you don't get caught off guard by them. One way I describe it to my patients is to think of it as being a snake charmer. You might be able to get the snake to dance by using the right movements and music, but you have to be ready for the snake to bite. It is up to you to know when to put the lid on the basket in the same way it is up to you to walk away from a difficult conversation, as Joe learned to do. When I see actors on talk shows being asked personal questions, I marvel at how they see them coming and answer with their limit by immediately shutting it down or shifting to another topic. That is exactly what I encourage my patients to be able to do: know the tough questions are coming, don't be naive and think the snake will no longer bite, and be ready. The fact is that you have to learn how to handle your difficult spouse.

When you are able to speak your truth, that is the emotional separating you need to give you the strength to take care of yourself. Think of it this way: you wouldn't go into a gunfight without a bulletproof vest, and you shouldn't go into a known-difficult situation with your controlling spouse without having the clarity of what you will say so you can stick to your facts, which will keep you sane and safe. As I told Audrey, you need to stay informed, and you need to know what your rights are. When you are in Denial, the simplest things don't occur to you.

When I first told Joe about some of the changes he could make, not responding to all of Ellen's texts, taking time before writing back, and holding on to some personal time, his first reaction was "she's never going to let me do that," similar to how Audrey thought any changes would be impossible when we first started to talk about them. They were already having the conversation in their head, and they knew exactly what their spouses would say.

"That's the big misconception everybody has," I said to Joe. "That he or she won't let me. Meaning that you believe you need their permission to do what you want because that's what their anger and your fear have kept you in line doing. You can and must give yourself permission and learn to tolerate their anger without giving in to it."

Joe could imagine the give and take; he wouldn't write and she would get angrier and angrier. I tell my patients to stop thinking of it that way and instead listen only to yourself and the conversation you need to have. For Joe that might be, "she is out of control and negatively affecting every corner of my life. I can't go on like this." Her biggest weapon toward him was that he was a bad father if he didn't do X, Y, and Z. Once he broke through his Denial of her Denial, he was able to see things clearly and he knew without a doubt he is a good father whether he answers every text or not.

Along those lines, I told Audrey that when she doesn't want to have sex with Nate it is that simple. She doesn't have to make excuses or get him to understand. She just doesn't have to do it. If she wants to, Audrey can relate to his disappointment and offer another time when she would be open to having sex. She might say, "I know you wish we could now, but tomorrow morning or tomorrow night would work for me," and hold firmly to her no. Using the skill *ADDRESS YOUR DISTRESS*, she has been able to stick to the facts, which, in this case, mean she is sad and upset about her mother, has no energy or desire, and doesn't want to have sex as frequently right now. She doesn't expect it to be a permanent situation. She has stopped trying to explain herself all the time. She is finally able to take her own needs seriously and that her need (to not have sex on a particular night) is as important as Nate's need (to have sex on that same night). She has put limits in place, saying that she wants to talk about it instead of having Nate assume they will have sex on a given night. That gives her the option to think it through, and not be thrust into the situation that is already in motion before she can consider what she wants to do. In the same way Eileen, Hope, and Lauren learned to take a breath and say they wanted to help, but maybe not completely. They can give something, but not the entire cake. Audrey learned that she could give a little to Nate without compromising herself. In a similar way that Eileen's mother, Hope's sister Maureen, and Lauren's friend Tiffany might not be happy when they did that, Nate was taken off guard and at first became angry and explosive or gave Audrey the silent treatment. However, now, because she had made a choice about what she was telling him, she accepted his anger, it wasn't so distressing or surprising, she wasn't frightened by it, and was finally able to move away from it and not feel like she was at fault or had done something wrong to cause it.

Another big problem of dealing with a *Dominator* is that your objective shifts from looking for compliments or loving moments, to instead just trying to getting rid of the negative behavior. It is no longer about sharing the good, but simply about stopping the bad. In other words, rather than looking for a supportive comment or a hug or kiss, you are just trying to eliminate the barrage of anger, verbal attacks, criticism, blame, and hurtful actions, which is not a healthy place to be in a relationship.

Audrey's realization of that and the skill gave her the courage to finally get a lawyer, get informed, and start to move toward filing for divorce. Initially, the practicalities of what that would mean overwhelmed her, as they often do for people. Where would she live? Would she have enough money? Would she have to go back to work? Audrey is stopped in her tracks like many people are, and these unknowns are so daunting that they eclipse the emotional anguish finally being confronted. In the end, now that she is able to see through her Denial of his Denial, the answer is clearly yes, it is bad enough to get out and she does.

In this chapter we have talked about shifting away from allowing a dominating spouse's unreasonable expectations of you to affect your happiness and confidence. In the next chapter, we are going to look at another aspect of Denial, with the *Stay-Stuck Complainer*, who repeatedly asks you for help; you give it; they reject it and don't use it at all to take any steps to improve their lives. It can be exhausting, frustrating, and seem like an endless cycle. I'll help you stop that, and, in the end, save you a lot of wasted time. Let's take a look.

CHAPTER ELEVEN

It's Always Yes, But, with You—

SONIA GLANCED AT HER RINGING PHONE. IT WAS RENEE. SHOOT. As usual, when her friend called, she felt paralyzed and didn't know whether she should answer or not. She had to leave her apartment in forty minutes to get to class, and she still had to curl her hair and clean up the dinner mess. She knew how hard it was to hang up when she was talking to Renee, seemingly impossible really, unless she wanted to be accused of rushing her off the phone and not caring enough to keep talking. But she also knew Renee was in a difficult relationship. *What if she really needs my help?* Sonia thought. *What if she is very upset and doesn't want to be alone right now? She's calling me for a reason; I should be there for her. She was there for me when my mom was sick.*

"Hello?" Sonia answered just before it went to voicemail.

"Oh hi," Renee said, sniffling. "I thought you weren't going to pick up."

"Sorry, my phone was just charging, and I had to get to it," Sonia said. "Are you okay?"

"Not really," Renee said. "Gavin promised this weekend was going to be just about us, since it's our anniversary, you know? We had the greatest plans. We were going to go to this hotel made up of cabins by the beach. There are kitchens and I was going to cook his favorite Bolognese. Anyway, he just called. His stupid ex

227

can't keep the kids this weekend like she was supposed to, so he has to cancel with me. I mean, I even said let's bring them. I don't really want to do that, but I like the kids; this isn't their fault. But he said no, he can't. They're too busy with soccer and dance and they need a routine."

"That sucks," Sonia said. "Isn't there anything you can do to convince him?"

"He promised this wouldn't happen," Renee said, a fresh round of tears beginning. "He said, 'Renee, my kids mean the world to me, but unless they are sick or in danger, I will never let them come between us.' I think those are his exact words. And yet here we are again."

"So, what if you plan an adventure at home? You could still make the Bolognese?" Sonia said, glancing at the time on her phone. She considered switching to speaker so she could at least curl her hair while she listened, but she knew Renee didn't like that. The few times she tried that in the past Renee would say she kept cutting out and could she please just talk into the phone. This had been going on for over a year now. At first, things seemed good with Gavin. There was always the potential for complications because he was divorced and had two relatively young kids, but those first two months or so he managed to make it work. Shortly thereafter, though, things went downhill and that's when Renee started to complain to Sonia quite regularly. Every single time Sonia and Renee were together it seemed to be all Renee could talk about: he is noncommittal, he changes plans constantly, he promised his ex-wife and kids wouldn't be a problem but they are. She would also call—all the time—when something went wrong and when Gavin disappointed her. Usually, like tonight, she would be crying, and Sonia would do her best to come up with solutions to help her, and then a day or two (or sometimes, if things went really well, a week) later they were right back in exactly the same place having the same conversation and Sonia would think, did I completely waste my time?

"No, that's no fun," Renee said in response to Sonia's suggestion to making the Bolognese at home. "I wanted a real adventure, and a cabin! And the beach!"

"What if you pretend?" Sonia suggested. "What if you do a clambake at home to evoke the beach? Maybe camp in the yard?"

"Really?" Renee said. "That would just make me more sad."

"Well," Sonia said, mentally giving up the hair curling it would just have to remain straight. And she could clean up the dishes later, she would just throw the leftovers in the fridge before she went to class.

"I don't need this," Renee said. "I say to him, 'let's go to the movies on Saturday night,' and he's like, 'let's see what the week brings.' What the week brings? What does he expect it to bring?"

"Do you ever talk to him about it? The way I suggested before?" Sonia asked. "To let him know that this is hard for you?"

"He doesn't listen," Renee said. "But honestly, I can barely stand it. I asked if he wants to think about a vacation, maybe in April. We could go to the Bahamas or something. I know the kids will be at Disney with his ex, so the timing is perfect. I tell him the flights are good right now, why don't we just buy tickets? And he smiles, like he likes the idea. But then he says he has to check with work, there might be a big meeting around that time. Can you believe it?"

"Well," Sonia said again.

"Who needs a man with a past?" Renee continued. "That was my first mistake. Oh wait, he's calling. Maybe he changed his mind. I'm going to take this."

The call ended. Renee was gone, and so was the forty minutes Sonia had set aside for herself. She felt agitated as she cleaned up quickly, but she couldn't quite put her finger on why. The next morning, she ran into Renee on the way to work.

"How are you doing?" Sonia asked.

"Great," Renee said. "Gavin promised we would take a trip to the cabins by the beach in a few weeks. We haven't set the exact date yet but it's going to be great."

"What about this weekend? Did you figure that out?"

"Forget about this weekend," Renee said, waving her hand as if to flick it away. "I'm focused on the future."

The next night, as Sonia was preparing to go to class again, Renee called. When she pressed Gavin, it turned out he couldn't find a weekend until late summer, at least four months away, and even then, he wasn't sure about it.

"I have no idea why I thought this was a good idea," Renee said through her tears. "I mean he says one thing and does another. I can't trust him or count on him."

Sonia settled in; she had about twenty minutes this time, and thank goodness she had already curled her hair. In the end she was late for class anyway.

I have seen this with many of my patients over the years. They have a friend or relative who has an issue; it could be anything—a bad relationship, a problem with their job or living situation, a health issue—but the thing they have in common is that they like to complain about it, and they do, seemingly endlessly. They talk about it whenever they are together, and they call frequently to vent. And each time, my patient tries to help by offering suggestions and ideas. Sometimes the friend or relative might listen; most often they will push back with an excuse about why that won't work for them, and almost always my patients find themselves in a loop of repeating the same conversation about the same things as if they never talked about it before. It feels oppressive and they feel burdened. They are always asking how much venting and complaining they have to listen to. How can the people they love be so out of tune with reality? Can they get out of these discussions? The real question is why they listen so much of the time and work so hard to try to get their friend or relative to see the reality of their situation.

I have a name for the people who vent endlessly, bombarding you with their negativity and putting you in a position where you feel as if you have to try to fix it, only to learn you have completely wasted your time. They are what I call the *Stay-Stuck Complainer*. They blame everybody but themselves, completely exhausting you, and never making an effort to change. Still, my patients stick around, feeling guilty about the possibility of letting the other person down and being in Denial thinking they can actually have a hand in changing their friend or relative's predicament. *Maybe they will listen to me this time,* they think, or *he's counting on me, he wants my help.*

"Sometimes I feel like I'm talking to a wall," Sonia said recently during one of our sessions. "Renee is a good friend. I really like her, but it's like she has blinders on and earplugs in. She calls, and there is the illusion that we are having a give and take, but she doesn't seem to want to hear anything I say. I just don't get it. There are very clear steps she could take to make things better, but she just says no, no, no. The other day, when she was talking, I kept thinking, I'm just going to hang up. And then I thought, *that would be so mean. She's alone. She already feels let down. I can't disappoint her, too.*"

"I understand that," I said. "When you are dealing with a family member's or a friend's Denial, which is exactly what is going on with Renee, you are fooling yourself, going along for someone else's ride, and you compromise your own peace and happiness. Case in point, you didn't get to take care of yourself the way you planned because you couldn't curl your hair, and the next time you were late for class. Plus, as you mentioned, you felt agitated and unsettled."

"I didn't feel like I had a choice," she said. "I saw her name come up, and I have this split second of wondering if I dare not answer—a million excuses run through my mind that I could text her later or the next day—and then I end up answering anyway. It's like I feel compelled."

"Listen, you're a good friend," I said. "What you mean is you feel guilty. Not only do you have to recognize that she is never going to hear you or absorb your advice; you have to shift to expecting that. When you say it feels like you are talking to a wall, you actually are. All she wants to do is vent, and then continue on as she is going. There is no way to get through to her."

"She is clearly unhappy. I think if she just reduced her expectations, like if being home with him and the kids could be enough, she wouldn't be so sad or disappointed all the time. Every time he offers something good, she grabs onto it and it's like she thinks it is really going to happen, but even when she tells me I think, he's never going to do that, he's never going to follow through."

"Did you hear what you just said?" I pointed out. "Now flip that around to you and Renee; every time she vents you grab onto it and try to offer help, like it might make a difference this time, but in the same way you know Gavin is never going to follow through with his promises, you should know Renee is never going to listen to you."

Sonia pushed right past that; she wasn't quite ready for it.

"And even worse," she said, "I have all these good ideas, but she acts like they are terrible ones, like I don't get it, like I'm dumb or something," Sonia said, clearly exasperated.

"Here is the thing," I said, reining it in a little so Sonia could catch up. "What you think might work and makes so much sense to you is very different from what she is looking for or even open to hearing."

I explained that I thought Renee was a *Stay-Stuck Complainer*, someone who voices the same complaint repeatedly but never does anything about it.

"What that means is that she is not open to your ideas," I said. "You could offer the best solution in the world, and it wouldn't make a difference."

"That's crazy," Sonia said. "Then why would she call me?"

"She wants to talk to you," I said. "She wants to say all the things she is saying. Basically, she wants to complain. Most people enjoy the act of venting. It has power and can be satisfying in its own right. It can be an outlet for stress and sadness. It is used to be able to move on to action. However, for some, the venting is the action unto itself. And of course, your knee-jerk reaction upon hearing all the things that are going wrong for her is wanting to help. But, from what you've told me, she's not looking to fix things. She's in Denial of her situation and continuing to stay steeped in wishing and hoping. In other words, her complaining is the end goal in and of itself, not a means to an end that, in your eyes, would be somehow eliminating the problems or helping to make her life better."

Sonia nodded as if she could finally see that.

"So, the result is you end up feeling as stuck as she seems to be," I said. "Because you feel you have no choice but to listen to her. Do you want to join her in wishing and hoping?"

"The way you make it sound is like anyone could be on the other end of the phone," Sonia said. "Like it doesn't matter that it's me with my ideas. I really could just put her on speaker then and let her talk away."

"Yes," I said. "Exactly."

I told her to pay attention the next time Renee called and see if she actually asked for help. Sonia said she would.

Another patient of mine, Don, was in a similar situation with his brother-in-law, Mike. At his wife's request, he had helped Don get the job he had as a floor manager at Home Depot, where Don worked in the corporate office. Mike had had a hard time keeping a job; he couldn't stand to be told what to do, but this seemed like a good fit because Mike liked moving around during the workday and would oversee his own department: lighting. The thing was, the top store manager was pretty hands-on and didn't let any of the floor managers make their own decisions; everything had to be cleared through him. It was true across the board, nothing personal, but Mike couldn't take it.

"You know, I had this great idea to do a display of holiday lights, it looked so good and brought so many customers to my aisle, and then he comes around the corner and says he doesn't like it, Christmas items have to remain in the designated section at the front of the store," Mike complained to Don on the phone as he did most nights. "I asked him to hear me out, but he said no, it was his way or the highway."

Don took a deep breath. He wanted to be with his family; his wife was reading to the kids and it was always so cozy, but almost every night Mike would call with one complaint or another and Don felt he had to talk him down off the ledge.

"Is there something else you could put on the display?" Don asked. "Maybe some environmentally friendly lights? Everyone likes those."

"No way," Mike said. "That's not going to draw people over. There's no color there."

"What if you tried to think of the other manager as part of your team?" Don threw out there. "You know, like not someone working against you but working with you to make the store a better place?"

"He's a jerk," Mike said. "We're not on the same team."

Don felt both sorry for Mike, who was clearly having a hard time, and also worried that his potential bad behavior would reflect badly on him because he had recommended him for the job. When he tried to get off the phone quickly, Mike was sulky about it. He lived alone and didn't have anyone to talk to. Plus, he figured Don understood the company culture.

When they go out to dinner or have family get-togethers, it is all Mike talks about. Even when Don tries to change the subject, Mike can't be swayed.

"He seems to have a one-track mind," Don said at our next session. "And I just don't know what I can do for him."

"It's hard," I said. "It's like you're a fish on the line. You feel forced to listen, you're drawn in, you offer feedback, but then you are thrown back into the lake like it never happened."

"Precisely," Don said. "And the worst part is if I try to cut the conversation short because I am either rushing somewhere or I just don't want to waste my time again, he gets so mad. He accuses me of not caring and says I got him into this mess in the first place. So, if I have already spent an hour on the phone with him, I get no credit for that, he just thinks I brushed him off."

I told him that I thought his brother-in-law was a *Stay-Stuck Complainer* and what went along with that.

"One of the hallmarks is exactly what you just said: no matter how much time you give to them it is never enough, and when you want to go or hang up they get mad," I said.

"I don't want him to think I'm insensitive," he said. "Or that I don't care."

"That's the problem," I said. "You're working too hard to try to get him to see your reality. You have to know in your own mind that you are tuned in to him, that you care, and that you are doing everything you can to show it; it almost doesn't matter what he thinks."

Don laughed.

"That's easier said than done," he said. "I'm better off listening than making him upset and worse, upsetting my wife, who is totally rooting for him and thinks things can get better. I mean, maybe he'll come around and calm down a little at work. Maybe if we talk about it more he'll be more on board with the idea of teamwork."

"That's your Denial talking," I said, wanting him to see it clearly. "You are blinded by the pressure and the idea that you can actually help him, guide him to better behavior. I just don't think you will ever achieve that, but you will waste a tremendous amount of time and also create a huge amount of stress for yourself trying."

"I feel it," Don said. "I feel the stress."

A third patient, Gabby, who was going through this exact same thing with her brother, also felt the stress. The only things that were different were the complaints. He was what she referred to as a medical nightmare and would call her weekly for a marathon phone session to talk about the health issues he had. She felt bad for him, as well as responsible, as if there must be something she could do to get him better or at least to get to the bottom of it, but every time he would reject her suggestions. The other day they spent well over an hour on the phone while he talked endlessly about feeling dizzy and light-headed, and going around in a circle trying to distinguish the difference between the two and repeating how awful it all was for him.

"I constantly feel like the floor is coming up to meet me," he said. "Like I'm off balance. I was walking into the pharmacy, and I had to stop to hold onto a shelf for a second. I didn't know which way was up. Everyone was looking at me. They probably thought I was on drugs or something."

"I know you said you don't want to," Gabby said for the twentieth time in that conversation, "but I really think you should see a doctor."

"I told you, they don't know what they're doing," he said. "They will just send me for endless tests that will lead to more tests. It will cost so much money, and then they will tell me it's a migraine or something. Oh, and I forgot to tell you about when I played tennis the other day. I was going for a ball, and I had to just stop, I felt so dizzy, or maybe it was light-headed."

"You know," Gabby said, gently interrupting him. "What about reading about it? Maybe you can distinguish the difference. I do think there is medicine for vertigo—if that's what it is."

"No way," he said. "I'm not taking any medicine."

When Gabby came to tell me about it, she had multiple examples of conversations like this, whether it was what sounded like IBS with his constant woes about diarrhea, constipation, gas, and indigestion, or a backache, or the dizziness that was always in there somewhere, ruining his day.

"Every time we talk, all he does is go through his ailments," she said in frustration. "And when I suggest he see a doctor, which is the obvious thing to do, he has every excuse in the book about why he shouldn't—they are quacks, they don't know what they are doing, they just want his money, and so on. It's excruciating."

I told her I understood, and she that is not alone in this situation.

"If you can believe it, yesterday he actually said to me, 'you don't understand the problem,' like I wasn't connecting the right dots or something," she said. "But I feel so guilty because he is suffering. I'm his sister. I want him to be happy and healthy."

"Of course, you do," I said. "And while it is concerning, there is only so much you can do. You can't physically make him move, or go to the doctor, and you could spend all your time trying with no result."

"What can I do, then?" she asked.

"Let me ask you this: does he ask for your help?" I said. "Is he saying things like, 'what can I do?' in the way you just did?"

"Uh, no, not in so many words," Gabby said with a furrowed brow.

I shared the important skill that I call *WAIT TO BE ASKED* with her, through which she can learn to put limits in place around a complainer, in this case her brother, and determine how and when to offer advice and when to stay out of it. The key is to find a balance between what you can put up with and what they need before it becomes toxic. You'll know you've reached that point when you feel desperate, hopeless, out of control, find yourself on the phone for hours with no satisfaction, or try to avoid answering the phone at all costs. The thing is, when people vent, they feel better, and when they feel better, they can tolerate the bad situation they are in a little longer. With that in mind, when you listen to them endlessly and offer solutions they won't take, you are actually enabling them to remain where they are. When you stop, it might feel as if you are abandoning them, but you are in fact taking away the release valve that allows them to stay put, or stay stuck as the case may be, and might therefore push them over the edge they need to finally make a change. Most people have a hard time stepping away—they feel too guilty. So, they continue to engage, as my patients did, and hope their friend or brother-in-law or brother will finally see it. The only way out of that endless maze is for you to recognize it and stop trying to help them.

Understand that they are never going to incorporate your suggestions into their life. They just want to vent to relieve their own anxiety. Your Denial around their Denial is that each time you find you are surprised when they are revisiting the same problem with the same distress and the exact same details as if they never spoke to you five times before. Once you can come to expect it, to know that is just how they are and nothing you do will change it, you will begin to see the situation more clearly. Your Denial also involves your believing they want to change and that you have to be a helpful facilitator to make that happen. In addition, when you do want to hang up or end a conversation, they bombard you with guilt and say you don't love them, that you are being a bad sister, friend, or brother-in-law, even though you are doing everything in your power to help them. So, the skill is to use the anger and frustration you inevitably feel constructively to set limits for yourself, so you are very specific about how and when you are going to be available to them. You can be helpful, but with limits in place; otherwise it will continue to be an endless outpouring of your time. You have to confront your own Denial about them— that's where you are stuck—because you are missing the signs of who they really are, wishing and hoping that they will change or be someone else entirely. Ultimately, they are not who you want them to be—a reasonable, caring friend, an accomplished and professional brother-in-law, or a physically and/or emotionally healthy brother. Instead, they are selfish, difficult to deal with, and they might even lie. With that in mind, you will have to deal with your own feelings of sadness, disappointment, and loss around recognizing and accepting that.

The name of the skill speaks for itself. You only want to give advice if it is asked for. And if they do ask, start with *have you ever tried this before?* whatever this might be. If they did, ask them *why didn't it work?* If they tell you why it didn't work, you can offer an additional suggestion or option. If they haven't tried that, take solace in knowing you have offered something new. You have to change your expectations so that you are prepared and expect them to tell you why it isn't a good idea. The harder you try to fix them, the more resistant they become. The most important piece is that you are not going to get them to understand the reality, so you have to surrender that as your objective. The goal is to be able to empathize with them. Instead of offering suggestions, simply let them know you understand how hard it is for them. You can say, "you know what, I feel so bad for you, and I don't really have answers. Maybe it's a good time to think about talking to someone professionally who can help you deal with this, since I'm not equipped." In that case, intentionally belittle yourself so they don't think you are brushing them off but simply that you are not the best person to talk to about it. That would be a win-win for both of you because they will be getting the help they need, and they will have someone other than you to talk to.

"Wow," Gabby said after I finished explaining the skill. "That's incredibly helpful."

"It is. And the first thing to recognize is that your brother is never going to take your suggestions to heart," I said. "He wants you there, and he wants to talk to you, but that is about all he wants."

"Sometimes I think he is going to do something," Gabby said. "He acts like he might, and then the next day or the day after that he is right back at it, his ear hurts, his eyes burn, etc., etc. I am so glad to have this skill and better understanding of what's going on with him."

"That is one of the things that happens with a *Stay-Stuck Complainer*," I said. "They make you feel that what you said just might make a difference—in some ways it is an attempt to keep you engaged—and then the next time they come back at you with the same complaints as if you never had the last conversation or the last thirty, as if everything you have ever said to them has evaporated and disappeared."

"It feels like that," Gabby said.

"Your own Denial is coming into play here, even though that might be hard to see. In believing your brother wants to change, that you can have a hand in it, that you can help make things better for him, you are in Denial," I said slowly, because this was a very important piece of the puzzle.

"But I can," Gabby said. "Isn't that what siblings are for?"

"Not necessarily," I said. "They are, under the best of circumstances, but in this case instead of helping your brother and lifting him up, you come away feeling as frustrated and defeated as he is."

Gabby nodded. She was beginning to get it.

The next time Sonia came to see me she was down. She said Renee was calling even more frequently. Her relationship with Gavin was so up and down, Sonia didn't know how she stood it.

"The worst part is I hear only about the down part," she said. "And lately she can go on for hours. Then he does something nice, and I don't hear from her again for a day or two. I dread seeing her name show up on my phone these days. I didn't use to feel that way."

I asked her the same question I had asked Gabby: had Renee asked for her help?

This stopped her.

"I'm not sure," she said honestly.

I shared the skill *WAIT TO BE ASKED* with her and everything that went with it, emphasizing the first rule, which was to never offer advice unless Renee asked for it.

"One of the most challenging pieces of this is that you have to go against your natural desire to be helpful and come up with solutions; you really have to contain that urge because most people jump in and problem solve and that is the worst thing you can do, the biggest mistake," I said. "The real objective is to steer clear of advice—to just be empathic."

I told her what I told Gabby: to try to forget about working to get Renee to see the reality of her circumstance and situation.

"When you do that, like when you suggested the clambake when she couldn't go to the beach, you're likely to make her feel misunderstood by you and she'll get more upset and angry with you," I said. "The only thing you can do is accept her reality, that he won't commit, that she is always on hold, that the kids can wind up ruining their plans at any minute. You can tell her you understand why it is so hard, why she feels let down. But try to stop feeling responsible to make it better for her and instead help her handle the feelings of what it is all bringing up for her. You want to say things along the line of, 'I hear you—it is awful—I wish it were easier—maybe things will get better soon—I wish I could stay on the phone longer, but I have to go.' Another thing you can do is limit plans so there is a designated end time, maybe you have to go back to work, or get to class, so Renee's complaining can't go on indefinitely and it won't seem like you are cutting it short unexpectedly. Build in your time limits so you don't feel guilty about disengaging," I said.

"That's a great idea," Sonia said. "I just don't want to completely let her down."

"You are an important part of this equation, too," I said. "This will help you look out for your own well-being. And keep in mind, she is never going to listen to you anyway, even if you take out a billboard with your words on it that she has to drive by every day—she will never see it."

"I am starting to understand that," Sonia said.

"The point is that you are not going to abandon her and never listen at all. You have to instead determine how much you are able to handle in advance. Will you go from three to two times a week? Will you go from an hour to half an hour? Figure out what you can manage. Knowing in advance will help you to be clear about the limits you set for yourself," I said. "Let her know when you have time to talk and when you don't. This is really about confronting your own Denial that you can help her. Think about where you are stuck and how to get unstuck. It's possible she is not the friend you think she is or want her to be, and there can be a sense of loss that goes with that once you accept it. Let yourself feel that."

When I saw Don again, I shared all of this with him. He was particularly moved by the skill.

"You know, looking back, I don't think he ever once asked me for help with his boss," he said. "He just kept talking, and I felt like I had to interject advice, like it was my job to get him out of that situation. I guess I just assumed that's what he wanted."

"Sometimes the hardest thing is realizing that your brother-in-law might not want to get out of what is so clearly to you a bad situation," I said. "It takes work, but if you can come to terms to accept him for who he is, and not who you want him to be, which might mean not getting involved next time if this job doesn't work out for him, it might make things easier for you."

In the end, each of my patients was able to finally leave their Denial in the dust and recognize that they were completely wasting their time—that nothing they said would ever make a difference. They were also each eventually able to take a step back and set limits, although that was most difficult for Gabby, who had to work extra hard to not feel responsible for her brother. Even she, though, was finally able to understand that by allowing him to continue to talk to her she was also letting him to remain in a holding pattern. Once she shortened the amount of time they talked each week, he finally sought out the help of a therapist, which was really the best possible outcome for him.

The bottom line is that a *Stay-Stuck Complainer* is not open to other people's words, and listening to one with no limits in place or recognition of what is really going on is an act of futility. If you want to eliminate your own frustration and stop feeling that you are wasting your time, start with understanding where they are. What do they want? What have they done before to try to fix something? Did any of it work, and if not, why? With all of that in mind, give advice only when they ask for it, not just because it seems obvious to you that they need it. If you can't stand being silent, ask if you can offer an option or a suggestion, but be prepared for their rebuttal or flat-out rejection. The harder you push, the more they will resist, so you have to let go, know you did your best, and shift to empathy. Think of yourself as oiling the tin man, holding their hand, and just generally offering soothing words. The fact is, you feel as trapped as they do when you are dealing with Denial—yours that you can help them and theirs that they are in trouble or in a bad situation that you might be able to resolve. Once you break through that and see things clearly, you will be in a much better and healthier position.

Conclusion

As we have seen in this book, Denial is everywhere. We all have a universal need to turn a blind eye to our problems and possible obstacles in an effort to shield ourselves and the ones we love from unhappiness and trouble. We change our stories, we make things up, we pretend everything is okay, and we refuse to see what is right in front of us. In the same way that our body protects us from a virus, our mind protects us from concerns and negative beliefs. Instead of facing the possibility that we will be failures or that things will go wrong, we spend far too much time deceiving ourselves into believing that everything is all right. The thing is, as we have observed, that only makes things worse and keeps us from working through the real issues. Luckily, you no longer have to live that way.

You now have a toolbox full of skills to combat Denial. These skills are interchangeable and can be used in a multitude of circumstances whenever Denial is present. If you have them all at your fingertips, you will be armed to find your way out of the darkness and into the clear light. They are like oars that enable you to row through the river of Denial to the other side, and no, it is not the river of De-Nile. Here is a quick recap of each skill that you can keep handy and pull out when needed, whether it is in a dating situation or when faced with a relative who expects more from you than you can ever give, or anything in between. You've been there with everyone in the book; you know how difficult it can get. Well, not anymore. Denial, let us show you out the door.

1. *READ THE SMALL PRINT—IT CAN BE HAZARDOUS TO YOUR EMOTIONAL HEALTH*: This skill teaches you not only to understand how important it is to pay attention to details, but that the seemingly small details that are usually dismissed as insignificant actually make a huge difference. It's easy to write them off as petty when comparing them to bigger things because they seem irrelevant, so you choose to ignore them. The most important thing about a pack of cigarettes is that it tells you smoking is dangerous and hazardous to your health, but it is in the small print. The little actions and behaviors that seem strange or odd but you choose to dismiss can add up to a barrel of potential trouble. The goal is to enable you to make wiser decisions and healthier choices. It will help you finally get off the up-and-down roller coaster ride Denial takes you on as you learn to focus on what is right in front of your eyes and truly important.

2. *DO THE EMOTIONAL MATH*: The goal of this skill is to enable you to know the truth so that you can lead with your head and not with your heart. In order to do this, you need to create two columns on a piece of paper. In the first column, list each excuse and reason that you've been told to justify their behavior. In the second column write down how it has made you feel, about them and about yourself. Emotion and Denial blind you to the facts and cause you to move forward with your feelings as your only guide. Using your head allows you to make decisions and choices based on knowledge. On paper, almost all the excuses might make sense, but coupled with the second column, you see the difference adds up to the true big picture. This skill teaches you to see the equation of what you long for versus what you are actually receiving, and how that all breaks down and then adds up to help you make important decisions based on

the reality of the situation, instead of how you wish it were. This can be applied to dating, but also to any relationship in your life.

3. *HOLD ON TIGHT*: This skill allows you to recognize the things that are essential to your identity and that you value the most. These can include lunch with a friend, talking to your mother on the phone, playing soccer on Saturday mornings, and many other activities. You want to preserve them instead of giving them up in order to keep your partner from being mad at you. The aim is to connect with the important parts of your personality that you will no longer sacrifice. It will help you spot the controlling behavior that blocks you and cuts you off from the person you are. The goal of this skill is to give you the clarity you need to stand up for yourself and break free.

4. *LOOK IN THE REARVIEW MIRROR*: With this skill you will learn to be aware of everything around you and be cautious even if you don't see something coming. In the same way that you feel safe because you can't see the car in the next lane, it doesn't mean you won't be blindsided. If you are changing lanes, you slow down, you put your blinker on, and then you give yourself time to double-check and be sure. If you suspect that something is off or detect clues or indicators that things are not right, you really need to investigate them. You want to take your concerns seriously and become open-minded, rather than staying in a single lane, so that you are finally looking out for yourself. The goal is to be careful and inquiring, and, most important, know that just because you are not seeing something, that doesn't mean you won't get hit.

5. *SET YOUR DATE*: This skill gives you the strength to figure out how long you will remain on hold, and what has to

happen for you to be willing to stay in a difficult relationship and continue to invest in it while you wait for change. You'll learn how to plan your timeline to take action—thereby gaining control and making it yours instead of theirs—while considering what your options are, such as seeking help through counseling, taking a temporary separation, or ending the relationship. This will make it so that you are the one calling the shots, and it is no longer about what works best for the other person. The goal of this skill is to gain a sense of control, rather than feeling stuck by the other person's timing.

6. *LEANING IN RATHER THAN LEANING BACK*: With this skill you will learn how to handle rejecting behavior and the anger and disappointment it causes by being proactive instead of withdrawing. The goal is to embrace your own sexuality instead of reacting to your partner and letting your anger disconnect you from your desire and sex life. You will see that taking the lead and initiating intimacy rather than sitting back and feeling bad about yourself is a healthy option because if your partner continues to be unresponsive, it will give you something tangible to address with them.

7. *THREAD THE NEEDLE*: This skill is about putting all the words, the promises, and the intentions of the person you are dealing with together with the specific actions and behaviors you actually see them display. You must keep track and make it real by writing it down and seeing it on paper in front of you. The goal is to overcome their negating and minimizing the severity of their behavior and how problematic it is so that you can take a pulse on how intolerable it really is for you. The objective is to tackle your guilt about not being a good enough wife, husband, daughter, mother, sister, or friend, in order to put boundaries in place and be true to yourself about what is acceptable. You will move away from

Denial and believing what they are telling you, to instead realizing that what they are saying and what they are doing are two different things.

8. *KNOW WHEN TO HOLD THEM, KNOW WHEN TO FOLD THEM*: This skill teaches you when and how to use empathy in the face of a judgmental stance to know if it is possible to have an open-minded conversation that can lead to a middle or common ground, or even a truce to just agree to disagree. Without that, you will find yourself continuously frustrated and feeling as if you are banging your head against the wall to get them to see your side. You can find yourself in this situation around differing politics as well as career choices, pandemic practices, marriage partners, having a baby or not, and much more. This will help you come to terms with what you can and can't accept—to know whether you can stay involved. The goal is to shift your intention to gaining understanding of where they are coming from instead of looking for agreement.

9. *USE WHAT YOU KNOW*: This skill will help you stop jumping through hoops to win approval from whoever is pulling on you for help. This will put an end to always feeling you are falling short. You will realize that whatever you do, they will always ask you to do more. The harder you try, the more they will demand because they are constantly testing you to prove your love. You will eventually be able to see them for who they are so that you are protected from the element of surprise and are no longer wounded by their negative responses. The goal is to see the total picture by recognizing the difference between a reasonable and an unreasonable request, so you have the power to respond accordingly, set realistic expectations for yourself, and allow you to effectively put boundaries and limits in place when necessary.

10. *ADDRESS YOUR DISTRESS*: This skill will help you stop making excuses for the other person and denying your anger. Instead, the aim is to handle that anger head-on in a healthy, constructive way by dealing directly with what is bothering you. The only one who can change is you; you want to stop justifying your needs and explaining why you do what you do. To achieve this, stick to the facts, don't explain yourself, validate your own needs, and take them seriously, knowing you deserve to have them met. By putting this into practice, you learn how to stop making excuses and giving in when you don't want to. Use your anger to fuel this change and figure out how you will handle things differently in the future. Make a plan and be clear about what your actions and responses will be when things become unbearable in the face of their controlling behavior. In this way, you will empower yourself. The goal is to break free of your victim role and find the courage to trust your gut and hold onto your truth.

11. *WAIT TO BE ASKED*: This skill will teach you how to put limits in place around a *Stay-Stuck Complainer*, as well as when and how to offer advice and when to stay out of it. Most importantly, it will allow you to stop expending energy that is never appreciated or reciprocated, and to learn to wait until someone asks for help before trying to assist them. The goal is to stop overextending yourself trying to make it better for the other person when they are not trying to make any changes or asking for your guidance. When they are complaining to you and you try to give them answers, the aim is to understand and accept they just want to vent and nothing more.

So, if you find yourself saying, *I can't believe it, that's not true, that's impossible, he or she would never do it, she's not that kind of person, how can that be? No way! It's not so bad! You're wrong, you don't know what you're talking about, that makes no sense, why would* *you think that? I have no problem, it could be worse, they are really* *trying*—all the things you tell yourself to let yourself or someone else off the hook and negate the truth as you know it to be—take a step back and consider whether you are in Denial. With the knowledge you now have after reading this book, along with all these skills you have developed, you will recognize the blinking lights that allow you to turn a blind eye to the truth and you will stop it in its tracks. You are ready; keep your eyes open and you can move toward a bright and happier life. If Denial were still in play, it would tell you don't believe anything you just read. However, as I promised at the beginning of the book, there is nothing left to hide behind. Are you lying to yourself? Not anymore.

INDEX

Address(ing) Your (His) Distress, 217, 218, 219, 220, 221, 224, 250

Believe/ed/ing What You Are (She Is/Was) Told, 29, 32, 70, 91, 125, 133, 140, 143

Cold War, 164

Demander's Denial, 194
Dominator(s), 66, 213–215, 221, 222, 224
Dominator Spouse, 206, 225
Do the Emotional Math, 36, 38, 41, 246

Emotional Acid Reflux, 222

Going Nowhere Relationship 23, 30, 38, 53, 66
Going Somewhere Partner, 66
Going Somewhere Relationship 36, 79

Hazard Light(s), 26, 28, 30, 32, 35, 37, 38, 40, 53, 66

Hold On Tight, 57, 58, 62–64, 66, 218, 247

Know When To Hold Them, Know When To Fold Them, 173, 175, 176, 178, 249

Leaning In Rather Than Leaning Back, 122, 128, 131, 248
Legal Emotional Blindness, 191
Look in the Rearview Mirror, 71, 74, 77, 247
Lose Yourself Relationship, 53, 65, 66

Me Versus We, 32
Missing the Signs, xv, 49, 70, 93

Not About You Guy(s), 10, 11, 12–13, 20, 22, 30
Not About You Relationship, 20, 23

Read the Small Print, 13, 15, 17, 18, 21, 22, 23, 246

Sexless Standoff, 119
Sexpectations, 125
Scheduled Spontaneity, 123, 132
Set Your Date, 98, 104, 105, 109, 247
Situationship, 19–20
Stay-Stuck Complainer, xiv, 225, 231, 232, 235, 240, 243, 250

Thread the Needle, 145, 150, 152, 153, 155–157, 248

Trust Factor, 72–73, 75, 84
Turning a Little Into a Lot, xv, 29, 34

Use What You Know, 193, 198, 201, 202, 203, 249

Wait To Be Asked, 237, 241, 250
Watch-Out Sign(s), 6, 7, 8, 9, 10, 11, 12, 14, 15, 20, 23, 26, 51, 52, 59
Wishing and Hoping, xv, 17, 70, 87, 90, 92, 95, 107, 109, 121, 123, 124, 133

About the Author

Dr. Jane Greer is a nationally known marriage and family therapist, psychotherapist, sex expert, author, and host of the "Doctor on Call" radio hour at HealthyLife.net, which features *Shrink Wrap on Call*, *Pop Psych*, and *Let's Talk Sex*. She has appeared on many popular television shows including: *The Today Show*, *Oprah*, *The Early Show*, *CBS News*, *CNN News*, *Anderson Cooper 360*, *Dateline NBC*, *20/20*, *Good Day New York*, and *The View*. She has contributed to magazines including *Cosmopolitan*, *Glamour*, *Self*, and has been interviewed for the *New York Times*, *The Wall Street Journal*, *USA Today*, the *Chicago Tribune*, *US Weekly*, *In Touch*, *Closer*, *Life & Style*, *Brides.com*, and *People*. Greer was a contributing editor for *Redbook* magazine, where she also wrote the "Let's Talk About Sex" column. She is the author of six books about navigating relationships. You can learn more about Dr. Greer at her website drjanegreer.com, or follow her on Twitter, Instagram, LinkedIn, and Facebook at Dr. Jane Greer.